Southern Literary Studies

Fred Hobson, Editor

The Novels of William Styron

The Novels of William Styron

From Harmony to History

Gavin Cologne-Brookes

Copyright © 1995 by Louisiana State University Press
All rights reserved
Manufactured in the United States of America
First printing
04 03 02 01 00 99 98 97 96 95   5 4 3 2 1

Designer: Amanda McDonald Key
Typeface: Trump
Typesetter: G & S Typesetters, Inc.
Printer and binder: Thomson-Shore, Inc.

LIBRARY OF CONGRESS CATALOGING-IN-PUBLICATION DATA

Cologne-Brookes, Gavin, date.
    The novels of William Styron : from harmony to history / Gavin Cologne-Brookes.
       p.   cm. — (Southern literary studies)
    Includes bibliographical references and index.
    ISBN 0-8071-1900-8 (alk. paper)
    1. Styron, William, 1925–   —Criticism and interpretation.
    2. Southern States—In literature.   I. Title.   II. Series.
    PS3569.T9Z6244   1994
    813'.54—dc20   94-19731
                                                                        CIP

For Nicki and Xenatasha and Philip and Bobbi

Compositional principles of a poetic work are
a manifestation of an author's view of life.
                    — Georg Lukács

Contents

Acknowledgments

My debts in connection with this project are numerous, but my thanks go first to James L. W. West III, of Pennsylvania State University, whose conversations with me in Cambridge in January, 1986, launched much of what has resulted. Jim West told me of a symposium on William Styron at Winthrop College in Rock Hill, South Carolina, and I am indebted to the many scholars I talked with there on the April weekend of 1986 when it was held, including those with whom I sometimes take issue. My specific gratitude goes to Eva B. Mills, who ran the conference, and to Melvin J. Friedman and Jackson R. Bryer, who edited a special issue of *Papers on Language and Literature* that included my article arising from the conference, "Discord Toward Harmony: *Set This House on Fire* and Peter's 'Part in the Matter,'" which evolved into the third chapter of this book.

I must also thank Thérèse de Saint Phalle for her kindness and infectious enthusiasm when I stayed in Burgundy, and Judith Ruderman for southern hospitality on my visit to Duke University in 1988. Thanks are due as well to Matt Martin and his family, ever ready hosts in Erie, Darien, and New York. For tremendous help on the trip of 1988, I am indebted to Robert Byrd and Patricia Webb, of the Manuscript Department at the William R. Perkins Library at Duke. For help during the later stages of the manuscript, I must mention Jan Beckett, librarian at Harlaxton College, the British campus of the University of Evansville. I thank my colleagues at Harlaxton and in the English department of Bath College of Higher Education for friendships that have created an atmosphere conducive to completion of the book.

William Styron himself has been more open, interested, and generous with his time than I at first dared to hope. I thank him not only for permission to publish our conversations and to quote from unpublished manuscripts but also, along with his wife, Rose, for times together in Roxbury, Vineyard Haven, and even the fog of Albion.

Much of the book would have been impossible but for the British Academy, which provided the bulk of the funding for the early stages of the study and for the trip to South Carolina in 1986; the British Association for American Studies and the American Embassy in London, which helped fund the trip in 1988 to Duke University and to Roxbury, Connecticut, where most of the conversations now in the Appendix took place; Peter Messent, of the University of Nottingham, who has given years of patient encouragement and advice during the first drafts of the manuscript; his colleague Richard King, who read parts of it; my parents, Philip and Bobbi, who have provided a stable base for so many years; and my wife, Nicki, who has been entangled with the project every sentence of the way.

The Novels of William Styron

Introduction

Shifting Patterns of Discourse in Styron's Novels

Despite some excellent criticism on William Styron's novels, books about them rarely stretch much beyond pamphlet length; few critics have managed to span wide and dig deep. They tend to offer partial views of the canon, studies of only one novel—as Albert E. Stone's *The Return of Nat Turner* does—or overviews that merely distill the main critical arguments. The want of sustained, comprehensive studies of Styron's novels in the United States—let alone in Britain, where scholarship about Styron has been oddly sparse in relation to the space allotted some of his contemporaries—contrasts with the strong interest evident in non-English-speaking countries. In France, Christine Chaufour-Verheyen's critical study *William Styron: Le 7e Jour* was published as a mass-market paperback. The aim of the present book, therefore, is to go some way toward filling this gap by combining close readings of each novel with an overall vision that acknowledges, encompasses, yet goes beyond, what is already familiar.[1]

Still, a Styron industry exists in the United States in periodicals, essay collections, dissertations, and brief book studies. But, of books devoted to all his novels, only Melvin J. Friedman's *William Styron* and John Kenny Crane's *The Root of All Evil*—the longest, at 168 pages—are more than introductory.[2] Friedman's assessment of one later work is that it "disappoints in essential ways." Judith Ruderman's *William Styron*, he says, "goes over familiar, undaring ground."[3] That book is

---

1. Albert E. Stone, *The Return of Nat Turner: History, Literature, and Cultural Politics in Sixties America* (Athens, Ga., 1992); Christine Chaufour-Verheyen, *William Styron: Le 7e Jour* (Paris, 1991).

2. Melvin J. Friedman, *William Styron: An Interim Appraisal* (Bowling Green, Ohio, 1974); John Kenny Crane, *The Root of All Evil: The Thematic Unity of William Styron's Fiction* (Columbia, S.C., 1984).

3. Melvin J. Friedman, "William Styron in Eden," *Papers on Language and Literature*, XXIII (1987), 544; Judith Ruderman, *William Styron* (New York, 1987).

indeed meant only as an overview, like those by Marc L. Ratner, Robert H. Fossum, Cooper R. Mackin, and Richard Pearce, the limited aims of which are implicit in the title they have in common, *William Styron.* The same is true of Samuel Coale's excellent but mainly reintroductory *William Styron Revisited.*[4]

Crane's *The Root of All Evil* is original and provocative. But that is partly because his main tenet, that selfishness is the "root of all evil" in Styron's fiction, is reductive. With little reference to the contexts of Styron's work, Crane collates, crushes, and compacts the novels' array of competing voices to impose a "thematic unity" on the work.[5] Stimulating as his insights have been to this study, the book leaves the impression of seeking to reduce Styron's canon to something like a color-by-numbers chart. The comment that resonates is Friedman's, reviewing Ruderman. "We have reached the point in Styron criticism," he writes, "when more daring assertions should be made, more sophistication should be expected."[6] Certainly, Styron's achievement seems to warrant an attempt at something rather more substantial than we have seen.

I have sought to combine an encompassing view with a specific approach. The overall view, that Styron's career develops from harmony to history, is broadly caught by a comment the writer made to his fellow novelist Philip Caputo in 1986: "I am amazed in retrospect that I am as political as I am, given the fact that I began as a writer who was totally ivory-tower oriented. *Lie Down in Darkness* is a book of very little political sensibility. . . . My statement is not regrettable, but I guess I have, over the years, almost unconsciously let my work be connected with politics, with politics in so far as they govern history and human affairs."[7] Styron here confirms what is evident from his novels, that his view of literature and of his role as a writer has changed radically during his career, and that this has resulted from his growing

4. Marc L. Ratner, *William Styron* (Boston, 1972); Robert H. Fossum, *William Styron: A Critical Essay* (Grand Rapids, 1968); Cooper R. Mackin, *William Styron* (Austin, Tex., 1969); Richard Pearce, *William Styron* (Minneapolis, 1971); Samuel Coale, *William Styron Revisited* (Boston, 1991).

5. See, for example, Crane, *The Root of All Evil,* 25, 6.

6. Friedman, "William Styron in Eden," 545.

7. Philip Caputo, "Styron's Choices," *Esquire,* CVI (December, 1986), 140.

interest and involvement "with politics in so far as they govern history and human affairs."

My specific approach to examining this overall picture is to focus on the evolving patterns of discourse from one novel to the next. Styron's first two works, his novel *Lie Down in Darkness* and his novella *The Long March*, are characterized by a discourse toward harmony— an impulse to harmonize the various battling voices they present. He told Caputo, "I thought of literature as just pure literature in the early days."[8] But, as his career progressed and he became more involved with historical and political issues, his vision—and thus the structure of his novels—altered. The notion of harmony jars with the political and historical issues he increasingly took on, and so it was dislodged from its central position in the novelistic structure. All the novels begin with discordant voices that the author or narrator orchestrates toward some form of mental, social, or aesthetic reconciliation. But once the issues shift away from the largely personal and narrowly artistic concerns of *Lie Down in Darkness* toward the sociohistorical concerns of *The Confessions of Nat Turner* and *Sophie's Choice*, the insufficiencies of the earlier kind of discourse toward harmony are revealed by the emergence of voices that contradict it. Styron's novelistic journey, in this sense, is from an aesthetic dominated by notions of harmony to one irretrievably intertwined with the realities of history.

The word *harmony* not only links with Styron's tendency to use musical analogies but is itself ambiguous. Harmony might take the form of genuine agreements or satisfactory solutions to conflicts among textual voices. But it can equally take the form, as in Peter Leverett's narration in *Set This House on Fire*, of a bald suppression of difficult elements. Similarly, a search for harmony can manifest itself in a legitimate attempt to flee to a new, perhaps more congenial setting, as in Peyton Loftis' unsuccessful escape to New York in *Lie Down in Darkness*, or in Cass's Carolina riverbank, yet it can also be seen, in Stingo's idyllic peanut farm, or in Peter's *use* of the riverbank setting in his narrative, as an attempt to evade the issues at hand.

Two particular theorists of the novel form—Mikhail M. Bakhtin and Georg Lukács—help articulate my specific approach and overall

8. *Ibid.*

view of Styron's work. Bakhtin's view of novels as arenas of clashing voices helps explain the multifaceted ways critics can interpret a novel by highlighting one aspect or voice among many and then claim, as Crane does, that hitherto "most, if not all, critics" simply "failed to recognize" the key themes.[9] For Bakhtin, language is "dialogic" and novels are a "contradiction-ridden, tension-filled" arena "of two embattled tendencies in the life of language"—the centripetal and centrifugal, or centralizing and decentering, forces of language.[10] His view of novels as having a general flow, rather than a wholly unified meaning, arms us against the fallacy of expecting thematic unity. The result is a greater openness to diverse interpretations within an overall, definable pattern.

Two observations by Lukács are especially pertinent to my analysis. One—that the "compositional principles of a poetic work are a manifestation of an author's view of life"—seems a fitting epigraph for this book, since Styron's changing vision has subtly affected the composition of his novels.[11] Of equal importance is Lukács' view that a "yearning for harmony" in literature and life "too often takes the form of a craven retreat or faint-hearted withdrawal before the contradictory problems thrown up by life." In that case, he argues, we bind ourselves to the "illusory and superficial," because "by seeking inner harmony men cut themselves off from society's struggles."[12] The evolving patterns of voices from one of Styron's works to the next signal a shift in his view of life and art. The shift partly reflects his recognition of the social and political consequences of his initial inclination to remove himself from society's struggles in endeavoring to harmonize conflicting voices within his art. Once his novels began to explore controversial matters in politics and history, they began to question this notion of harmony. The later novels show that—as desirable, artistic, and human as the urge to reconcile voices may be—the notion of harmony runs counter to our experience of life. It can lead, in Lukács' words, to

9. Crane, *The Root of All Evil*, 6.
10. Mikhail M. Bakhtin, *The Dialogic Imagination: Four Essays*, trans. Michael Holquist and Caryl Emerson, ed. Michael Holquist (Austin, Tex., 1981), 288, 272.
11. Georg Lukács, *Writer and Critic, and Other Essays*, trans. Arthur Kahn (London, 1978), 140.
12. *Ibid.*, 89.

a "faint-hearted withdrawal," to imposed agreement, or even to an abdication from responsibility that worsens a situation. Apparently unproblematic on a personal or aesthetic level, a search for harmony is at best naïve. At worst it is insidious, as in the context, say, of the Holocaust.

Part of the shift in the patterns of discourse in Styron's work connects with his relationship to his high modernist precursors, one thread of whose work often stressed how the alienated artist turns to art as a way to order the world. It is not necessary to share what Jerome Klinkowitz calls Lukács' "embattled anti-modernist position," which reproaches modernism for ahistorical tendencies, to follow Lukács' implicit idea that art can become more vital by setting the viewpoints of social and historical debate against one another.[13] Styron's more direct engagement with historical issues results in a greater narrative and linguistic complexity even though he seems to move in the later work from modernist formal experimentation to a more direct narrative style.

Although my aim is for an encompassing study of Styron, I have given fullest attention to Styron's four novels and his early novella. Styron's essays, especially from *This Quiet Dust and Other Writings*, his shorter fiction, including that in *A Tidewater Morning: Three Tales from Youth*, and the play *In the Clap Shack* all help shape my view of his novelistic journey. So does his account of his struggles with clinical depression, *Darkness Visible: A Memoir of Madness*. His experience of that illness, indeed, has brought a new kind of reflection—for Styron, as he acknowledges, as well as for the reader—on the development of his vision. But because he is primarily a novelist, anything other than his novels is always seen here as subsidiary.

Equally, since several aspects of Styron's writing have been the frequent subject of previous study, the Freudian, existentialist, and southern qualities in his work enter the discussion only when relevant to the overall argument. But that said, I must also acknowledge that the examination of existentialist elements in Styron's work by, among others, Sidney Finkelstein and David D. Galloway and Rhoda Sirlin and

13. Jerome Klinkowitz, "The Extra-Literary in Contemporary American Fiction," in *Contemporary American Fiction*, ed. Malcolm Bradbury and Sigmund Ro (London, 1987), 56.

of Freudian elements by, among others, Crane and Richard W. Noland reveals the wealth of voices that make up the novels and fits with my general view of the novels as arenas of clashing voices.[14] I shall make specific reference to Styron's use of Albert Camus in *The Long March* and of Erik H. Erikson in *The Confessions*, but for the most part the study explores less traveled paths.

As for the South, my emphasis is less on Styron as a southern writer—as one centrally concerned with southern themes—than on him as a writer influenced by his "southern roots."[15] His position relative to southern writers is often a critical focus, and much interesting work on him is by southerners or southern specialists like Louis D. Rubin, Jr., James L. W. West III, and in Britain, Richard Gray. But other approaches offer more scope for original discussion.

Moreover, such critics aside, the idea of Styron as a southern writer has contributed to detrimental criticism, and to a certain amount of pigeonholing. In Rubin's view, much of the negative reaction to *Set This House on Fire* resulted from its being "simply not a 'Southern' novel at all, in the way that Southern novels had been written by his predecessors."[16] Regionalizing a writer can allow critics to marginalize him. Walker Percy saw that as a special problem for southern writers and objected to the "undue attribution of a particular sort of regionalism which the expression invites—regionalism in the bad parochial

14. See Sidney Finkelstein, *Existentialism and Alienation in American Literature* (New York, 1965), 211–42; and David D. Galloway, *The Absurd Hero in American Fiction* (London, 1981), 51–81. For Freudian analysis, see especially Richard W. Noland, "Psychohistorical Themes in *Sophie's Choice*," *Delta* (Montpellier), XXIII (1986), 91–109.

15. "I feel myself to be an American writer with southern roots, but I don't feel regional about the South. I don't feel that the South informs my sensibility at this moment" (William Styron, "Styron's Cycle," BBC Radio Four interview by Paul Bailey, August, 1982). On Styron's southernness, see also his comments in "A Voice from the South," in *This Quiet Dust and Other Writings* (Rev. ed.; New York, 1993), 52–62. For critical views, see especially Richard Gray, *The Literature of Memory: Modern Writers of the American South* (London, 1977), 284–305; Valarie M. Arms, "William Styron and the Spell of the South," *Mississippi Quarterly*, XXXIV (1980–81), 25–36; and Jane Flanders, "William Styron's Southern Myth," in *The Achievement of William Styron*, ed. Robert K. Morris and Irving Malin (Rev. ed.; Athens, Ga., 1981), 106–23.

16. Louis D. Rubin, Jr., "Notes on a Southern Writer in Our Time," in *The Achievement of William Styron*, ed. Morris and Malin, 70.

sense, not the good universal sense in which the best writers are all regionalists. Even William Faulkner is generally thought of as a Southern novelist. But Hemingway and Bellow are not thought of as Northern novelists. Cervantes is not thought of as an Andalusian novelist. Cézanne is not thought of as a Provence painter."[17] Styron is rightly seen by most southern specialists as something other than a southern writer, but he is then labeled with the regionalist tag by critics eager to shunt him into a parenthetical siding.[18] One cannot properly discuss *Lie Down in Darkness* without reference to Faulkner, nor *Sophie's Choice* without reference to Stingo's southern background. Too, if C. Vann Woodward is right to argue in *The Burden of Southern History* that southern preoccupations are "with guilt, not with innocence, with the reality of evil, not the dream of perfection," southern threads are clearly evident in Styron's work. But since it is over thirty years since Woodward in the same book asked if it was time for the southerner to question "whether there is really any longer very much point in calling himself a Southerner," such associations will receive limited attention.[19]

Taking the major fictional works chronologically, each of my chapter starts with a close reading of the voices in dialogue at the level of the characters before examining external voices—other texts—in dialogue beyond that fictional world. The external voices often clarify the overall argument but at times account for inconsistencies evident at the level of the story. Chapter 1 focuses on the way the characters' struggles in *Lie Down in Darkness* are manifestations of the centripetal and centrifugal forces of language, with the effaced narrator using minor characters to offset the failures of the main characters and to ensure a discourse toward harmony. Beyond that, Peyton's struggle against her parents parallels Styron's struggle to quell the voices of his modernist precursors and to assert a voice of his own.

17. Walker Percy, *Novel Writing in an Apocalyptic Time* (New Orleans, 1986), 2.

18. See Fred Hobson, "Casting a Long Shadow: Faulkner and Southern Literature," in *American Literature*, ed. Boris Ford (Harmondsworth, Eng., 1988), 476–77, Vol. IX of *The New Pelican Guide to English Literature*, ed. Ford. Mailer and Bellow are elsewhere examined simply as novelists, but Styron and Percy are mentioned as "Southern writers."

19. C. Vann Woodward, *The Burden of Southern History* (New York, 1960), 3, 21.

Chapters 2 and 3 trace similar movements toward harmony in *The Long March* and *Set This House on Fire*. Between these two works, however, the inadequacies, and questioning, of such a discourse grow more apparent. Culver's personal need for harmony, and his detached, artistic role as harmonizer, prove ambiguous in the context of a more political subject. Seemingly a passive mediator in the conflict between Templeton and Mannix, he in fact affects it in such a way that the movement toward harmony jars with the political struggle portrayed. In *Set This House on Fire*, the movement is dislodged as the main discourse. Like Culver, Peter tries to harmonize conflicting voices, but unlike Culver he is an autonomous narrator, whose outlook is challenged by Styron's now centrifugal presence. In Bakhtin's phrase, the narration is thus "double-voiced."[20] The decentering of the discourse toward harmony coincides with an increased concern with political and historical issues. *Set This House on Fire* is thus a pivotal novel. In it, Styron looks toward the more sophisticated uses of language and dialogue of his later work.

Chapters 4 and 5 examine *The Confessions of Nat Turner* and *Sophie's Choice*. Launching, first, into the historical, political subject of slavery and race, Styron in *The Confessions of Nat Turner* puts into prominence questions of language and the textuality of history to create a far more complex novel than its predecessors. Again the discourse toward harmony is dialogized by a gap between narrator and author, as well as between the older and younger Nat. But such are the subject and context that the urge to harmonize remains evident. The use of sources like James Baldwin, Frederick Douglass, and Erikson leads to some jolting of 1831 against the 1960s, thereby contributing to the ensuing public controversy. *Sophie's Choice* is also based on a crucial matter of historical debate. Styron here fully decenters the urge to escape into a private, art-centered, harmonious world. Through Sophie's story, he connects Stingo's attitude with wider issues, suggesting the ambivalence, even danger, of such personal quests for harmony. Styron thus comes full circle. Entering political and historical precincts, he doubles back to satirize the discourse that began as the fundamental shaping pattern of his novels. The invocation of George Steiner, Rich-

20. Bakhtin, *The Dialogic Imagination*, 355.

ard L. Rubenstein, and others underlines the move away from the pure notions of novel writing with which he began his career.

In conclusion I look briefly at Styron's work in relationship to his contemporaries and to his more recent writing, in particular *Darkness Visible*. I also include an appendix of extracts from recorded conversations I had with him in 1988 and 1991. These serve as reference and support for my argument. In the earlier extracts, Styron outlines, reads, and discusses parts of his novel long in progress, *The Way of the Warrior*, as he conceived of it at the time of the conversations.

1

Inheritance of Modernism: *Lie Down in Darkness*

The real task of stylistic analysis consists in uncovering all the available orchestrating languages in the composition of the novel.
                    —*Mikhail M. Bakhtin*, The Dialogic Imagination

"Inheritance of Night," Styron's original title for his first novel, reflects Peyton Loftis' doomed struggle to escape parental influence and find personal identity.[1] Her struggle and her parents' equally unsuccessful attempts to unify the family yet, paradoxically, to assert their own contradictory viewpoints is one story in *Lie Down in Darkness*. Still, as Roland Barthes says, "To understand a narrative is not merely to follow the unfolding of the story, it is to recognize its construction in 'storeys.'" And on a different level, another struggle parallels Peyton's: that of the young Styron's "anxiety of influence" (Harold Bloom's term) as he seeks his own voice amid those of his illustrious literary precursors.[2] It is to these two battles involving heredity that I turn.

On both levels, the struggle is to harmonize various voices into an apparently unitary whole. The narrator—effectively the young Styron—tries to efface himself but remains the orchestrator of the struggle. He begins by stressing the social, mental, and verbal discord that has torn the Loftis family apart, then traces the clashing voices of Milton, Helen, and Peyton in their ill-fated search—through memory and in the recollected events—for personal and social reconciliation. All three ultimately fail in their quest, but the narrator uses minor characters like Ella Swan, Carey Carr, and Peyton's husband, Harry

1. See James L. W. West III, "William Styron's *Inheritance of Night:* Predecessor of *Lie Down in Darkness*," *Delta* (Montpellier), XXIII (1986), 1–17.

2. Roland Barthes, *Image-Music-Text*, trans. Stephen Heath (1977; rpr. London, 1982), 87; Harold Bloom, *The Anxiety of Influence* (New York, 1973).

Miller, to bring out how an overall movement toward harmony prevails. On the second level, Styron seeks not only to close the novel but also to harmonize the voices of his modernist forerunners in the apparent unity of his own literary voice.

Participating in the shaping of both textual "storeys" are the centripetal and centrifugal—the centralizing and decentering—forces of language. On the first level, the Loftis parents construct bulwarks—birthday celebrations, family traditions, weddings—for holding their world together. Scenes and episodes amount to microcosmic distillations of how these structures momentarily unify the family. But as much as the main characters struggle to hold their world together, the family members' urges work to undermine their attempts at unity. Milton's memories of early married life, for example, reveal how his sense of dissatisfied security in the unifying structures of family, social, and religious life leads him to undermine them. Only later, when that world is disintegrating, does he strive to restore its order. Helen's voice, in contrast, is predominantly centripetal, asserting order on her and others. What she says, however, turns out to be a symptom of a growing inner disarray that, no less than what Milton does, helps tear the family apart. Peyton, too, while striving for a coherent identity, undermines the family unity through her search for freedom. If all three strive toward mental or social reconciliation, in each episode their conflicting efforts combine to ensure that their attempts fail.

The dynamic of centripetal and centrifugal forces also manifests itself on the second level. The young Styron tries to break free from the voices of his precursors or to suppress them—often unsuccessfully—in an apparent unity of narrative voice. The complexity of the textual battle is greater still because the novel's movement toward harmony is a legacy of high modernism's view of art as functioning to order a chaotic world. Styron, in seeking to quell the voices of others and assert his own, thus does not break with one of the most fundamental patterns evident in the very writers who dog him.

If, then, Peyton's and Styron's stories relate—if both strive to escape external influence and to find voices of their own—the question is whether Styron succeeds where Peyton fails. According to Mikhail M. Bakhtin, there is in "literary language" a constant struggle "against various kinds and degrees of authority" and each age "reaccentuates in its own way the works of its most immediate past."[3] Can it be said that Styron reaccentuates his modernist forebears? On the novel's second level, a movement backward seems to occur, not only into the characters' pasts but into a literary past. Richard H. King's description of Faulkner's structures as taking "us back, then through, and out the other side—which turns out to be the way we came in, only at a different level"—is as true of *Lie Down in Darkness*.[4] But if the characters yearn for an idealized past, so that the novel moves backward into memory, at the same time Styron himself, nervously glancing back to literary predecessors, tries to struggle forward, imitating yet also exorcising his modernist precursors in search of his own literary voice.

The novel opens with verbal and social discord. This is largely the result of a complete breakdown in communication between Helen and Milton as they wait for Peyton's body at the Port Warwick railroad station, but it pervades the whole scene. Awaiting Peyton's body with Helen and Milton are the undertakers Casper and Barclay, the cleric Carey Carr, who is with Helen, and the couple's black housekeeper, Ella Swan, and Milton's mistress, Dolly Sclater, who are with Milton. The scene evolves by way of isolated utterances, jarring sounds, and strangled cries. Closed in by "sulphurous" air and dust clouds "spread against the sky,"[5] the characters' attempts at dialogue compete with a constant cacophony. Above an "incessant whistle" of steam and the "rattle and hum of an electric crane" (12), Casper tries to tell Barclay why the hearse has stopped, but he is drowned out by the roar of coal being "swallowed up in a ship's hold with a hollow, booming noise . . . *Ree-ee-eep. CaaaaARWONG!*" (18).

Milton and Helen meanwhile remain apart, but his and Casper's memories of the days leading up to the funeral reveal the couple's mental disparity. Milton is near collapse. Close to "hysteria" (19), he faces

3. Mikhail M. Bakhtin, *The Dialogic Imagination: Four Essays*, trans. Michael Holquist and Caryl Emerson, ed. Michael Holquist (Austin, Tex., 1981), 345, 421.

4. Richard H. King, *A Southern Renascence: The Cultural Awakening of the American South, 1930–1955* (New York, 1980), 10.

5. William Styron, *Lie Down in Darkness* (New York, 1951), 32, cited in the present chapter by page number, without title.

the "evidence of all his errors and all his love" (14). "I won't think too much," he decides, imagining that then "the train won't come at all" (13). But even that evasion, like the hearse, has broken down. As if in sympathetic echo, so too has his syntax: "I can bear . . . WON'T!" (19). His voice is incomplete and unanswered because Peyton, the focus of his love, is dead. As in Allbee's depiction of widowerhood in Saul Bellow's *The Victim*, Milton is like half a man. "Dead is dead. Finished," says Allbee. "She bends to you and you bend to her in everything, and when she dies there you stand, bent, and look senseless."[6] Worse still, since by loving Peyton as "more than a father" (286), Milton has loved "too much" and the wrong way (291), he faces a tragedy he has helped create.

Others offer him comfort, but to no great effect. Casper's words— "All right, old trouper" (19)—are platitudes. In the café, Hazel, the girl behind the counter, chatters on at Milton "above the droning fan" (37), her mouth seeming to Dolly, outside, to move "rapidly, soundlessly" (40). Dolly herself offers "tender whisperings" (12), but anything she says "sounds so inappropriate" (44). Voices, indeed, never seem appropriate as the novel opens. They are fragmented like Milton's, bemused like Barclay's, empty clichés like Casper's, or like Hazel's, a stream of drivel. Communication has effectively collapsed.

Helen at first seems altogether composed. She strives for a social and personal harmony built not on casual indulgence but on the oppression of others and the suppression of her own feelings. Milton's early view of her as "strait-laced" and "severe" (16) is recaptured by Casper's comment that she seems "devoid of feeling." When he visits them to discuss funeral arrangements, Helen is impatient—"If you'll just sit here," she clips (21)—whereas Milton sounds "husky and tired." In contrast to Helen's brusque manner, Milton has "crumpled clothes" and "bloodshot eyes" (22). The basic lineaments of Milton's sloppy evasion and Helen's demand for order emerge. If Milton has loved too much, and perversely, Helen has loved "so little" (291).

But the traits they share have contributed as well to the breakdown in communication that opens the novel. They are both vain. Milton has "rarely worn a hat," because he thinks his gray streak attracts "ad-

6. Saul Bellow, *The Victim* (1947; rpr. London, 1965), 65.

miring glances" (13); Helen pulls "the skin of her face taut" to look younger in the mirror (24). They also have selfishness and self-pity in common, traits linked to their drug dependency. If Milton's alcohol keeps him from hearing others, Helen's Nembutal immures her like a "marble sepulcher" (157). A paradigm of the "suffering woman" (274), Helen has become wholly wrapped up in herself. Their deafness to others is reflected in their choice of companions. Milton's affair with Dolly is mostly a "one sided communion" in which "usually she agreed with him" (71). Helen has first Maudie, who says little except, "Yes, Mamadear," and then Carey "as long as he agreed with her" (143). So when Milton does try to talk with Helen, he fares no better than with Dolly or Hazel, repeating, "Why don't you say something?" but getting no response (26).

The couple, then, are "like the negative poles of a magnet" (93). Helen builds defenses to hide inner turmoil, and Milton confuses freedom with self-indulgence. Despite their sporadic urges for mutual understanding, their outlooks have become irreconcilable. There is not just a clash of "different values" (66), as Helen asserts, but a field of forces that stirs their personal traits into conflict.

Peyton is dead now, but in life she was caught between the conflicting viewpoints of Helen and Milton. Though she is absent from much of the text, her view, like Addie Bundren's in *As I Lay Dying*, is felt through its absence, before pouring out in her final monologue. But we hear her briefly in the first chapter, in her letter to Milton. The letter reveals her derangement as she too strives, but for reasons different from her parents', to preserve coherence and find meaning. Her confusion is evident in her language: "The trouble is that they don't—these thoughts—seem to have any distinctness." It is just as evident in the thoughts themselves, as she edits them: "it's (*something crossed out*) wings it" (39). But the "Mozart concerto" (37) she buys is testimony to her attempts to find harmony, as is her alarm clock, a recurring symbol of harmony, with its "precisely moving wheels" (370).

Also appearing in the discordant opening scenes are the voices of blacks. Like Peyton's, these are largely silenced or ignored by more dominant voices. When Ella tells Milton that she "and Miz Bonner take keer of things," Dolly tells her to "Shh-hh" (14). But the black discourse, by remaining in the background, can offer an ironic, if sympathetic, commentary on the family's predicaments. From the start, when the narrator imagines two Negroes watching the train from the woods, blacks are portrayed as present yet detached. When the hearse breaks down, for instance, a Negro's casual remark, "Dead wagon, man!" (19) offers a different, undercutting perspective through the pun on *dead* and through the slang use of *wagon*.

Ella Swan, who, with her daughter La Ruth, is the novel's main black presence, is seen by Milton as another prop. She is a stereotype from what King calls the Southern Family Romance: a stock, surrogate-mother figure who takes the place of the shadowy, sexless white mother in the southern mythical structure.[7] She is, as critics often note, distinctly like Faulkner's Dilsey. For Milton, she is a figure to be ribbed, or to comfort him, depending on his needs. The night he hears of Peyton's death, he hurries to Ella to "communicate his distress." But her response "Lawd have mercy!" (27) is a banal one that shows Milton once again to be left without real communication. Since Milton has no faith, Ella's words are no comfort. Though the two live almost in each other's pockets, there is little genuine dialogue between them. In the society portrayed, black and white live, as Styron has written of his own upbringing, "firmly walled off from each other."[8] Whatever the black discourse offers, it is between the text and the reader, not between the characters, since the whites, stuck in self-imposed sorrows like "flies in amber" (32), are deaf to any voices but their own.

Overall, then, the novel's opening holds a combination of despairing confusion and disjunctive voices. With memories of previous attempts to find personal or social harmony, the characters will pursue the goal once again. But Peyton is dead, and it is a doomed effort for Milton and Helen. Their reminiscences chronicle a growing failure that is confirmed, near the end, by Milton's attempt to strangle Helen before disappearing into the rain. Preoccupied by their own sorrows, they have used Maudie and Peyton as weapons in a fight. Between Milton's evasions and Helen's control, their attempts to unify the family, or to come together in bereavement, will have all collapsed.

The novel traces the growing conflicts between Milton, Helen, and Peyton, mostly through the parents' memories of the family's life.

7. See King, *A Southern Renascence*, 35–37.

8. William Styron, "Social Animal of Manic Gusto," *Observer*, December 6, 1987, p. 10.

Framed by the funeral—a last attempt to affirm order where there is confusion—the portrayed struggle builds in the main around five recollected attempts to "hold together the formal things" (159): during a family Sunday, on Peyton's sixteenth birthday, at Christmas two years later, at a college football game, and at Peyton's wedding. Each time, Milton and Helen try to uphold the structures that give family life coherence, yet because of conflicting interests they each time end undermining what they seek to uphold.

Just as the parents in their reminiscences attempt to reassess the past and discover mental harmony, so, within the recollected episodes, the characters try to build up the structures of decorum. At the same time, however, their differing attitudes undermine the verbal and social unity they seek. Each of the five events recalled in the novel is more structured than the one before it, and in each the failures of the characters grow more conspicuous.

The traditional structures offer the momentary illusion of family unity. But the underlying clash of language always reveals in advance the centripetal and centrifugal forces that will thwart the effort. In the first recollection, when Peyton is aged nine, both Milton's and Helen's language reveals their attempts to ensure family harmony. Helen insists on family tradition: they have, she says, "got to go to church" on Sunday (53). Milton corrects Peyton when she wants the newspaper comics, making her say, "let me," instead of, "gimme," and he reminds her of family hierarchy: "children," he tells her, "should respect their parents" (47). The way Helen's and Milton's attitudes conflict, however, ensures that harmony will not prevail.

Despite ostensible attempts to unify the family, Milton's main role on this remembered Sunday is centrifugal. In contrast to the desperation that prompts his reflections, here he has a Faustian confidence. Feeling secure enough to boast that he will live "any goddam way" he pleases, he pokes fun at the pieties of traditional family life (54). The trouble is that when he mocks Ella's faith, Pookie's stupidity, and Helen's drive for order, he has nothing he wants to put in their place. Much of his mockery has institutional Christianity as its target. When Helen says the family must go to church, the deliberate joke in his reply "Church? Oh yes. Hell" (50) degrades his positive answer. Helen's stress is on "propriety" (94), and his mocking what she cherishes contributes to the breakdown of dialogue. The breakdown is foreshadowed by her literal failure to hear his decision not to go.

"What—"
  "No church—" he began again.
  "What—" she seemed to say. (50–51)

Milton's attitude is similarly revealed in his parodying of Ella's language. "Here's looking at you, Ella," he teases.

"Ain't nobody lookin at me," she snuffled, "leas'wise not today. Know who's lookin at you, though. Good Lawd's lookin down, He says, 'I am de troof and the way and de life,' good Lawd's sayin. . . ."
  "All right, Ella," he said. "That's fine. That's fine. No sermons. Leas'wise not today . . . for Christ's sake," he added deliberately, smiling. (51)

Mimicking her diction, Milton enjoys making fun of the Christian discourse that is insincere on the lips of Helen but sincere on Ella's. The novel hardly upholds conventional Christian morality: Carey Carr, its representative, is ineffectual and unsure of his own faith. But Christian morality furnishes one among the several discourses dialogized in a novel that seeks on all levels to compose conflicting discourses in the interest of harmony. The closest Milton comes to Ella's spiritual harmony is through alcohol, which lends him—in a no less borrowed diction—a "state of palmy beatitude," a "misty Eden" (55) where his surroundings "take on the quality of perfection" (51).

"Alongside the centripetal forces," Bakhtin asserts, "the centrifugal forces of language carry on their uninterrupted work."[9] Milton, secure in his family life, indulges himself in ways that undermine his security. If at the start of the novel he strives to rediscover verbal coherence, in this remembered scene he plays with language's centrifugal potential. He further compromises the fragile harmony of this family Sunday when he introduces the outsiders Pookie and, especially, Dolly, the ideal receptor for Milton's verbal games since she has "always identified him with talk, speech" (71). But if his knack for twisting "words into grotesque parodies of themselves" (71) impresses Dolly, on the whole his activities betray a lack of the underlying beliefs that are needed to give language meaning.

9. Bakhtin, *The Dialogic Imagination*, 272.

After the tenuous harmony of this family Sunday is utterly destroyed, the brunt of Helen's wrath is borne by Peyton. Helen slaps her for helping tie up Maudie, and calls her a "little devil" (63). The epithet is in keeping with Helen's general tendency to label Peyton rather than let her develop her own identity. Not inaccurately, Helen and Milton blame each other for the day's events: though Helen's determination to impose order is a cover for the "infirmity and disorder" (65) suggested by her room, Milton's mockery has played its part as well.

The second recollection is Helen's. All seems well again as Peyton's sixteenth birthday party looms. But a party harbors both the centripetal and the centrifugal. It is a form of carnival, in which otherwise suppressed, dissenting tendencies are allowed, for a while at least, to undermine the normal hierarchies. So it can be seen as either a safety valve for hierarchical pressures or an opportunity for subversion—as an excuse to release centrifugal impulses or a means of containing such forces in a governable sphere. Moreover, a sixteenth birthday party combines traditional forms with youthful rebellion, marking in some states and in Britain, for example, arrival at the age of consent.

While Milton drinks and flirts, Helen is intent, it is clear, on verbally and socially containing events. The laughter and music "splintering the air" fill her "with anxiety" (80). If, in the first recollection, Milton undermines family harmony, here Helen is its destroyer. She tries to end the party and threatens to take Peyton home. Purportedly, this is for drinking, but the threat really springs from her jealousy over Milton's flirting, and from Peyton's enjoyment of youth.

"Your father gave that to you, didn't he?"

"Yes," Peyton said meekly. "He said that for my birthday—" She was beautiful, she was young, and these two things together caused Helen the bitterest anguish.

"I won't have it," she said. "I've seen your father ruin himself with liquor and I won't have it. Do you understand?"

Although she tries to cut off Peyton's explanation, Peyton finally gets her word in. "I despise you!" she says (82)—the first sign of her conscious attempt to be heard. But since she is still young enough to control, Milton and Helen are able to avoid violent or prolonged conflict. They agree to "be ladies and gentlemen" (94), so outward decorum is restored. The family unity, however, is further undermined, and tension increases.

The pattern of centripetal and centrifugal interaction recurs in scenes between those in the primary recollections. Soon after the party, Helen is gardening, caught up in tasks that help her feel "rooted to something firm and substantial" (121). She thinks about future reconciliation, when she and Milton will be "old but happy" and Peyton will love her. But, lost in thought, she slices a "pomegranate root right in two" (122). Alongside the centripetal forces, the "uninterrupted" movement toward disunity indeed continues, as Bakhtin affirms.

Tension increases in the Christmas reminiscence, with Peyton aged eighteen. More than ever, Helen seeks to "pick up those fallen pieces" and unify the family with the "decorous masonry" (115) of a traditional family occasion. But Peyton's self-assertion now threatens to negate Helen's unifying discourse. Helen has spent days "fixing things up" (155) for Christmas, but Peyton arrives wanting to go to a party. Helen's struggle to envelop Peyton in the family, and the collapse of her discourse at Peyton's challenge, are distilled in a short scene relayed to us through Milton, with Peyton's voice—now that she clearly is wielding it—ironically absent:

Helen had said, Peyton you must stay home. Had said, Christmas Eve is no time for parties, Peyton dear: Uncle Edward is here, you and Dick stay downstairs and I'll get up and get Maudie dressed and we'll all have a nice party right here. We'll open all the presents. . . .

No, then? No? Oh, you've promised? (Sinking back onto the pillow.) All right, all right, have it your way then. (Turning to look at her for a moment, bitterly, then gazing away at the ceiling, perhaps with her breath now coming in long, pained gasps, or then again, naturally and easily, being mistress of her emotions.) All right then. I guess your father thinks it's all right. Go out, do what you want then. (162)

Helen begins in the role of the caring mother, but always uppermost is her determination to impose social order. She combines "we'll all have a nice party" with "Peyton you must stay home. . . . Christmas Eve is no time for parties." Even the first of these comments, expressed as a statement not an option, contains in the word *we* an attempt to bring Peyton's dissenting voice within a unitary discourse.

We should take into account that this is Milton's perhaps unfair reconstruction. Certainly his own limited insight is evident; we know that Helen is *not* "mistress of her emotions" from her recent confrontation with Dolly, whose spirited response to Helen's challenge leads quickly to Helen's distraught recognition of "how disordered she had become" (137). But the pattern remains. Christmas Day itself is "pure hell" (163), with Helen ignoring Peyton's attempts at dialogue. Milton's jaunty mockery gives way to bleak parody. At dinner, which is eaten "under a fog of hostility," Helen imposes a militaristic order in which, thinks Milton, all is "present, accounted for" (168). Helen still strives for unity through family tradition, dusting off Maudie's xylophone "to tie together the passing years," but instead of producing harmony, the "insipid knocking notes" only echo the domestic and social discord—the "inept clashing of pots and pans," and the "undertone of furious, obsessed whisperings" (166). The day ends with Peyton running out and Milton trying to comfort her, but the situation is exacerbated by his more overt sexual interest. "Fascinated and confused" (165), he has earlier watched her undress until she shouted at him to leave. From now on, Peyton must escape not only her mother's attempts to mold her but also her father's smothering love.

The fourth memory, of the football game, is marked by a further increase in Milton's desire for Peyton, and her more desperate attempts to escape his perverse love and Helen's bitter hatred. With Maudie critically ill in the hospital, Milton is lured to the fraternity house in his search for Peyton, and then to the game, and he gets drunker than ever. Like the birthday party, the traditional festivities accompanying the game are as fraught with centrifugal forces as they outwardly suggest ritualistic coherence. But the episode also reveals a drastic change in Milton's mood. With his drinking beyond control and family unity near to lost, his once carefree, centrifugal voice is genuinely striving for order: "It occurred to him first, prime and foremost (*order, order,* he found himself pleading) that he was not properly articulating" (209). "Out of place" amid the "waves of laughter" that compete with the phonograph and the "persistent off-beat" of the piano (198), Milton meets Pookie. He tries to maintain a polite decorum, but—whisky bottle crashing and spilling across the floor—he insults him instead. Images of disorder flooding out of containing structures abound.

At the game itself, still searching for Peyton, Milton evinces his struggle for order in the way he collects paraphernalia, including a "container of coffee," a program, whisky, a "pillow he had rented," an umbrella, an "orange badge," and a "huge banner" (206). He gains limited insight into the "apathy" (209) that has led to his plight, and his vain struggle against a current he initiated is at least marked by a renewed effort of will: "I *will* become sober" (191), "I will be strong" (213). But he also reaches the despairing realization that, in his goal of an "indissoluble, perfect" union with Peyton, he has "expected too much" (215).

The emptiness of Peyton's borrowed language, when Milton does find her, confirms the failure of her search for an identity beyond the roles imposed by her parents. She asks "darling" Milton what he is "trying to *convey*" (215). That her classmates also now label her— "The Body!" "Lover!" (198–99)—underlines the failure. The shattered family is briefly reunited when Milton and Peyton join Helen and Maudie at the hospital. But the reunion's emphasis is on the memory of what is now "beyond recovery" (225). Helen uses the occasion to accuse rather than reconcile. More "rigid and tense and exact" than ever, she asserts her separation from Milton and Peyton (217). "I'm the only one that knows," she says of Maudie's illness (193). If the family is "made briefly whole" (225), the unity is only one of art, foreshadowing further collapse.

But the family can make one last stab at reconciliation. Peyton marries Harry Miller, the artist she thinks can bring her world into coherence in much the way he aims to harmonize his own through painting. The wedding her parents give her is the most ornately developed of the traditional structures relied upon to unite the family, so its collapse is all the more cataclysmic. All the ingredients for disaster—Milton's drinking, his love for Peyton, Peyton's recognition of her mother's facade, her own determination to speak out—combine, and the wedding disintegrates like the cake itself. With "golden insides exposed" and "white frosting crumbling," the bride's cake looks like a "snow-covered mountain" that has had "one slope blown away by dynamite" (287).

Before the wedding, Carey Carr sees "promise of improvement, if not of perfection" (246), in the apparent changes in Helen and Milton.

Milton, for his part, feels that, having given up Dolly and drink, he has at last found a "state of tranquility" (253). Both thus look forward to a ceremony that Carey sees as the "symbolic affirmation of a moral order" (248). But what they witness is just an "illusion of serenity" (266). Helen wants Milton back only "to watch him plead and grovel" (273). She has "falsified her true feelings" so as to appear a "successful mother" who has "brought together the broken family" (274). Seemingly having lost the battle for her own coherence, she struggles all the harder to affix labels and impose external order. Peyton herself is now a fully dissenting voice. She shatters Milton's hopes for reconciliation by saying that she knows Helen is a "faker . . . flaunting the blissful family" (268) and by insisting that Milton himself not "smother" her (267). Refusing to be "part of the spirit of the day," she begins "to destroy it," determined finally to escape Helen's thinly masked hatred and Milton's "jealous tenderness" (270). The episode ends with her using her fingernails on Helen's cheeks and with Milton, once more drunkenly inarticulate, insulting Harry and calling Helen a "monshter" (312).

Milton's journey to the despair we see at the start of the novel reveals a shift in his language from centrifugal parody to centripetal desperation. He begins as a "spendthrift with words" (254), mocking structures of suburban life and turning, in his apparent security, to womanizing and alcohol. But as the structures he helps undermine go into collapse, he begins to strive centripetally to reorder his world, recover family unity, and rediscover "ar-tic-u-la-shun" (209). His conflicts with Helen, however, turn him toward Peyton, whom he smothers with love. Peyton says to him, "You'd love me half to death if you could" (268), which in effect he does. Helen's "*loathing*" (274) drives Peyton the rest of the way. For the more "haywire" (238) Helen becomes, the more she tries to reorder, suppressing her own feelings and attempting to suppress the dissenting voices of others. With Peyton dead and the individual reminiscences of Milton and Helen at an end, Milton tries to strangle Helen, before stumbling out of sight. So each parent ends the novel, literally and verbally, with "nothing" (389).

Throughout, Peyton is caught up in her parents' struggle. Her attempts at self-assertion are at the heart of their failure to find long-standing personal or family harmony of the kind they strive for. If her death is determining in that her funeral frames the novel, her absent viewpoint helps distance her from the often cartoonlike activities of those around her, adding poignancy and a tragic quality to her fate. No one lets her voice be heard. She is desperate not only for a hearing but also for an identity not imposed. Fastened down by Helen, smothered by Milton, and labeled by her friends, she pretentiously uses the "tones of Tallulah Bankhead" (163), and when she tells "darling" Milton in her "new sprightly voice" that she has the "vastest capacity ever" (164), it is partly adolescent role playing but also part of her struggle to discover a new identity. That she ends up dying naked and unidentified and being buried in Potter's Field, an island reserved for the "nameless" New York dead (327), might be taken either as the measure of her failure or as a final ironic image of shedding all the roles and voices imposed or adopted.

When, in her monologue near the end, we at last hear her voice at some length, it has become confused and largely incoherent, as in the letter Milton could not finish reading. What comes across is less her assertion of freedom—after all, the novel's opening tells us that she dies—than her lack of direction and her entrapment in the discourses she seeks to escape. As in the letter, her disordered mind is reflected in a struggle to retain syntactic order. If the ultraformal "I stopped brushing my hair, for I was angry" (343) betrays her through overcompensation, elsewhere she fails totally: "I wanted to cry. This mustn't" (345). Striving for coherence, she borrows a range of verbal forms in search of her own: the language of fairy tales, in "Yet *alas*, and I knew *alas* for it was what they said in the fairy books" (363); literary language in the form of Dante, Browne, Dickinson, and others; Ella's idiom, as in "the rest I disremember, as Ella used to say" (362); and even an "English accent" (349).

Indeed, her monologue is really a heteroglossia of the voices and attitudes of others. Although the shift into her monologue takes us into what Bakhtin would term a new chronotype—a new time-space unity—she is forever "drowning" (348) in voices from other contexts, including that of Port Warwick (348). Her mother's diction is especially evident. Just as Helen and Milton are briefly reconciled when Helen decides he does "understand" her and has, she says, "learned what I need" (256), so Peyton tells Harry he has "never understood" her (381) and talks of her "need," not love, for him (320). If her cast of speech is Helen's, so is her attitude. As Harry says, Peyton is partly a "Helen with her obsessions directed in a different way" (353). Peyton remembers how she once "cried out voiceless" (362) when Helen shut her in a room. In her monologue, suffused with Helen's locutions, there is still no coherent voice properly hers.

Her choice of Harry as partner is connected with her search. She recognizes that he, at least, has found the kind of coherent identity she lacks. Having apparently managed to digest other voices and find his own, he is *"right* inside" (263). Peyton buys the alarm clock believing that they can "coast among the bolts and springs and ordered ticking wheels, riveted to peace forever" (345). That Harry is an artist is of the essence, since art, for Peyton, is one of the few ways to find harmony— whether through painting, literature, or the "ordered and proper" music of Mozart (344)—and her search for identity is bound up with a struggle for personal and social harmony. The clock's "accomplished harmony" (345) offers what she cannot attain elsewhere and stands less for time than for structure and purpose. It symbolizes the ideal relationship she sees for Harry and herself—a harmony that, like the clock's ticking, will be "perfect and ordered and eternal" (340): "Once I'd had a dream: I was inside a clock. Perfect, complete, perpetual, I revolved about on the mainspring forever, drowsing, watching the jewels and the rubies, the mechanism clicking ceaselessly, all the screws and parts as big as my head, indestructible, shining, my own invention" (335). When Harry criticizes her purchase, her vision collapses. The clock becomes potentially chaotic, "he and I crushed and ruined amid all the fiercely disordered, brutally slashing levers and wheels" (375).

All else failing, she translates death itself into a vision of harmony: "Will I not rise again at another time and stand on the earth clean and incorruptible?" (358). Through a Christian discourse of resurrection, she links death with cleansing, and dies believing that "all souls must go down before ascending upward" (385) and expecting to wake in a "far, fantastic dawn" (382). But always her efforts toward wholeness are frustrated. She envisions her self "all shattered" (386) after her fall, but she is already verbally broken. Like the "flightless birds" who she thinks "have suffered without soaring" (386), she cannot take flight and escape the way Stephen Dedalus envisions doing in *Portrait of the Artist*. Despite her vision of falling "toward paradise" (386), she makes no verbal headway. If her comment early in her monologue "I don't have enough time" (335) echoes Harry's "I don't have much time" (377), her final word, *must*, echoes both Milton's struggle to reorder his world and Helen's authoritarian "must be proper" (386). To the very end, Peyton remains engulfed by the voices of others.

Although the major characters fail to attain personal or social reconciliation, the novel is artistically organized from discord toward harmony. That design is partly effected through the minor characters, such as Maudie, Carey Carr, Ella, La Ruth, and Harry Miller, and it is advanced by the primitive religion of Daddy Faith's revival meeting. If Peyton is talking of a friend called Laura when she says that "maybe the key to happiness" is "being sort of dumb" (39), she might as easily have been speaking about Maudie. During the family's confrontations, Maudie alone remains "tranquil and unmoved" (83). Her wordless meeting with Bennie, who knows the "secret heart of this girl" he has "never even spoken to" (223), offers Maudie "understanding," says Helen, a "lover, father, magic—something" that, however momentary, is more genuine than anything the other three can know (225).

Not unlike the Loftis family, Carey Carr struggles to find certainty and stability. A failed poet who once wrote "a sonnet a day" (106), he looks to religion for the cohering power he has encountered in art. But he still suffers because he cannot "attain a complete vision of God" (107), and he is, at base, inadequate as a clergyman, "tongue-tied in the presence of those stricken by grief" (108). He resorts to his creative aptitude, such as it is, to bolster himself against uncertainty. Unsure "of the worth of his judgments," he quotes "imaginary sources to lend an air of authority" (126). Where he differs from the Loftises is in his selflessness. With Milton and Helen, he is most of all concerned to "bring her and him together again" (109). That they both end the novel with the word *nothing* may reflect his inadequacy as much as theirs, but he at least has found a degree of personal stability by directing his efforts outward. As Shaun V. O'Connell writes, however incomplete Carey's vision, "he finds himself a meaningful life."[10]

10. Shaun V. O'Connell, "Expense of Spirit: The Vision of William Styron," *Critique*, VIII (1965–66), 24.

Like the black spectators at the start, Ella and La Ruth counterbalance by their comments the melodramatic suffering of Helen and Milton. Ella has her say on the remembered Sunday. La Ruth first appears as a "huge, slovenly Negro" with an "air of constant affliction" (56), but her dignity surpasses anything Helen displays. Helen may try to prevent true dialogue—interrupting La Ruth's commiserations with the command to "go get me a glass of cold water" (144)—but La Ruth's revelation that she has lost "two of her three children" (144) puts Helen's grieving in perspective. Ella and La Ruth speak in behalf of spiritual, mental, and social harmony. Like Carey, they try to restore family harmony. La Ruth pleads with Helen that "Mama says dat ain't right. 'Take him back,' she says" (148). Like everyone else's efforts to hold the family together, theirs too fail, but they themselves find personal harmony in their religious faith.

Styron uses the black discourse—rather obviously echoing the end of *Soldiers' Pay*—to suggest that personal and social harmony is still possible.[11] After Peyton's monologue, the novel ends with Ella and La Ruth at the revival meeting. If Styron here falls into primitive stereotypes pitting simplicity against neurotic sophistication, he avoids offering the blacks' faith as ideal, by suggesting that Daddy Faith and Gabriel may be less than they appear. Had Daddy Faith "been white, he might have been mistaken for a senator" (396), and his announcer, Gabriel, has eyes that suggest "arrogance and contempt" (395), presumably for the naïveté he exploits. Nevertheless, Ella's eyes reflect "a perfect peace, a transcendent understanding" (396), and La Ruth's belief in Daddy Faith, unlike Carey Carr's in God, is held "with every part of her soul" (144–45). In contrast to Milton, Peyton, and Helen, they find a father figure whose word, as Styron portrays it, seems adequate to their needs. The voices of both Daddy Faith and Gabriel offer a sense of wholeness that the three main characters do not share in. Gabriel's "orotund, massive, absolute" voice has a "quality of roundness that was the roundness of the infinite" (394), and Daddy Faith's voice and gestures are "in perfect harmony" (397).

The affirmation we witness here stands side by side with the negation at the end of the Loftises' story, sustaining the movement toward

11. See William Faulkner, *Soldiers' Pay* (New York, 1926), 318–19.

harmony. With the train rumbling nearer, Ella whirls about, "finger upraised to the sky," and cries out, "Yes Jesus! I seen him! Yeah! Yeah!" Her voice is "almost drowned out" by the train, but her affirmations compete successfully with its roar (400). The suppressed black voices finally are dominant. There is still a clash between the human voices and the train's "clatter" (400), echoing the struggle of voices against the noisy mechanisms of the novel's opening. But these later voices, far from being fragmented or despairing, make defiant affirmations— helped along by the narrator's religious imagery. The night into which the train speeds is offset by both the human fellowship and the air "of expectancy and hope" (391) of the revival meeting.

Peyton's husband, Harry, models yet another route toward harmony. An artist, he also constitutes a transition to the next level of competing voices, that of the author's against his literary forebears'. Like the other minor characters, Harry countervails the failures of the main characters. When Peyton dies, it is he who exhumes her body and assures a decent burial. If she and her parents are torn by inner conflicts, Harry is "*right* inside," and if Carey, having failed to become a poet, has inner doubts about the vocation he has chosen, Harry will, Peyton believes, "be a great painter someday" (263).

Harry turns to art to order existence. He becomes an onlooker who, like Stephen Dedalus, adheres to a religion of art: "I don't know what good it'll do anyone but me, but I want to paint and paint and paint because I think that some agony is upon us. Call me a disillusioned innocent, a renegade Red, or whatever, but I want to crush in my hands all that agony and make beauty come out, because that's all that's left, and I don't have much time—" (377). A young artist like Styron at the time, Harry is also a survivor whose viewpoint is never undercut. No one questions his choice of art over people or his notion that art is about a movement toward harmony. He thus seems to hold the young Styron's own view of the artist as excluding social relations so as to devote himself to beauty. Harry's rationale is that because he does not have "much time" he must paint not just to record the "agony" but "to crush" it all "and make beauty come out." He takes art to be centripetally occupied in forcing chaotic events into artistic shape. An artist, in his view, can retreat into art as a transcendent form of harmony and so stand apart from society, pursuing art for its own sake. Peyton thinks that Harry's painting of an "old man," of "an ancient monk, or a rabbi" who lifts "proud, tragic eyes toward heaven" amid a "landscape dead and forlorn" (374), is a portrait of Harry himself. It is a vision of the heroic dignity of the isolated artist who, monklike or rabbilike, upholds the religion of art as the only effective tool for ordering a chaotic world.

The suggestion is that Harry succeeds where the main characters fail. Shutting himself off from society and from Peyton's troubles, he can create harmony through art. This is just the view Stingo starts with in *Sophie's Choice* and that the older narrator satirizes. For it is a view Styron rejected as his career developed, his novels entered historical arenas, and their political implications became clear. In the second "storey" of *Lie Down in Darkness* we have a balance between Peyton's failing to find her own identity and Harry's availing himself of art as the only way outside of idiocy or naïveté—as Styron then thought—of moving toward personal harmony. That harmony is the end to pursue is barely questioned despite Helen's experience. On Harry and Peyton rest the centripetal and centrifugal impulses warring in Styron himself as he strived both to create order through art and to wrench free of his predecessors in gaining his own voice.

Peyton and *Styron:* a phonetic connection is obvious, and indeed Peyton's struggle indirectly parallels that of Styron, the young novelist; her search for identity is analogous to his search for a literary voice. On examining the author's struggle, it becomes evident that the novel is less a unified work than an unfinalized, layered conflict of discourses involving the personality of Styron's supposedly objective narrator as he seeks to appropriate but also circumscribe the voices of his modernist precursors, to redirect their legacy and so find the path of his own career.

Styron has spoken of how he tried to avoid writing a "young first novel" and sought to avoid the trap of autobiography by effacing the *I* who edits and narrates the story.[12] At first glance, he succeeds; the narrator seems to fit Joyce's ideal of the "invisible" artist, "indifferent, paring his fingernails" while the story unfolds.[13] But on a closer look,

12. Conversation, Roxbury, Conn., April, 1988.
13. James Joyce, *Portrait of the Artist as a Young Man* (1916; rpr. London, 1985), 195.

the narrator shows himself to be a young man—really a Stingo-like young Styron—who tries to compose a harmony of voices from the conflicts of the start. That he is young and male is shown in several details during the train travel opening the novel, not least in his expectation that on arriving "you" will be met not by your children, wife, or husband but by "your girl or your friends" (11). The supposedly objective, effaced voice of narration is quickly revealed to be no such thing.

The narrator's general identity alerts us to the likely centripetal shaping that a close reading confirms. That is most evident in the portrayal of Helen, who for whatever reasons is portrayed with much less sympathy than Milton. By the end she is the crazy mother, erecting a formal sense of order to hide the "little hatreds" (111) that culminate in her "loathing" of Peyton (286). Identification with her is sure to lessen once she tells Carey that he should "die of shame" for conspiring with "that little whore" Peyton (300) and after we observe her alone "clutching her throat with nerveless fingers in a spasm of soundless, hysterical laughter" (273). We come to see her as the true destroyer who drives Milton to drink and to the comfort of Dolly. As her views grow more extreme, we are swayed in the direction the narrator wishes.

The problem is that for this to happen Styron contorts the story to make Helen's failings stand out while largely suppressing other possible explanations of the events. Given Milton's general irresponsibility in the name of living "any goddam way I please" (54), the reader is likely to begin with more sympathy for Helen. So a chasm develops between the narrator's—and some of the characters'—condemnation of Helen and the reader's awareness that Helen has more of a case than we get to hear.

The novel leaves clear that Helen's disposition is linked to Milton's activities, but it tends to favor scenes with details that load the case against her. She does become unreasonable and destructive, but to ensure that portrait of her, Styron not only resorts to having her laugh alone but also has others confirm her guilt in events that, if we look elsewhere, largely begin with Milton. Carey, for instance, emphasizes that Helen "would make no concessions. Which was bad, wrong" (141). When reconciliation seems possible, his focus is again on her failings: "I can't understand why . . . he would stay with her," says Carey. "I wouldn't, I know. As a husband" (248). Such comments fuel the idea that Helen is unbearable to live with, which may be so but is only part of the story. No one offers quite so unqualified a comment about what it might be like to live with a womanizing lush. Here and elsewhere, Styron steers the text so that the stress falls heaviest on Helen's failure to "compromise." The question left begging is, Why should she? Why is it any more "bad, wrong" for Helen not to make concessions than for Milton?

A prime example of such narrative manipulation occurs in a passage we saw earlier, in the straightforward explication of the text. "Your father gave that to you, didn't he?" says Helen.

> "Yes," Peyton said meekly. "He said that for my birthday—" *She was beautiful, she was young, and these two things together caused Helen the bitterest anguish.*
>
> "I won't have it," she said. "I've seen your father ruin himself with liquor and I won't have it. Do you understand?" (82; my italics)

Note the clash between the characters' dialogue and the narrator's judgment, in the unconvincing attempt to sway the reader. Helen's point is not unreasonable, but the narrator's suggestion that her motives are a jealous desire to curb her daughter's fun directs the reader away from the legitimate issue—Milton's drinking—to reinforce our sense of Helen's personal limitations. Elsewhere the narrator, Carey, Dolly, and Milton all imply that Helen has driven Milton to Dolly, though the evidence is that that is not so. When, for example, Milton hears of Peyton's death, he walks straight past Dolly to be comforted by Sylvia Mason. Milton, as the text shows despite itself, does not want Dolly for comfort and is not driven to her by Helen's coldness, at least not initially; her coldness stems, in part anyway, from his drinking and chasing Dolly.

The issue here is not moral but textual. The novel has internal contradictions arising from prejudiced orchestration by Styron's ostensibly objective narrator. As a result, gaps appear between his implicit judgments and the reader's view of events. Beneath a convincing veneer, there is a distinct young male personality betraying at times a less neutral voice than his masquerade pretends, one insinuating the idea that Helen's breakdown is worse than Milton's dipsomania. Prejudice is also evident in the portrayal of Pookie and Dolly as members of a lower, and unliterary, class. The narrator's mockery of their common man-gling of Frost's meter—Pookie's version of Dolly's version: "Where'er you walk I'll think of you because there are miles more for both of us before we go to sleep" (203)—smacks of Stingo's disdain for the "club-footed syntax" of the manuscripts he reviews in *Sophie's Choice*.[14] Lit-erary language receives preferences in this highly literary novel. But that is unsurprising, for the novel is partly about its author's struggle against youthful prejudices as he strives to assert his voice amid others but, above all, somewhat paradoxically, tries to avoid detection.

Revealed, however, as a personality who shapes the story he tells, he has an effect, like Harry's, that is mostly centripetal. He guides the various voices but also engages in a battle to mute or reaccentuate voices that exist in a world beyond the characters, where he skirts, parries, plays on, and alludes to writers who influence him. Styron's struggle and Peyton's, similar but on different levels, mingle in Pey-ton's cry that the Lost Generation "weren't lost. What they were doing was losing us" (235). If Peyton struggles against her parental legacy, Styron struggles against a literary one.

The obvious question is whether Styron succeeds where Peyton fails. That *Lie Down in Darkness* is highly derivative is well docu-mented. There are multiple echoes of modernist writers, especially Faulkner. From *The Sound and the Fury* alone the characters of Dilsey and Benjy are redrafted as Ella and Maudie. Peyton owes something to both Quentin and Caddy Compson—and her alarm clock to Quentin's watch. Faulknerian themes of guilt, time, and incest have all been ap-parent to critics. Peyton, whose funeral is at the center of the novel's structure, is, like Addie Bundren—or Caddy, in Richard Gray's words—a Faulknerian "absent presence."[15] The black revival meeting echoes the end of *Soldiers' Pay*. Other southern voices are also audible. Like Carson McCullers' characters, the hearts in *Lie Down in Darkness* are lonely hunters, and the understanding, silent form of Bennie is a ver-sion of John Singer. The opening derives from Robert Penn Warren's *All the King's Men*, and the exiled, alienated Peyton, like Thomas

---

14. William Styron, *Sophie's Choice* (New York, 1979), 5.

15. Richard Gray, *Writing the South: Ideas of an American Region* (New York, 1986), 209. Gray sees Peyton as "modeled on Temple Drake in *Sanctuary*" (*The Litera-ture of Memory: Modern Writers of the American South* [London, 1977], 289).

Wolfe's protagonists Eugene Gant and George Webber, can't go home again. Nor are the voices only southern or American. If the parties spill over from F. Scott Fitzgerald, Peyton's final burst is Joycean, and the interweaving of viewpoint is reminiscent of Virginia Woolf's *To the Lighthouse*. As pervasive as any influence is that of, in Mary Ann Caws's phrase, the "proto-Modernist" Gustave Flaubert.[16] As we will see, the rhythm of yearning and disintegration, the repetition of social structures, and the seriocomic characters that help condemn the heroine to suicide all owe something to *Madame Bovary*.

Derivation is evident not only in structure, characterization, and theme but also in the novel's diction. Just as Peyton's final monologue is shot through with others' voices, so Styron teeters on the edge of others' phrases, occasionally getting wet. The description of dust clouds "spread against the sky" is only one word off T. S. Eliot's *Prufrock*, and when Peyton talks of a "land lost to me, unvisited, irretrievable," where, "bulbs hung at every landing and around them, as if borne back ceaselessly to the light of their beginning, fluttered a cloud of moths" (385), Fitzgerald's phrase "borne back ceaselessly" occurs in the same breath in which Gatsby's irretrievable dream is evoked, a dream that focuses on the green bulb at the end of Daisy's different kind of landing. Peyton's monologue is, on another level, dialogic, with her yearning for an irretrievable past simultaneously Styron's anxious pastiche of Fitzgerald. This kind of thing is frequent in the novel, with the voices of Fitzgerald and Faulkner in particular.[17] If lines between pastiche, allusion, and plagiarism are hard to draw, a conscious if anxious flirtation with other literary voices is nevertheless apparent in the novel.

Melvin J. Friedman and Marc L. Ratner judge *Lie Down in Darkness* a form of pastiche, a characterization that fits with the idea that it is partly about trying to deal with modernist influences. Styron does

16. Mary Ann Caws, "Gestures Toward the Self—Representing the Body in Modernism: Cloaking, Remembering, and the Elliptical Effect," in *Modernism: Challenges and Perspectives*, ed. Monique Chefdor, Richard Quinones, and Albert Watchel (Urbana, Ill., 1986), 238.

17. See T. S. Eliot, "The Love Song of J. Alfred Prufrock," in *Selected Poems* (1954; rpr. London, 1961), 11. As examples of a Faulknerian idiom, consider *tableau* (93) and *vanquished* (288).

seem deliberately to draw attention to the voices of others: the enlargement of Quentin's watch into Peyton's alarm clock suggests the urgency of the struggle for him. He baldly borrowed Fitzgerald's technique of the guest list, and Helen and Milton's recuperative week takes place in, of all places, Wolfe's Asheville. But Styron has asserted, "I never knew what the hell I was up to," throwing his preconsideration into question.[18]

The author's intertextual concerns have a bearing on how some passages are read. Seen purely in the context of the story, Peyton's view that the Lost Generation were "losing us" has to do with her attempt to escape the influences of others and ignores the different levels on which the remark can have meaning. John W. Aldridge goes so far as to say that it is a direct authorial comment. He cites the passage in accusing Styron of having a "derivative imagination." Given Aldridge's intertextual emphasis, his thinking is worth understanding:

> [Peyton's] remark is appealing, of course, not only because it is Fitzgeraldian, although one cannot discount the immensely pleasurable effects produced when a novel reminds the reader, regardless of his age, of emotions he got from books earlier in his life but which he despaired of ever getting from books again. It is also appealing because it seems to offer a simple and familiar explanation for much that is opaque and confused in the motivation of the Loftis family. In fact, it seems to represent an effort, however uncalculated, to replace that motivation with a romantic reading of the old *Zeitgeist* theory of human behavior, in much the same way that the Faulknerian overtones of the style seem to represent an effort to replace it with dark intimations of ancestral blood-guilt and transcendent damnation. For the remark appears to suggest that the Loftises are tragic and lost not merely for psychological reasons but because they are victims of the moral breakdown supposedly suffered by the Lost Generation.[19]

But, claims Aldridge, however lyrical the style, "the *Geist* in this case as clearly belongs to another *Zeit* as the style belongs to another man."

---

18. Appendix conversations, 217. On pastiche, see Melvin J. Friedman, *William Styron: An Interim Appraisal* (Bowling Green, Ohio, 1974), 2; and Marc L. Ratner, *William Styron* (Boston, 1972), 19. Both Friedman and Ratner refer to J. D. Scott's comments in "New Novels," *New Statesman and Nation*, April 19, 1952, pp. 472–73.

19. John W. Aldridge, *The Devil in the Fire: Retrospective Essays on American Literature and Culture, 1951–1971* (New York, 1972), 207.

In his view, the "middlebrow reading public" warmed to Styron's writing because it "sounds like the serious literature they have been taught to admire." One could "easily imagine" Styron's books "as big sprawling houses of language, crammed with antiques passed down to him by beneficent forebears named Wolfe, Faulkner, Fitzgerald, and Hemingway," he maintains. He finds Styron's work a clever melding of the styles of others, containing the "stock situations and emotional stances" that seem valid not "because of their relationship to actual life and observed experience but because of their relationship to past literature." He goes on, "In meeting them again in Styron's work, one has the feeling of having met them before, not necessarily in any specific book, but in the whole of modern literature, the feeling of being on familiar ground without the feeling of having detected a plagiarism."[20]

But Aldridge, caught up in his lyrical flow, misreads a comment made by a distraught young girl as the unqualified opinion of the author, when clearly it is distanced by irony. Peyton is pretentious, romantic, confused, and searching for something to cling to, whether Harry, an alarm clock, or art. Here, Aldridge simply misses the context, and so the point. Unsurprisingly, then, he also fails to consider the possibility that satire, or pastiche, might be involved. Still, inasmuch as Aldridge was writing prior to *The Confessions of Nat Turner*, he had a point. The writer of *Lie Down in Darkness* was obviously trying to find his voice, uneasy about his influences, and he was still seeking direction in what at the time of Aldridge's assessment was his latest novel, *Set This House on Fire*. But Aldridge's conclusion that the influence of other authors made Styron at that stage no more than imitative is unearned. All discourse is derivative; there is no discoverable underived origin, and even if there were, it would not, as Aldridge seems to assume, be with high modernism.

Echoes of other texts are present in any work, surfacing in different ways. If an author has yet to reach literary maturity, the echoes are stronger, as witness the early work, even best work, of both Faulkner and Fitzgerald. Some of Faulkner's own early stories, like "Red Leaves," have the clear imprint of Ernest Hemingway; Joseph L. Blotner, in his biography of Faulkner, talks of the impact of Sherwood An-

20. *Ibid.*, 207, 202, 203, 204.

derson, and Hugh Kenner discusses the "highly 'literary' convention of *The Sound and the Fury*, a book written by a man who had just read *Ulysses*." Fitzgerald, too, aged twenty-one, wrote to a friend that he was writing a novel that had "traces of Tarkington, Chesterton, Chambers, Wells, Benson (Robert Hugh), Rupert Brooke and includes Compton Mackenzie—like love affairs." Even Flaubert had to react to the influence of Balzac.[21] Since all discourse is social and acquired externally, there is no such thing as an entirely self-generative imagination.

A dialogue exists in all literary texts, indeed all utterances, between the author and his precursors. Insights derive from a synthesis of existing ideas, whether it is Marx's use of Hegel, Styron's use of Fitzgerald, Warren, and Faulkner, or even, perhaps, as Styron has wryly noted, Faulkner's use of Styron. Son can influence father, as vice versa. There is, as Styron has remarked, "no formula," only an arena of discourses in which texts cluster.[22] Mature writers shake off crude influence, or grow more cunning in their synthesis of ideas. If anything, originality, so called, involves an explosion of energy out of contact with others' ideas. As Theodor Adorno writes, if nothing new exists under the sun, there are "thousands and thousands of combinations which have never been invented."[23]

So if *Lie Down in Darkness* owes much to *The Sound and the Fury*, the latter also owes much to *Ulysses*, and *The Great Gatsby* to *Heart of Darkness*. The context of novels, as Bakhtin, Bloom, and others say, is, first of all, other novels. "Every age," writes Bakhtin, "reaccentuates in its own the way the works of its most immediate past."[24] Derivation of itself is not distinguishing. On the arena's edge, of course, is Eliot's dictum "Immature poets imitate, mature poets steal."[25] In keeping with the idea of dialogue and synthesis, I suggest that the vital question with *Lie Down in Darkness* is how well it reac-

21. Joseph L. Blotner, *Faulkner: A Biography* (2 vols.; New York, 1974), I, Chaps. 22–23; Hugh Kenner, *A Homemade World: The American Modernist Writers* (London, 1975), 207, 34. Maurice Nadeau talks of Flaubert's debt to Balzac. See his *The Greatness of Flaubert*, trans. Barbara Bray (London, 1972), 135.

22. Appendix conversations, 227.

23. Theodor Adorno, quoted by Anna Balakian in "A Triptych of Modernism: Reverdy, Huidobro, and Ball," in *Modernism*, ed. Chefdor *et al.*, 156–57.

24. Bakhtin, *The Dialogic Imagination*, 421.

25. T. S. Eliot, "Philip Massinger," in *Selected Essays* (London, 1951), 206.

centuates, rather than imitates, the works that clearly influence it. What, in other words, is the overall relationship between *Lie Down in Darkness* and literary modernism? Does Styron, anywhere in this novel, break free?

As Michel Décaudin writes, definitions of modernism present a "confusion worthy of Babel," perhaps because modernism itself is such a heteroglossia. At worst, as Joseph D. Singal argues, modernism may be "too amorphous ever to be susceptible to definition" unless, following Malcolm Bradbury, we acknowledge not *a* modernism at all but "modernisms."[26] Our question can therefore concern only a few threads apparent in some versions of modernism. Even so, it is clear that the fundamental discourse toward harmony in *Lie Down in Darkness* ties it to aspects of high modernism that endow writing with centripetal objectives. M. Pierrette Malcuzynski argues that the stream-of-consciousness technique, in particular, works to contain dialogue so that "everything is ultimately resolved in one single consciousness," and David Murray echoes this in seeing modernism itself as a "series of strategies to contain carnivalization."[27]

Two commentators, Georg Lukács and John Barth, while discussing modernism from different directions, reach similar conclusions. In "The Literature of Replenishment," Barth refers to the modernists' "celebration of private, subjective experience over public experience" and their romantic insistence "on the special, usually alienated role of the artist in his society, or outside it." He couples this with their "fore-grounding of language and technique" at the expense of "traditional 'content,'" suggesting that the "preoccupation" with the artist's alienation leads to accomplishments in technique but also to a "relative difficulty of access." For Barth, modernism lends itself to artistic elitism, in that its subjective experimentation is "at the frequent expense

26. Michel Décaudin, "Being Modern in 1885; or, Variations on 'Modern,' 'Modernism,' *Modernité*," in *Modernism*, ed. Chefdor *et al.*, 25; Joseph D. Singal, "Towards A Definition of American Modernism," *American Quarterly*, XXXIX (1987), 7; Malcolm Bradbury, "The Nonhomemade World: European and American Modernism," *American Quarterly*, XXXIX (1987), 36.

27. M. Pierrette Malcuzynski, "Mikhail Bakhtin and Contemporary Narrative Theory," *University of Ottowa Quarterly*, LIII (1983), 57; David Murray, "Dialogics," in *Literary Theory at Work: Three Texts*, ed. Douglas Tallack (London, 1987), 131.

of democratic access," with the result of a relative unpopularity outside "intellectual circles and university curricula."[28] He sees modernism as incorporating three salient features: a sense of the artist's "special, usually alienated role," a preference for the personal over the public, and an elitism with its own centripetal tendencies. Malcuzynski's and Murray's imputation to modernism of such tendencies is relevant to its elitism, since that facet of modernism is about closing off possibilities for dialogue: the less accessible the work, the fewer the voices capable of challenging it.

Modernism's elitism does not seem to offend Barth, and his own postmodernism takes modernist cerebral experimentation as a starting point. But Lukács' orthodox Marxism leads him, in *The Historical Novel* and *The Meaning of Contemporary Realism*, to view modern writing from Flaubert onward as a deterioration into subjectivism. He thus calls for a return to nineteenth-century realism, a move Barth spurns.[29] The difference between Barth's and Lukács' positions is, however, largely in their evaluation, rather than their description, of modernism. Both perceive in it artistic alienation, a partiality to the private over the public, and an emphasis on the centripetal. Lukács argues that for modernists alienation is a "universal *condition humaine*": "Man, for these writers, is by nature solitary, asocial, unable to enter into relationships with other human beings."[30] Like Barth, he believes that modern writing from Flaubert tends "to make history private," severing "all possible ties between historical events and private destinies" so that the historical events are "no more than a decorative scene." For Lukács, too, the modernist "yearning for harmony" is evasive since it leads to a "withdrawal before the contradictory problems thrown up by life."[31]

28. John Barth, "The Literature of Replenishment," *Atlantic Monthly*, CCCXIIIV (1980), 65–71.

29. "I deplore the artistic and critical cast of mind that repudiates the whole modernist enterprise as an aberration and sets to work as if it hadn't happened" (Barth, "The Literature of Replenishment," 70).

30. Georg Lukács, *The Meaning of Contemporary Realism*, trans. John Mander and Necke Mander (London, 1963), 20.

31. Georg Lukács, *The Historical Novel*, trans. Hannah Mitchell and Stanley Mitchell (1962; rpr. Harmondsworth, Eng., 1981), 237–39; Georg Lukács, *Writer and Critic, and Other Essays*, trans. Arthur Kahn (London, 1978), 89.

Obviously, history or a mythic version of it is crucial for Faulkner, but Barth's and Lukács' observations hold in varying degrees for writers like Joyce, Hemingway, Woolf, and Eliot. They plainly apply to the Styron of *Lie Down in Darkness*, whose characters are solitary and alienated personally—and apparently universally—in justice to what the narrator calls "our strange solitary state" (264). The upholding of art as a way to redirect centrifugal voices toward harmony clearly stems from the modernist emphasis on art as "the one dependable thing,"[32] and from the modernist's in effect religious devotion to art in general. In *Lie Down in Darkness*, Harry is content to mold order through art—retreating into his painting while Peyton kills herself—just as Styron begins and ends the novel with the aesthetically satisfying train travel that brings him and the reader into the churn of events but also safely transports them both out again.

Lie Down in Darkness also exemplifies the modernist separation from history. The characters are isolated from one another, and the novel is about their private activities. The war is seen by Milton as little more than a place to escape to: "If he could get off to war, he thought, get a commission, everything would be solved" (173). As Lukács puts it, "History shimmering colourfully in its distance, remoteness and otherness has the task of fulfilling the intense longing for escape from the present world of dreariness." Harry, true to Lukács' description of the modernist hero, is the "individual retreating into himself in despair at the cruelty of the age."[33] His desire "to crush . . . all that agony and make beauty come out, because that's all that's left," is typically modernist. Art is in this novel a point of order, an end in itself. At the start of Peyton's monologue, which lays stress on her separateness from those around her even as she seeks to escape their voices, her basic wish is *"that my words were now written oh that they were printed in a book. That they were graven with an iron pen and lead in the rock forever"* (335). Harry, by painting her, and Styron, by writing the novel, both oblige her, ordering her chaos through art.

Lie Down in Darkness appears to mesh with the modernist style, structure, language, and preoccupations. But what is important for Sty-

32. Virginia Woolf, *To The Lighthouse* (1927; rpr. New York, 1955), 224.

33. Lukács, *The Historical Novel*, 246; Lukács, *The Meaning of Contemporary Realism*, 38.

ron's later direction is that it is largely because the events recounted are private, in the main divorced from any historical particularity, that the movement toward harmony that Styron pursued confronted him with no apparent problem. The ahistoricity is something he inherited but, since he had yet to find his own subject or voice, he had not so far thought it through. His gradual shift into a historical mode, because of the subjects that truly interested him, was to force him to reexamine the drive toward harmony, until in *Sophie's Choice* it is precisely Stingo's notions of the separation of the artist from society and his idea of personal harmony that are satirized.

Louis D. Rubin, Jr., has cataloged several differences between Styron's first novel and Faulkner's *The Sound and the Fury*, but he offers as the main divergence that "whereas the tragedies of Caddy and Quentin are *dynastic*, not personal," and "are caused by *history*," in *Lie Down in Darkness* "the historical dimension is almost entirely absent." Rubin argues that "the Loftises exist entirely *in the present*" and are involved in "not a community tragedy but a private one." He comments, "There is little sense that what has happened to Milton, Helen, and Peyton Loftis is symbolic of the historic decline and fall of the Tidewater Virginia gentry."[34] In accepting that one major difference between Styron's first novel and Faulkner's plainly influential work is that *Lie Down in Darkness* is personal rather than historical, however, the reader may come to think of the novel as less Faulknerian but as even less a breaking free from modernism or as Styron's own reaccentuation of modernism's themes.

But if *Lie Down in Darkness* is mostly unconcerned with history, where and how the novel does depict it is where the reaccentuation occurs. For in later novels, Styron departs from Faulkner's influence even as historical concerns become more important to his work. Faulkner's novels, though concerned with history, remain predominantly intent on unification. "Faulkner's onward going voice," as Eric Mottram puts it, "holds together the energy of events, which continually threaten to refuse boundary and cause chaos." According to Murray, Faulkner's work reflects "the desire to hold" the various voices "and his fictional world together by a style which overrides these voices and

34. Louis D. Rubin, Jr., "Notes on a Southern Writer in Our Time," in *The Achievement of William Styron*, ed. Robert K. Morris and Irving Malin (Rev. ed.; Athens, Ga., 1981), 70, 81–82.

a myth which contains their history."[35] Faulkner's writing reflects his political conservatism by remaining largely centripetal even while relating to history, whereas Styron's work, which is here predominantly centripetal and concerned with private matters, later decenters centripetal inclinations as it takes on sociohistorical concerns.

Styron's move into history in his later novels involves a move away from Faulkner even as, on another level, he appears to come to share Faulkner's concern with history. His reaction to his historical material, and its effect on his narrative structure, take him away from what was Faulknerian in his first novel. The increasingly centrifugal nature of Styron's work remains for me to elaborate upon. But if, at the present stage, the notion that Styron can move into history but away from Faulkner seems paradoxical, that may be because the blanket word *history* can cover many things. Styron's historical interests are very different from Faulkner's preoccupation with southern myths. If Styron grapples with the race question, he also addresses American foreign policy, World War II, and the Holocaust—in ways that bear no deep relation to Faulkner's Yoknapatawpha sagas. In *Lie Down in Darkness*, Styron echoes Faulkner partly because, with his private and literary preoccupations, he has not yet come to terms with the implications of the centripetal movement of his narrative. He only begins to do that in *Set This House on Fire*, after the clash between his subject matter and narrative movement in *The Long March*.

Whereas Faulkner burrowed into the South, encapsulating the past by means of different lenses and voices, Styron in *Lie Down in Darkness* was extricating himself from southern history, and in the latter parts he shows signs of his eventually wider historical concern. That he was already less consumed than Faulkner by the South is apparent in his characterization, as Rubin suggests, but also in his setting and historical focus. In an early interview, Styron said that he thought his "people would have behaved the way they did anywhere," and the setting could certainly be outside the South.[36] Parts of the novel, of course, take place in New York, but even the temporal and spatial pat-

35. Eric Mottram, *William Faulkner* (London, 1971), 1; Murray, "Dialogics," in *Literary Theory at Work*, ed. Tallack, 132.

36. Peter Matthiessen and George Plimpton, "The Art of Fiction V: William Styron," in *Conversations with William Styron*, ed. James L. W. West III (Jackson, Miss., 1985), 11.

terns of the Port Warwick scenes derive less from Faulkner than from *Madame Bovary.*

Styron once described Flaubert as at least as influential on him as Faulkner, and *Madame Bovary* as "one of the few novels that moves me in every way, not only in its style, but in its total communicability."[37] In *Lie Down in Darkness*, Port Warwick owes much to Flaubert's setting of provincial tedium, dreams, and frustrations. This is Bakhtin's description of Flaubert's chronotope, his spatiotemporal placement of the novel: "In Flaubert's *Madame Bovary* the *provincial town* serves as the locus of action. . . . Such towns are the locus for cyclical everyday time. Here there are no events, only 'doings' that constantly repeat themselves. Time here has no advancing historical movement; it moves rather in narrow circles: the circle of the day, of the week, of the month, of a person's entire life."[38] For Styron too the locus of action is a provincial town—or its suburb—and the constant rhythm of centripetal and centrifugal, where repeatedly structures erected by the characters disintegrate, is similar to the cyclical tedium portrayed in Flaubert's novel. Like Emma Bovary, Styron's characters live out their constricted lives amid romantic dreams and yearnings doomed to decay and disappointment. Each episode, with its interplay of centripetal and centrifugal, is in tune with this "cyclical everyday time," which constitutes the "circle of the day, of the week, of the month, of a person's entire life." This is pinpointed by the imagery of the wedding:

The ceremony had been the spring part of the affair, it had passed; that was all innocence and had withered like April. Then there had been the summer, the season of nonchalance, easy acquaintance, the first mellow glow, through which the guests had drifted (alcoholically speaking) as through a mist of August sunlight. Now early autumn of the reception had come, and if you closed your eyes you could hear it sound: the loose, high, windy laughter of the women, the male voices filled with a sudden, hoarse bluster, like the rattle of leaves. Thus do all parties move toward the cold of winter and a final numb extinction. (283)

Lie Down in Darkness dramatizes the idea that "in each act of creation" we commit ourselves "to the last part of the evolutionary cycle"

37. *Ibid.,* 12.
38. Bakhtin, *The Dialogic Imagination,* 247–48.

(367)—and thus also the idea that to live, as the book's epigraph from Browne's *Urn Burial* suggests, is eventually to "lie down in darkness." Clearly, in that respect, Styron's concerns, notwithstanding the Virginia setting, are hardly as concentrated on the South or southern history as Faulkner's; certainly the ideas in the novel bear little relation to W. J. Cash's notion, resonant in Faulkner's work, that the southern mind has a "profound conviction that the South is another land."[39]

Moreover, the historical references in the novel are only peripherally southern. Southern history and southern Civil War rhetoric appear only as a parodied sideline. A drunk begins a "long story, mostly incoherent," of how "his grandpappy fit with Mosby in the Valley and if there were any bloody Yankees around he'd vivisect them alive" (200), and the football crowd is described as an army retreating: "Virginia had been defeated, but who cared? They trooped back to the fraternity houses in twos or threes. . . . A few sang songs, others kept on drinking, and those who fell were not left to lie there, but were carried away by two friends, in the spirit of brotherhood" (210). In contrast, when the novel begins, in the final sections, to bring in serious, if perhaps gratuitous, historical references, they have to do not with the South at all but with Hiroshima and the "one hundred thousand lives" that were "snuffed out by the great American commonwealth" (377). If the war is merely a backdrop to the characters' personal concerns, confined to a voice on the radio in a suburban living room, or an attempt to universalize what is essentially a private story of neurotic anxiety—personal for Peyton, literary for Styron—it also suggests the direction that Styron was to take. Although both the American Civil War and World War II are at the margin of the text, southern history is receding from the page while a wider field of concern emerges.

Styron was showing signs of moving, in Warren's phrase, "out of history into history"—out of the South into a wider historical awareness—but the influence of high modernism and Flaubert meant that his characters, and his view of art, connected mainly with the personal and the ahistorical.[40] Only in the final part, written when Styron found himself recalled by the marines because of the Korean War, and hence

39. W. J. Cash, *The Mind of the South* (1941; rpr. New York, 1983), vii.
40. Robert Penn Warren, *All the King's Men* (London, 1948), 447.

pulled out of his ivory tower and back into history, do historical references steadily punctuate the text.

Soaked with the influence of Faulkner, Fitzgerald, and others, *Lie Down in Darkness* embodies a struggle between borrowed voices and Styron's own emerging voice. Whichever way Styron turned, he was hemmed in. When he differed from Faulkner by attending to the personal rather than the historical in his characters' lives, he negated history in the very way Lukács claims modern literature from Flaubert so often does. So, like Peyton's, Styron's attempt to break free of one influence led him into the path of others. Right to the end of this first novel, the various voices refuse to be wholly subsumed.

What *Lie Down in Darkness* amounts to is a highly literary novel with largely literary concerns. But in it there are suggestions of Styron's eventual engagement by subject matter more than style. In Styron's view, most of his generation were "subtly traumatized" by the events of a world war, and that, he suggests, is one of the reasons that he, at least, retreated into ivory-tower notions of art in his first novel.[41] Like Milton as much as Peyton, he had to come to terms with his past, his background, and the authoritative discourse of his dead "father." For Styron, the "fathers" are literary, the authoritative discourse being that of Faulkner, who was—in Marcus Cunliffe's phrase—the "embodiment of the idea of the South in literature."[42] Above all, it was Faulkner whom Styron had to imitate or reaccentuate. But far from feeling, like Milton, "defeated" by his father's words (14), or avoiding the challenge of Faulkner's discourse by steering clear of him, as Flannery O'Connor did for fear that her "little boat would get swamped,"[43] Styron confronted the words. Like Peyton, though, he had to fall to "rise at another time" (386), committing figurative suicide by stabbing at the authoritative discourse of high modernism that began as his lifeblood.

41. William Styron, "My Generation," *Esquire*, LXX (October, 1968), 123. See also appendix conversations, 213–14.

42. Marcus Cunliffe, *The Literature of the United States* (Harmondsworth, Eng., 1985), 359.

43. Flannery O'Connor, *The Habit of Being*, ed. Sally Fitzgerald (New York, 1979), 273. Styron quotes O'Connor's remark that "no one wants to get caught on the tracks when the Dixie Special comes through" ("My Generation," 124).

"One's own discourse," says Bakhtin, "although born" or "dynamically stimulated by another, will sooner or later begin to liberate [itself] from the authority of the other's discourse."[44] Inevitably, traces remain, but the high modernist voices are never as influential again in Styron's work. Searching for direction, he began to absorb other voices that less directly, yet significantly, influenced him. As Styron tackled such subjects as slavery and the Holocaust, the external discourses became myriad, as well as less literary.

In particular, however, he has talked of the influence of writers like Albert Camus, André Malraux, George Orwell, and Arthur Koestler, who stand in contrast with the high modernist devotion to art.[45] The commitment evident in the work and lives of such writers influenced Styron's rejection of the ivory tower, where the centripetal desire to quell clashing voices and crush them into harmony can remain largely untroubled by the historical and political world. Certainly there is less aesthetic experimentation in Styron's later novels, less of the high modernist emphasis on form and more emphasis on what King, writing of Orwell, calls "language's ability to clarify and illuminate rather than to obfuscate."[46] Styron may look to language to clarify, not instead of but as well as obfuscating. He continued to challenge the boundaries of the novel, but as Orwell says, awareness of the "injustice and misery of the world" and a "feeling that one ought to do something about it" can make it harder to engage in play or to devote oneself "to literature as single-mindedly as Joyce or Henry James."[47] A real sense of direction is not fully apparent in Styron until *The Confessions of Nat Turner*, but *The Long March*, and more radically *Set This House on Fire*, offer pointers to the voice that Styron, in decentering the discourse toward harmony, eventually achieved.

44. Bakhtin, *The Dialogic Imagination*, 348.
45. Appendix conversations, 222–23.
46. King, *A Southern Renascence*, 74.
47. George Orwell, *The Collected Essays of George Orwell* (London, 1948), 428.

2

Signs of a Shift: *The Long March*

Soon now we shall go out of the house and go into the convulsion of the world, out of history into history and the awful responsibility of Time.
—*Robert Penn Warren*, All the King's Men

As Styron's career progressed, the discourse toward harmony was dislodged from setting the underlying direction of his fiction to being one part of a more complex dialogue. *The Long March* shows signs of this shift, since a conflict emerges between the textual movement toward verbal and social reconciliation and the novella's subject matter. As in *Lie Down in Darkness*, a struggle is waged between the centripetal and the centrifugal, this time with Tom Culver, as a "critic" ostensibly on the margins of the conflict, having a personal interest in—and as a lawyer, a professional disposition toward—finding a stable outcome.[1] Since the novella continues the shift toward social and historical preoccupations that was incipient in the latter parts of *Lie Down in Darkness*, a conflict arises between Culver's personal drive to harmonize voices—the text's fundamental shaping movement—and the political struggle between Mannix and Templeton.

To an extent, *The Long March* is about the "intrusion of history" into private lives—as Roger Asselineau puts it—and certainly the novella embraces a wider social outlook than was apparent in the private neuroses of the Loftis family.[2] Essentially a war novella, it fits Frederick R. Karl's description of such novels as *Catch-22*, *The Naked and the Dead*, and *From Here to Eternity* as being "about a societal equiva-

---

1. William Styron, *The Long March* (New York, 1952), 14, cited in the present chapter by page number, without title.

2. Roger Asselineau, "Following *The Long March*," trans. W. Pierre Jacoebee, in *Critical Essays on William Styron*, ed. Arthur D. Casciato and James L. W. West III (Boston, 1982), 54.

lent found in the military" as much as about military life.[3] Culver suffers acutely from the "perpetual apprehension" that, in James Jones's novel, is seen as the lot of modern man.[4] In *The Long March*, an increased engagement with society and history begins to reshape the fixation on individual and artistic harmony in *Lie Down in Darkness*. The shift is still small, but it is enough to create tension between the discourse toward harmony and the novella's subject matter. Culver, as one critic says, tries "to put the pieces into some pattern" by attempting to reconcile the warring discourses of Templeton and Mannix.[5] But for that very reason he becomes a destabilizing figure in his overall effect on events. If in one sense *The Long March* springs from an age of conformity, of the retreat into concerns that produced, in Morris Dickstein's words, the "narrowly personal" art of *Seize the Day* and *The Assistant*, in which "the only salvation is individual or religious," at the same time the events portrayed call into question the centripetal, harmonizing measures by which Culver seeks an intermediate perch between Templeton and Mannix for personal peace.[6]

An examination of Culver's personal and social effort toward harmony reveals that he is not merely the "passive but sympathetic observer" of the struggle between Templeton and Mannix that some critics see him as.[7] Rather, whether Styron intended it or not, the seemingly straightforward discourse toward harmony is complicated by Culver's effect on events. If it is partly true, as Marc L. Ratner says, that Culver "cannot bring himself to act," his inaction is itself a form of action.[8] As in *Lie Down in Darkness*, the conflicting discourses of the work occur on two levels. I will deal first with the clash of voices within the story itself. Then I will offer a brief comment on one exter-

3. Frederick R. Karl, *American Fictions, 1940–1980: A Comprehensive History and Critical Evaluation* (New York, 1983), 93.

4. James Jones, *From Here to Eternity* (New York, 1951), 342.

5. Irving Malin, "The Symbolic March," in *The Achievement of William Styron*, ed. Robert K. Morris and Irving Malin (Rev. ed.; Athens, Ga., 1981), 179.

6. Morris Dickstein, *Gates of Eden: American Culture in the Sixties* (New York, 1977), 13, 52–53.

7. Marc L. Ratner, *William Styron* (Boston, 1972), 10. See also Samuel Coale, *William Styron Revisited* (Boston, 1991), 21. Coale sees Styron's narrators as "clear-eyed witnesses": "ineffectual, passive, but often sympathetic observers."

8. Ratner, *William Styron*, 64.

nal voice that can also be heard in the text, that of Albert Camus, and on the rather different way in which it contributes to the disaccord in textual discourse.

At the heart of *The Long March* is the conflict between Colonel Templeton and Captain Mannix, with Mannix struggling to draw Templeton, and the authoritative discourse he upholds, into dialogue. But the conflict between Templeton's centripetal voice and the dissenting, suppressed voice of Mannix has to be seen through the figure of Culver. Thrown into turmoil from the outset, Culver is uncertain and uncommitted. He seeks to reconcile the warring voices he is caught between, as well as to reassert a sense of personal stability. The subject of the novella—a recall of Culver to the marines that alters his understanding of the kind of society he lives in—plainly relates to the threat that hung over Styron during the last stages of writing *Lie Down in Darkness.* Culver and Mannix have alike been wrenched from their domestic lives and personal ambitions and thrown into military life. Culver, however, persists in trying to find personal and social harmony, and the novella's movement reflects his aim. At the same time, the implications of his attitude—and of Styron's aesthetic—become especially apparent in virtue of the subject matter.

Bakhtin's concept of the chronotope, touched on in the last chapter, can illuminate the novella's opening and overall pattern. Just as any novel is shot through with forms of language and voices, so it is also furnished with chronotopes—with spatiotemporal patterns that are the "organizing centers for the fundamental narrative events" and that "are *dialogical* in the broadest sense of the word."[9] If the chronotope of the provincial town permeates *Lie Down in Darkness* in a way that links the text, beneath surface detail, as closely to Flaubert as to Faulkner, in *The Long March* two key chronotopes are those of domestic well-being and the military. The immiscible merging of the domestic and military worlds is at the bottom of Culver's initial distress. His mental dislocation has an underlying cause in his literal dislocation. The incommensurability of the two worlds is apparent from the start:

9. Mikhail M. Bakhtin, *The Dialogic Imagination: Four Essays,* trans. Michael Holquist and Caryl Emerson, ed. Michael Holquist (Austin, Tex., 1981), 250, 252.

"One noon, in the blaze of a cloudless Carolina summer, *what was left of eight dead boys* lay strewn about the landscape, among the poison ivy and the pine needles and loblolly saplings. *It was not so much as if they had departed this life but as if,* sprayed from a hose, *they were only shreds of bone, gut, and dangling tissue to which it would have been impossible ever to impute the quality of life, far less the capacity to relinquish it*" (3; my italics). Here one set of chronotopic details competes with another, the pleasant or pastoral giving way to the ugly reality of the military world. The details expressed by "a cloudless Carolina summer," "strewn about the landscape, among . . . the pine needles and loblolly saplings," and even "sprayed from a hose" belong to pastoral or suburban relaxation; they might be part of a summer picnic or a day lounging in a Port Warwick garden. But interspersed with these—like poison ivy, as it were—and irreversibly altering the picture are the disruptive and eventually dominant details (the phrasing of which I have italicized) of random, violent death. The remains "strewn about" are not those of a picnic—or not only of that—but of "eight dead boys": "shreds of human bone, gut, and dangling tissue." The two sets of details intermingle further in the description of human carnage literally mixed with food: a "welter of blood and brain, scattered messkits and mashed potatoes, and puddles of melting ice-cream" (4). The unblended merging of the two chronotopes is coupled with the dialogic nature of the language, which mingles the specific, descriptive language of the dead bodies with abstractions like "departed this life." The passage is structured out of linguistic and chronotopic clashes.

The discord situates a fundamental part of Culver's sense of confusion as the story opens. "After six years of an ordered and sympathetic life," he finds himself wrenched from domestic contentment back into military life, a "new world . . . of disorder" (36). As Ratner says, there is the "contrast between the apparent harmony of civilian life for Culver and the chaos and disorder of the present."[10] Culver's particular need for harmony is evident in the "moderation" of his "sensible" home life (8). Finding himself in a world where his idea of normal relationships between time, space, and human beings is shattered, he

10. Ratner, *William Styron*, 60.

feels "disoriented," as if in "another dimension of space and time" (34). He struggles to reorient himself.

The same chronotopic conflict continues to be a major cause of Culver's early sense of disorder. He feels "adrift at sea in a dazzling, windowless box, ignorant of direction or of any points of the globe." His sense of reality is so shaken that not only does his former life of "wife and child and home" seem unreal but so does his present existence. He moves from a "strange thicket to a stranger swamp and on to the green depths of some even stranger ravine," as if in the nonsequential "dream of a man delirious with fever." For him, "all time and space" seems "enclosed within the tent, itself unmoored and unhelmed upon a dark and compassless ocean" (34–35). His disorientation is literally and figuratively chronotopic, and his bearings are at this point absolutely lost.

Some critics have seen little relation between the scene of the dead boys and the rest of the march, but the march too reflects the discord that Culver will try to harmonize.[11] Culver senses a disparity between military and civilian life, and within the military world there is the further unsettling contrast between the static, dead bodies and the constant movement of the march, an entrapping pattern of perpetual, perversely ordered movement set against chaotic stasis. In the latter, space and the time exist as a frozen instant, whereas on the march, the two are concretized in a single continuity. Templeton asserts that a certain place means a certain time, and, having begun at "nine on the dot" (74), the group reach the highway "at ten o'clock, almost to the minute" (74). But so imposed, so rigid is this chronotope that Culver's normal sense of spatial and temporal orientation—his memory of domestic life—is undermined. The "constant movement" makes the sun seem to come from "ever-shifting" points, so he suffers from "displacement" and "confusion," never sure if it is "morning or afternoon" (37). His confusion amid order is worsened by the shock of seeing the human remains, which stays with him in a lingering memory that blocks any recovery of stability. If the opening explosion replays the suddenness with which Culver has been slung into this other world, the

---

11. Cooper R. Mackin calls the link "tenuous at best" (*William Styron* [Austin, Tex., 1969], 14).

march itself functions as the novella's central chronotope; it is what moves the plot along, what brings to a head the conflicts of the participants, and what determines the outcome.

Thrown from a relatively unstructured environment into a world of strict hierarchy, Culver suffers a disorientation that is compounded by the apparent perversity of the order he observes. Like Mannix, he has a "violent contempt for the gibberish, the boy-scout passwords" that replace "ordinary conversation in the military world" (43). The menacing childishness of those in authority is illustrated by Templeton's cowboy poses: his "pearl-handled .38 revolver" (66), his "thumbs hooked rakishly in his belt," and his casual, squinting eyes (67). His cowboy mentality finds an outlet in the constant order to "saddle up" (70). Culver and Mannix not only are in a setting that is strange to them but have to respond to, and use, a language they despise.

As the novella begins, Culver is in a state of confusion: a combination of disorientation, exhaustion, and shock only deepened by such discordant sounds as the "multitude of wails" that crackle through his radio headphones like a "jungle full of noise" (41). Not least of these, for Culver, is the voice of Mannix himself. "Recklessly vocal" (17), Mannix constantly feeds Culver's apprehension. But Culver is trying to bring his several vortices of verbal, chronotopic, and mental conflict under some kind of control, to rediscover orientation and stability.

If the chronotopic disorder serves as a narrative device to motivate Culver to make sense of events, it also suggests both ontological and epistemological concerns. Culver asks, How? and, Why? (4), yet his underlying need is to connect one reality with another, civilian with military, and to make sense of his existence. In that regard, *The Long March* foreshadows Styron's concern in *Sophie's Choice* with differing simultaneous experiences of a single thing, as when he broaches George Steiner's idea of "time-relation" in musing about the widely differing experiences of Stingo and Sophie.[12] The contrast between Stingo's and Sophie's fortunes, and the effect of differing chronotopes on the human image, engender wider moral, historical, and political questions about our sense of identity, but the same concerns appear in *The Long March* in embryonic form. The ontological concern also

12. William Styron, *Sophie's Choice* (New York, 1979), 215–19.

comes across in the textual suggestions that *The Long March* is as much about the absurdity of existence as about that of the march—an aspect of the novella that depends on Camus' voice being heard.

If the chronotopic conflicts help determine the novella's structure, its narrative interest and Culver's anguish are prolonged by the struggle between Mannix and Templeton. Their largely verbal battle, representing in microcosm the war beyond, is a struggle between the centripetal voice of Templeton and the centrifugal voice of Mannix, with Culver seeking to reconcile the two. If Templeton upholds, in a sense embodies, the authoritative discourse of the military, Mannix struggles first to bring this discourse into dialogue and then, in his frustration, to overthrow it. The irony, for Culver, is that in pursuing "individual" action, Mannix himself becomes a centripetal voice at the height of his "rebellion in reverse" (73), when he tries to coerce others to follow his lead and carry out Templeton's orders in full.

Much of the conflict between Templeton and Mannix flows from their different dispositions toward authoritative discourse. To the degree that discourse is authoritative, any challenge to it is taboo; the authoritative word, as authoritative, is an object of reverence, a vessel of truth, beyond questioning. It might include sacred texts, the law, literature of the canon, social etiquette, or other codes of conduct. The portrayal of military discourse in *The Long March* makes it appear quasi-religious, and some of the characters, such as O'Leary and Hobbs, uphold it unquestioningly. Mannix, on the other hand, and at times Culver, try to resist its authoritative claim. But since it remains sacred for the marine regulars and rules the actions of Culver and Mannix, they can do no more than mock, parody, and profane it. They are unable to reduce its grip.

For Templeton, O'Leary, and others, marine regulations are the "special script" that governs their world view.[13] Templeton's adherence to the word of the military is backed up by his use of a special language. But it is also apparent in his name, which reinforces the idea that military discourse is a form of religion and signals his devotion to it. Culver likens Templeton to "certain young ecclesiastics, prematurely aged

13. Bakhtin, *The Dialogic Imagination*, 343.

and perhaps even wise" (18). Templeton helps sustain, but also as a commanding officer embodies, an institution that does not doubt its possession of the truth and that thus smothers any possible dialogue. Templeton expects "to be obeyed" (18). Referred to by the regulars as Old Rocky, he has a world view that precludes dialogue. The word *old* associates him with tradition, and the image of a rock captures his adamantine temperament.

Throughout there is in evidence Templeton's suppression of any true dialogue between his own voice, a vehicle for military discourse, and any voice seeking seriously to challenge it. Like Helen in *Lie Down in Darkness*, Templeton hews to the centripetal not only with others but also internally, avoiding even self-reflection unless it, like his external speech, is rigorously stylized. This is evident in his rationale for the march: "I said to myself, 'How's the battalion doing?' I mean, 'What kind of an outfit do I have here? Is it in good combat shape? If we were to meet an Aggressor enemy tomorrow would we come out all right?' Those were the queries I posed myself. Then I tried to formulate an answer" (26). His stilted thoughts show how riddled he is with the military value system. Everything is in abstract concepts and Latinate diction. In trying to "formulate" an answer, he leaves no space for emotion but limits himself to logical, abstract thought. His Latinate diction is a way of seeking to reinforce the authority of his decisions by wrapping them in the cloak of objectivity. His internal dialogue occurs only within the bounds of his own narrow code and, unlike Culver's, is not concerned with the tension between discourses.

Any discourse that has appeal for being unified or that is vested with a monolithic truth is open to attempts by centrifugal voices to undermine it. Where such attempts seem to occur but do not is in Templeton's stylized external dialogues with regulars. O'Leary supposedly questions the decision, but his demur is mere ritual since it takes place only in the bounds of marine discourse, offering no serious challenge. O'Leary, says Culver, is "inextricably grafted to the system" like "flesh surgically laid on arm or thigh." Since he performs with "devoted, methodical competence," he can "say sarcastically, 'The Colonel's really got a wild hair, ain't he?' but shrug his shoulders and grin, and by that ambivalent gesture sum up an attitude which only a professional soldier could logically retain: I doubt the Colonel's judgment a little, but will willingly do what he says." Like the radio man Hobbs, he has "immunity," because his voicing of doubt is merely a stylized part of the system (22–23).

Mannix, in contrast, is a reluctant reservist thrust back into a military he despises. The words he utters as a partial outsider unwilling to accept the role of subordinate marine threaten to break through the accepted code. Whereas O'Leary's "incredulous whistle, right in the Colonel's face," only elicits an "indulgent smile," Mannix' murmur of "Thirty-six miles, Jesus Christ" in a tone "laden with no more disbelief or no more pain than O'Leary's whistle" brings to the colonel's face a "delicate shadow of irritation" (24). Templeton's reacting at all opens the possibility that he will enter into dialogue with Mannix and offer some vent to the latter's frustration. But his reply "You think that's too long?" is again delivered as "merely a question candidly stated"— *stated* being the operative word. In truth, the colonel still brooks no response, and his face, having found "absolute repose" (25), reflects this no less than his voice.

Templeton's indifference causes Mannix to look for release by trying, again and again, to engage Templeton, and in him military authority, in dialogue. The struggle advances from Mannix' comic mockery, in the early stages, to his reverse rebellion of carrying out orders even after they have been countered. But the revolt, despite Mannix' efforts, never gets beyond verbal challenge for long, since behind the colonel's indifference lies the brute force that authority can bring to bear. This is underscored by Culver's description, however satiric, of the colonel's cowboy gesture of reaching for his pistol when Mannix swears at him. Mannix, largely restricted to verbal weaponry, moves ever more recklessly from a centrifugal parody unheard by authority to outright defiance. At first he is merely "more noisily frank" than other reserves about his dislike of the Marine Corps. His antagonism comes out only in odd comments, such as his deliberately testy, colloquial reply to one of Templeton's orders: "Jesus, lemme digest a bit, Jack." At that stage, his comments, if "too often audible" for Culver's taste, are "frequently comical" and keep Culver "in a constant state of mild suspense—half amusement, half horror" (19). They comically undercut authority but have no further effect.

Even this early there are hints that, in Culver's opinion, Mannix' revolt is doomed. Mannix seems halfway to failure already because he has begun to speak "like a marine." Thus, though Templeton can detect an extra edge to his complaints, he fits within the pattern of those whose function is to obey (17). Though he is trying to stand outside the stylized question-and-answer system, the seeds of his eventual capitulation are evident in his diction, for cursing and groaning serve as safety valves rather than challenge authority.

When Mannix goes on to question the length of the march, the colonel interrupts again, his voice "anticipatory, as if it already held the answer to whatever Mannix might ask" (27). True dialogue still does not occur, and Mannix is provoked to more reckless action. Templeton remains intent in his centripetal determination to arrest any attempt at dialogue and to reposition it within the order of the discourse he adheres to. His Latinate diction, shed of emotive content, assists him in this: "They're *marines. Comprehend?*" he says. "They're going to *act* like marines" (28). His voice again echoes Helen's, intent on keeping Peyton in a role. Each time Mannix starts to question authority, Templeton closes up, returning "once more to that devout, ordered state of communion," with his preordained script, that Mannix' "words had ever so briefly disturbed" (29).

The sham dialogue of authoritative marine discourse is most starkly exposed by Mannix' bid to enter into it during one of the "compulsory lectures." Lectures being, in any case, the perfect monologic structure to buttress authority, these seem specifically designed for the purpose. With "appallingly familiar" outlines, they are "doggedly memorized" ways to deliver a preset message (46), and they leave no room for innovation or discussion. Like Templeton's speech, they are dressed out in Latinate terminology and abstract concepts like that of "amphibiously integrated" group destinies, and are supported by "reams of printed and mimeographed tables and charts and résumés" (48). The lectures may prefigure Major Danby's "monotonous, didactic" descriptions of the "heavy concentrations of flak" awaiting Yossarian in *Catch-22*, but Mannix' disruptions are far more muted than those by Yossarian, whose groans set off groans and laughter from others and put the room in uproar, until the officers unwittingly groan themselves.[14] Yossarian succeeds in humbling the authoritative struc-

14. Joseph Heller, *Catch-22* (New York, 1961), 216–17.

ture—albeit by a nonlinguistic stratagem—and gains a limited coup. Mannix is less successful and gets less open support and reaction from those around him. Most of the marines are content to discard the printed matter or simply not to listen. Mannix has to make a gesture. Parodying the "grandiose doctrine" and "aping" the young colonel, he mutters, "Corporal, kindly pass out the atom bombs for inspection" (48). But he does this beyond the hearing of authority, and so without engaging it in dialogue.

Later, during the question-and-answer part of the lectures, however, he exerts pressure directly on the stylized dialogue by answering "some generalized, hypothetical question" (50) by saying that he does not have the "faintest idea" (51). Faced with Mannix' freewheeling, the young colonel retreats deeper into formality: "I stated earlier, Captain, that I wanted some sort of answer. None of you gentlemen is expected to know this subject pat, but you can essay *some kind of answer.*" Yet the questioner clearly does not want just some kind of answer—which would allow escape from the codified marine discourse. So for a moment Mannix succeeds and the colonel is "at a loss for words" (52).

The victory, though, is minor, a successful skirmish that punctuates overall failure. Mannix still cannot engage authority in genuine dialogue. His insistence on preserving his identity as an individual, moreover, is ironically debilitated, since the more he asserts his right to challenge, the further he reveals his adherence to the system. Becoming "more in need to scourge something" (52), he turns to direct action but even then can only act within the code and language he is trying to fight. It is here that Culver's indecision grows problematic.

Culver has an ambivalent attitude toward both the authority of Templeton and the recklessness of Mannix. This is the strength and the weakness of his outlook. When he describes the colonel as being like "certain young ecclesiastics," he tails off with the concession that the colonel is "perhaps even wise" (18). Culver has doubts about the worth and legitimacy of rebellion. Certainly he is skeptical of, and—when personally affected—appalled by, Templeton's fixation on order and his suppression of dialogue. Watching the colonel "squint casually into the sun" when news comes of the accident, as if he were "receiving the most routine of messages," Culver wonders "what interior struggle" has gone into the "perfection of such a gesture" (14). In Culver's view, Templeton's stability has been bought at the price of losing the ability to feel, and so to be fully alive. "A man to whom the greatest embarrassment would be a show of emotion" (18), he has become less a person than a "quantity of attitudes" (117).

Still, Culver is envious of the certainty Templeton has found in accepting a code to live by. Notwithstanding that Templeton suppresses inner contradictions and bothersome emotions, Culver is drawn to the sense of order the colonel displays. Seeking stability himself, he has a kind of "respect" (30) for the man—though he puts the word in quotation marks to distance it from his own discourse. He is caught between the language of Mannix, whose rebellion upsets his desire for harmony, and the language of the military, which reinforces Templeton's authority. Sympathetic to Mannix' viewpoint, Culver is also wary of it. In order to go along with a system he dislikes, he seeks to reconcile the opposing views. That, we will see, is also the basic reaction of Peter Leverett to Mason and Cass in *Set This House on Fire*, but that novel subjects the attitude to a more critical scrutiny, questioning the conviction that art should seek to move toward order. In Peter's case, a liberal acceptance of something repugnant threatens to leave the existing conditions intact. In Culver's case, it leaves them intact.

It is not that Culver lacks insight or fails to question authority. But he sees that Mannix is unknowingly caught up in the system he is defying, and so realizes that the battle Mannix thinks he is engaged in is partly illusory. Culver tells himself that he despises not the "man," Templeton, but "the Colonel, the marine" (89), since Templeton is "not himself evil or unjust" (30) but just devoted to regulations. He is aware too that the colonel's regular subordinates have no wish to question the authority and that military speech conventions reinforce it. He sees how the major bestows on Templeton a "third person flattery," as if the colonel is beyond direct address, let alone challenge (16).

Since Culver's thoughts are the filter for our view of events, he does, for us, subvert Templeton's authoritative discourse. Whereas Mannix seeks to undermine Templeton through parody and then action, Culver employs irony. His narrative viewpoint supplements Mannix' actions, as when he describes the colonel's false display of emotion as "good grade-A Templeton." He sees through the "performance," and to this extent, is a centrifugal voice (14). In that role, he appears as an observer who, recognizing how Mannix' individualist rebellion is doomed to fail, offers sympathetic commentary on it—a commentary that makes fun of Templeton's pretensions.

But this leaves aside that because Culver never acts on his dislike of the system, he limits the shape of the action that Mannix can take and helps ensure his defeat. Culver's strength is his critical awareness, which allows him to recognize that Templeton is impervious alike to true dialogue and to Mannix' heroic challenges. What is less laudable, however, is the way the pose of critical detachment allows Culver to avoid confronting an authority he himself is unhappy with. His weakness is an ironic use of language that ends up misrepresenting the contest between Templeton and Mannix as a personal, equal one to which he is merely a detached bystander rather than letting him understand its broader, political implications.

The cowboy imagery of Culver's ironic commentary displays the conflict as a duel between individuals, even a shoot-out:

The Captain got up, limping off toward his company, over his retreating shoulder, shot back a short, clipped burst of words at the Colonel—whose eyeballs rolled white with astonishment when he heard them—and thereby joined the battle.

"Who cares what you think," he said. (90)

Culver here casts the conflict of voices in terms of men in equal combat rather than as a broader social fray of which Culver himself is integrally a part. At a moment when Mannix, however recklessly, finally gets through to the colonel, Culver, the detached, passive critic—or artist—is taking a neutral stance, paring his fingernails. When he satirizes Templeton, he includes the deluded, grotesquely limping Mannix in the satire. Mannix becomes a "mammoth, gyrating" parody, with the "suffering face of a clown" (114), who for all his heroism fails to comprehend that "the hike had nothing to do with courage or sacrifice or suffering." Culver is content to think of Mannix' rebellion as "individual" and "therefore hopeless, maybe even absurd" (55–56).

Culver's aloof complacency ensures that the dominant power remains intact. The net result of his liberal pluralism is to entrench the status quo as effectively as O'Leary or Hobbs. We are left to ponder whether it is because of him that Mannix' behavior is absurdly futile and that Templeton has his victory. Culver's chief criticism—that

Mannix' actions are "hopeless" because they are "individual"—invites the obvious rejoinder that had Culver himself, and others like him, acted with Mannix, the actions would have been neither individual nor necessarily hopeless. Culver may profess sympathy for Mannix' viewpoint, but he in practice ends up supporting authority. His inaction means that he is not merely a passive witness but an active shaper of the unfolding events. At times he does physically act to shape events— when, for example, he stops Mannix from burning down the mess— but even his apparent passivity helps steer the course of the action toward the ultimate renewal of social stability.

The extent to which Styron was aware of Culver's ambivalent role is unclear. Culver is a detached artist trying to harmonize the world, and the conflicts in his role may arise from the clash between Styron's own disposition to harmonize voices and the more problematic subject matter he was canvassing, a clash not wholly muted here. Culver is distanced from the author not only because he is described in the third person but also in virtue of his job as a lawyer, which, as for Peter Leverett in *Set This House on Fire*, signals that he is disposed to seek order. At this stage, however, the author's dialogizing of the discourse toward harmony is not explicit, nor perhaps conscious.

Nevertheless, it is clear that the pursuit of harmony grows more questionable when, as begins to happen here and as is increasingly the case, Styron's works leave the domestic world of the larger part of his first novel and enter political arenas. The danger in trying to reconcile warring discourses is that to compromise may leave the authoritative discourse, or the power that is, intact. In *The Long March*, that is not perhaps an obvious concern, and there may be a case for arguing that, given what Mannix is up against, Culver is right to react as he does. But the political moral beneath the skin of *The Long March* rises to the surface in subsequent novels and has a bearing on some of the public controversy that attended *The Confessions of Nat Turner*.

Like *Lie Down in Darkness*, *The Long March* ultimately moves toward a reconciliation of conflicting voices. But a displacement in the harmonized voices reflects the discongruity between Culver's, and perhaps the author's, discourse toward harmony and the social and political questions raised by the struggle between Templeton and Mannix.

Culver's viewpoint remains ambivalent to the end. He tells how Mannix himself, striving to instill marine pride in his men, becomes a centripetal voice as he works to ensure that they survive the whole march and so defy Templeton. The description of Mannix as "rocklike" (45), indeed, invites comparisons with Templeton. Culver thus continues to mediate, wishing "to caution" Mannix about the futility of the rebellion (72) and to show the extremity of both men's positions.

Consumed with "one idea"—to last through the march and so defy Templeton—Mannix lets his discourse become, ironically, monologic (72). Coercion replaces persuasion as he proceeds to "sting and flay" his men "with the merciless accents of a born bully" (77). As Culver sees it, Mannix' actions are part of the problem, a "part of the general scheme" (78). It is "useless to reason" with him, since he matches Templeton in resisting dialogue:

"See, that little jerk wants to make a name for himself—Old Rocky Templeton. Led the longest forced march in the history of the Corps—"

"But—" Culver started.

"He'd just love to see H & S Company crap out," he went on. (82)

Seeing Mannix' actions as unavailing and even dangerous, Culver becomes all the less inclined to condemn Templeton. Realizing—or rationalizing—that the colonel is "as far removed from the vulgar battle" as the "remotest stars" (111), Culver doubts that a struggle is possible and wonders if O'Leary "could be right, and himself and Mannix, and the rest of them, inescapably wrong" (101). Subdued by weariness, he begins to fear that Mannix may instigate something worse than what he rebels against.

Mannix, for his part, battering against the impregnable wall of military discourse, becomes a caricature, "toiling down the road with hobbled leg and furious flailing arms" (97). Physical disfigurement is matched verbally: "Let them crap out! I've did—done—" he sputters (107). As Ratner says, he "has been talking to his men in the brutal clichés of the march" but now "becomes inarticulate."[15] His language, even in rebellion, remains in the military mode he despises; outside it, his revolt loses coherence. He and Culver are, in Culver's view, above

---

15. Ratner, *William Styron*, 67.

all marines, doomed to rebel only in terms of the system. Not only is Mannix' failure to breach authoritative discourse confirmed but so too, when he tells Templeton to "fuck" off (112), is the true nature of Templeton's discourse: "I'm not *interested* in your observations," he tells Mannix. "*Keep your mouth shut!*" (113). After all the rhetoric, Templeton bares his intention to suppress challenging voices. What he wants from those below him is, if not stylized quasidialogue, silence.

The novella's ending, where mental and social harmony gain a hold, must be seen in light of Culver's attitude. The march seems to be a journey toward insight. Culver accepts that he cannot reconcile the interests of Mannix and Templeton, but he turns to a form of understanding between voices in the final scene, when a Negro maid asks him and Mannix, "What you been doin'? Do it hurt?"

"Oh, I bet it does. Deed it does." Mannix looked up at her across the short yards that separated them, silent, blinking. Culver would remember this: the two of them communicating across that chasm one unspoken moment of sympathy and understanding before the woman, spectacled, bandannaed, said again, "Deed it does." (120)

The black voice, wheeled on at the end as in *Lie Down in Darkness*, may evince a dubious attempt to parallel the suffering of the marines with that of American Negroes. But in the movement toward harmony, the maid's appearance signals a merging of voices. The "moment of sympathy and understanding" culminates, in the last line, in Mannix' echo of the woman's words, "deed it does." By using her language, he reaccentuates it, so that it links her historical situation with his immediate struggle against authority. In doing so, he invests the phrase with a new meaning that is harmonious rather than antagonistic, signaling mutual understanding. Thus the moment fulfills Culver's need to reconcile voices and end with a semblance of harmony. By using the black maid's language, Mannix suggests that they share in a struggle; the "it" that hurts transcends Mannix' situation.

The phrase is also a pun, signaling a return to the humor Mannix lost at the peak of his rebellion. The use of black discourse is integral to this since it introduces an open-ended quality. In *Black English*, J. L. Dillard discusses the ambiguity latent in black dialect. He quotes the English wife of a plantation owner, who recorded "that 'spect meaning *expect*, has sometimes a possible meaning of *suspect*, which would give the sentence in which it occurs a very humorous turn."[16] Although it is the author here, rather than the black woman, who uses the dialect this way, *deed* offers a similar ambiguity, both suggesting the need to act and confirming that the struggle is unwinnable. *Indeed* confirms the pain and unendingness of the struggle, merely consoling through verbal alliance. But *deed* can be taken as reiterating the need for the kind of action Mannix takes.

The introduction of the woman's dialect allows for an ambiguous ending. The phrase flickers between pessimism and optimism. The struggle continues, but defeat is as elusive as victory, so hope is never lost. With the return of humor, both Mannix and the tone of the novella return to a healthier condition. Mannix can resume his subversive role as an overturner of language, if not, for the moment, of authority itself. Culver's movement toward harmony, and the novel's overall movement toward a reconciliation of voices, seem realized.

The verbal and social harmony reached, however, is ultimately an evasion, for to bring it about, Culver—or the author—refocuses the narrative, displacing mutual understanding from where it was originally sought, between Mannix and Templeton, to only between Mannix and the maid. The political harmony achieved permits the retention of military hierarchy. The harmony achieved on a personal level simply changes the outlooks interacting. If we see the crucial conflict as one between discourses in a society—a view encouraged by the self-containment of the world portrayed—Mannix' failure to overturn Templeton's authority through anything except parody is bleak enough. Culver's attitude near the end makes it bleaker still. If Mannix seems to Culver to prove himself part of the system he seeks to subvert, Culver himself settles for Templeton's authority, however unwanted, to achieve a "quality of repose" (117). In other words, Culver is willing to compromise for a quiet life, content to see Templeton as someone "remote from [his] world" (117). His personal need for harmony takes precedence over even justifiable challenges to perverse forms of authority.

16. Frances Anne Kemble, *A Journal of Residence on a Georgia Plantation in 1838–38* (New York, 1863), 118, quoted by J. L. Dillard in *Black English: Its History and Usage in the United States* (New York, 1972), 22.

The whole narrative of events shows that Culver ends up deluding himself. When he is flung from one "world" into another, where Templeton's power over him shows itself, his sense of civilian life as somehow illusory is more honest than the harmony he eventually settles for. The military, after all, has always been able to propel him out of his normal surroundings. That Templeton, contrary to Culver's conclusion, does not belong to another "world," and hence cannot be discounted, is shown in the way Culver suddenly finds himself part of Templeton's world.

Culver's thinking is dubious in a number of ways. His belief that Mannix becomes as bad as the authority oppressing them draws on one of the classic forms of argument against rebellion—a form of argument used by the lawyer Gray to Nat Turner. Culver's conservative, uncombative stance ensures that the authority rankling him remains. If Mannix is reckless and lacks reflection, Culver lacks the boldness to translate reflection into action. One way or another, both try to undermine authoritarianism but neither is able to cut loose from the system. The attempts to dialogize military discourse fail because Mannix and Culver are caught up in that discourse. But they also fail because, while Mannix strives to rebel by using a marine code of heroic perseverance, Culver's urge to restore stability leads him to do what he can to quiet the centrifugal voice of Mannix, so ensuring that change does not come. The long march is to nowhere not only in that the physical journey is circular but also in its concrete results. Culver and Mannix remain firmly stuck in the hierarchical structure. If anything, Mannix will end up worse off, since the threat of court-martial hangs over him.

This relationship between the self and its sociohistorical context figures in all Styron's work from this point on, becoming a preoccupation that led to his attempt to consider two social and historical realities that have beleaguered the modern mind: slavery and its heritage, and the Holocaust. The value of Styron's voice, we can begin to see, may be precisely that it is not that of the historical or social victim—though any voice is of a potential victim—but rather that of one relatively privileged, situated somewhere between authority or power (Templeton, Mason) and the struggle of those beneath (Cass, in some ways Mannix), seeking to find his own, and by inference many of our, relationships to evil done in his, and our, name. The Long March involves a clash that, in *Set This House on Fire,* became a more conscious dialogue between the author's urge to harmonize conflicts and the urge to face social, historical, and political issues. Questions of wider scope began to compete with the largely personal and artistic concerns of Styron's earliest fiction.

In *The Long March,* later themes appear in embryonic form. Disjunction and discord move toward harmonious interaction, but Culver's personal and artistic commitment to such harmony results in a perpetuating of what is objectionable. His focus away from the struggle with authority is symptomatic of an attitude that gives the personal precedence over the social. His choices thus are a good illustration of what Lukács means when he says that a "yearning for harmony" can amount to a "faint-hearted withdrawal before the contradictory problems thrown up by life." Since the harmony achieved depends on Culver's cutting himself off "from society's struggles," it is "illusory and superficial" (see pp. 4–5 above).

The Long March shows few obvious signs of the Faulknerian influence that is evident in *Lie Down in Darkness.* Among high modernist writers, Hemingway might be canvassed for influences upon the novella; the line "none of this Hemingway crap for me, Jack" (43) at least suggests that Styron, who wrote the piece in Paris, had Hemingway on his mind. But the voice that clearly stands out is that of Albert Camus. The way Camus' sense of the absurd manifests itself, moreover, indicates that Styron was here at least entangled by, rather than in control of, the problematic aspects of the discourse toward harmony. At the same time, Camus' influence constitutes further evidence that Styron was moving away from the largely literary concerns of *Lie Down in Darkness.*

In *The Absurd Hero in American Fiction,* David D. Galloway at some length discusses Mannix as a Camusian hero. Styron has acknowledged that this "bleak, bleak view" of man's condition "helped form" his writing. Galloway's treatment, however, only partly covers the effect of Camus' voice in *The Long March* and—to reiterate a point made earlier—highlights a single aspect of the work rather than considering the heteroglossic whole. Although certain structural aspects confirm the existential theme Galloway ascribes to the novel, the confluence of metaphysics and politics causes an imbalance between diction and subject matter that relates to the incipient shift in the underlying pattern of Styron's novels to one in tune "with politics in so far as they govern history and human affairs."[17]

The Long March is not an absurdist work but intermeshes the absurdist voice with others. Mannix may suggest a Camusian hero, but ontological concerns offer only one of a number of possible entrances upon the novella, not least because the social struggle that makes up the text sits uneasily with metaphysical reflection. Because, seeing the work solely in existentialist terms, Galloway is persuaded that "Mannix knows, as the true absurd hero always knows, that he has virtually no chance for victory, but he must be true to his intentions," he maintains that Mannix' rebellion is "limited but successful."[18] Looking at the overall pattern of voices, however, we can recognize that Mannix' rebellion is fundamentally unsuccessful; he never really pierces the authoritative discourse beyond impelling Templeton to take the time to say outright what he has implied all along: Shut up. Only when seen solely in Camusian terms can the rebellion look like even a limited success—as a heroic metaphysical rebellion against an absurd universe. Galloway's observations persuade only by neglecting the sociopolitical aspects of the rebellion.

The existentialist reading gains credibility, however, if we consider some of the other details Galloway passes over. Camus' influence is apparent in the novella's very diction. Words like *absurd, will,* and *rebellion* come from an unmistakable source. But what really discloses the text's concern with the metaphysical is the universal character of what it portrays. Numerous aspects of the novella's world suggest it to be at a remove from the flux of experience and all-enveloping. The chronotopic structure places the events over twenty-four hours, from noon to noon. The march is thirty-six miles long. The multiples of twelve help suggest inclusiveness, and Culver's feeling that his civilian life is dreamlike, or nonexistent, enhances the suggestion. Phrases like "universe of the tent" (40) reinforce it. The novella seems to unfold its

17. Appendix conversations, 223; Philip Caputo, "Styron's Choices," *Esquire*, CVI (December, 1986), 140. For an overview of the way Camus is present in Styron, see Coale, *William Styron Revisited*, 27–31.

18. David D. Galloway, *The Absurd Hero in American Fiction* (London, 1981), 90–91.

war within a war as a figure for our metaphysical condition. If the march is an example of Bakhtin's "chronotope of the road"—in that the road here is a "place for events to find their denouement"—it is also a significant departure from it. For Bakhtin, the road chronotope usually provides a basis for a meeting.[19] But conspicuous in *The Long March* is the lack of meetings. A car passes by, but its occupants seem "unaware of the shadowy walkers," as if in another world, and the juxtaposition of civilian life with the march only adds a "new sensation of unreality to the night" (83). Styron's road chronotope is set apart and self-contained.

The novella's themes are also universalized by its structure, and by incidental references. The march has marks of an unending history, with Culver remembering the dead bodies as being "weeks, years ago, beneath the light of an almost prehistoric sun" (93). Like the cosmic journey alluded to, the novella begins with a big bang: the explosion that leaves eight dead. Those marines who collapse lie by the roadside "in attitudes as stiff as death" (44), and the marchers are driven by an "old atavism" (69). Besides that, there are references to Mannix' nakedness, not only in the image of him hanging naked, screaming, upside down in the night—an image of birth, as Welles T. Brandriff points out—but also at the end, when the towel slips from his body.[20]

Mannix' actions can thus be seen as dramatically rendering the artistic revolt in Camus' *The Myth of Sisyphus*, man's "dogged revolt against his condition." As such, they would commend themselves as "perseverance in an effort considered sterile" that at least allows a person the opportunity "of overcoming his phantoms and approaching a little closer to his naked reality." Mannix' revolt would be a Camusian "encounter between human questioning and the silence of the universe,"[21] with Templeton, remote as the "most distant stars," alternately a "priest" who is "leading a march to some humorless salva-

19. Bakhtin, *The Dialogic Imagination*, 243–44. For Bakhtin's comments on the "close link between the motif of meeting and the chronotope of the road," see *The Dialogic Imagination*, 98.

20. Welles T. Brandriff, "The Role of Order and Disorder in *The Long March*," *English Journal*, LVI (1967), 58.

21. Albert Camus, *The Myth of Sisyphus*, trans. Justin O'Brien (London, 1955), 93; Albert Camus, *The Rebel*, trans. Anthony Bower (1953; rpr. Harmondsworth, Eng., 1986), 14.

tion" (87–88) and an unhearing "creator" of a "wild and lunatic punishment" (101).

On this reading, Mannix, like Camus' hero, is "defeated in advance." But if the novella is about social as well as metaphysical revolt, a Camusian understanding of the novella is incomplete. Although Culver convinces himself that defeat is predestined, he is wrong. It may be that mankind can merely revolt with doomed dignity against what Camus calls our "ineffectual condition," but it does not follow that political revolt need be ineffectual.[22] Styron has used social revolt as a metaphor for metaphysical revolt, but the two discourses he tries to bring into relationship are incommensurable.

The result is a clash between the novella's subject and its language. Vernon Scannell mentions that the march stands for a "situation of extremity, an event where human resolution and endurance are tested to the limit." But, he remarks, for the march to be capable of the role Styron allots it, it would have to be "literally a matter of life and death, not a matter of a comfortable ride in a truck, or badly blistered feet."[23] Scannell does not address the novella's existential dimension but simply observes the poor fit between the social struggle and Styron's attempts to imply wider significance. Part of that broader import is, we have seen, itself social. The existential discourse confuses rather than clarifies the larger social ramifications by countenancing hyperbolic language at odds with the events portrayed. The rather tame trials of Culver and Mannix collide with the language of metaphysical struggle. The emphasis on Mannix' suffering and Culver's age—he is not even thirty—comes across as a glaring stratagem for making the march appear worse than it is. Styron seems constantly trying to add weight to the pack, as it were, on Mannix' and Culver's backs, with such details as the nail in Mannix' boot (in more top-heavy religious symbolism) and Culver's anguish at the explosion. The metaphysical load of the novella explains rather than justifies this.

The novella hovers between being a serious story of pain and pathos and being cartoonlike elsewhere.[24] Styron's ironic description of its fic-

---

22. Camus, *The Myth of Sisyphus*, 77, 75. There is, of course, a sociopolitical side to Camus' writing, and that, as I suggested in Chapter 1, is significant for Styron's adoption of an increasingly committed stance as his career develops.

23. Vernon Scannell, "New Novels," *Listener*, April 19, 1962, p. 701.

24. See Ratner, *William Styron*, 89–90.

tional counterpart in *Sophie's Choice*—"a taut, searing book eviscerating the military in a tragicomedy of the absurd"[25]—intimates awareness of its limitations. In any case, a conflict of discourses is evident again, not only in the story but also in the author.

Even in the novella's metaphysical contentions, Styron differs from Camus, for he portrays the rebel as less an individual than someone formed by others' codes. Mannix and Culver are, first of all, marines. Camus suggests that the individual can transcend his fate, but in *The Long March* individualism is delusory. Instilled with marine pride, neither Mannix nor Culver has "enough free will" (102) to defy marine dictates. To commit the suicide of crapping out would, for Camus, be to admit that "life is too much."[26] But not to do so is, in the case of *The Long March*, to adhere to the system despised.

Styron, however, was moving away from such defeatism. He was increasingly questioning the dubious position of Culver, and the underlying idea that art should move toward harmony. And in place of the idea that individuals are constituted by the codes of others, there was emerging the conviction that individual behavior, as *The Long March* implies perhaps despite itself, can indeed affect events. In his next novel, *Set This House on Fire*, he still seemed to be trying to define his subject and voice, and his endeavor at that, together with his conscious dialogue with other writers—including the still looming figure of Faulkner—remained as evident, and as interesting, as the ideas the novel bore. But, though Peter Leverett is similar to Culver, a gap had more plainly opened between the author's position and the narrator's as the movement toward harmony was becoming dialogized.

25. Styron, *Sophie's Choice*, 450.
26. Camus, *The Myth of Sisyphus*, 12.

3

The Mind in the Act of Finding: *Set This House on Fire*

To live *is to war with trolls*
in the vaults of the heart and the brain.
To write: *that is to sit*
in judgment over one's self.

—*Henrik Ibsen, letter to Ludwig Passarge*

Chaque notaire porte en soi les débris d'un poète.
—*Gustave Flaubert*, Madame Bovary

A movement toward harmony shaped Styron's early work. *Lie Down in Darkness* and *The Long March* involve a centripetal molding of clashing voices that supposes an artist is somehow separate from society and can use art as a way to order a chaotic world. But emerging in the same work has been a conflict between the movement toward harmony and Styron's interest in sociohistorical matters. If signs of a change of emphasis appear in the latter part of *Lie Down in Darkness*, Culver's artistic quest for personal and social harmony in *The Long March* leads to an aloofness that helps the authority figure, Templeton, retain control. Styron's attachment of existentialist ideas to the social struggle adds to the textual discordance. His conflict eventually led to a radical shift in the pattern of his work.

In *Set This House on Fire*, the problems besetting a discourse toward harmony receive more conscious attention. Whereas Styron's voice in *Lie Down in Darkness* was both coincident with the narrator's and largely centripetal, here Styron, as author, acts centrifugally. This is first evident in the title; in contrast to the downbeat phrases "Lie Down in Darkness" and "The Long March," Donne's reference to the human soul, "Set This House on Fire," suggests a new awareness of the centrifugal potential novels can have. *Set This House on Fire* still includes a movement toward harmony, but the movement is tested by the significant gap Styron created between himself and the narrator, Peter Leverett. Styron calls Peter's role as a centripetal artist into question in a way that anticipates the author's open rejection in *Sophie's Choice* of his early artistic notions.

In *Set This House on Fire*, Styron was questioning the implications and discovering the inadequacies of his role as a creator of meaning and a harmonizer of voices. The house set on fire is not merely Cass's soul but also the underlying pattern of Peter's narrative and the harmony that, as a lawyer and would-be "composer," he orchestrates.[1] Thus the novel is at once centripetal and centrifugal; it questions the notion of seeking order through art even as its narrator, Peter, adheres to the idea.

If in tracking the shift of attitude concerning the movement toward harmony, we take Peter to be not—as most critics see him—a secondary but the primary figure of the novel, *Set This House on Fire* sheds light on the path of Styron's career. Styron has said that the novel has a "transitional quality" because he was "trying to feel [his] way in certain directions" without fully understanding "what those directions were."[2] His uncertainty allows critics to find plenty to criticize in the novel's less disciplined aspects. But our concern here is with the overall clash of voices, not with easy targets. As the epigraph from Roethke between the halves implies, *Set This House on Fire* is about an awakening not just for Peter and Cass but for Styron. It is, in a phrase of Wallace Stevens', both about and suggestive of the "mind in the act of finding."[3] Its flaws owe partly to the new directions Styron was taking, including the fundamental reexamination of, and judgment on, the objective of having a narrative move toward harmony.

The critical estimate of *Set This House on Fire* is remarkable for its diversity. The novel has received a large measure of praise in Europe

1. William Styron, *Set This House on Fire*, (New York, 1960), 5, cited in the present chapter by page number, without title.
2. Appendix conversations, 221.
3. Wallace Stevens, "Of Modern Poetry," in *The Collected Poems of Wallace Stevens* (London, 1955), 239.

from Georg Lukács, and in France especially from, among others, Robert Kanters, Jacques Cabau, and the novelists Thérèse de Saint Phalle and Michel Butor.[4] But Anglo-American critics have for the most part been disparaging from the outset, their criticism dissipating more recently into neglect. There were early attacks from, in particular, Richard Foster, who called it (in a negative sense) an "absurd book" lacking in "sincerity," and from Norman Mailer and John W. Aldridge.[5] In Britain, reaction has in the main been limited to the poor reviews.[6] The novel has been widely seen by the English-speaking establishment as Styron's weakest, and even those who defend it tend to see it as having, in the words of Louis D. Rubin, Jr., a "grievous structural flaw" relating to the supposedly dual narration.[7]

The critics broadly accept, however, that the novel is about Cass. Peter, whom David D. Galloway sees as the "only uncorrupted male character in the book," is regarded at best as Styron's "clear-eyed"

4. Georg Lukács describes the "theme" of "alienation" as exemplifying what "links significant writing in our time with the great literature of the past" (*Writer and Critic, and Other Essays*, trans. Arthur Kahn [London, 1978], 18). See also especially Michel Butor's preface to the French edition, "Oedipus Americanus," trans. Ahmed Amriqua, in *Critical Essays on William Styron*, ed. Arthur D. Casciato and James L. W. West III (Boston, 1982), 138.

5. See Richard Foster, "An Orgy of Commerce: William Styron's *Set This House on Fire*," *Critique*, III (1960), 59–70; Norman Mailer, *Cannibals and Christians* (1966; rpr. London, 1967), 102–105; Norman Mailer, *Advertisements for Myself* (1959; rpr. London, 1961), 400–401; John W. Aldridge, *The Devil in the Fire: Retrospective Essays on American Literature and Culture, 1951–1971* (New York, 1972), 209–16. If Mailer's rivalry is well known, light is shed on his and Aldridge's criticisms by the comments of George Plimpton and Larry Alson in *Mailer: His Life and Times*, by Peter Manso (1985; rpr. Harmondsworth, Eng., 1986). Plimpton talks of how "[James] Jones sided with Styron" in a row with Mailer; "then, of course, Norman ripped them . . . in *Advertisements*" (p. 247). Alson describes how Styron "found a house" for Aldridge in Connecticut. "A whole bunch of people were up there, part of the group, and then Styron somehow put Aldridge into coventry, so ostracized him that he was forced to leave" (p. 239).

6. See, for example, the anonymous reviews, "New Fiction," *Times* (London), February 16, 1961, p. 15; and "What Happened at Sambuco," *Times Literary Supplement*, February 17, 1961, p. 101. For a more recent British view, see Richard Gray, *The Literature of Memory: Modern Writers of the American South* (London, 1977), 290.

7. Louis D. Rubin, Jr., "An Artist in Bonds," in *Critical Essays on William Styron*, ed. Casciato and West, 94.

spokesman—his language, solutions, and evasions being seen as the author's—and at worst as an extraneous nuisance to the narrative.[8] In contrast, I will focus on Peter as both the unifying voice and a deliberately problematic figure.

Although the story may be about Cass, the novel is about Peter. Whereas Peter needs to write the account, he sees Cass as having found some stability prior to the writing. One of Cass's last comments, in the context of Peter's composition, is that he can at least choose being over nothingness, "not for the joy of being, or even the love of being, much less the desire to be forever—but in the hope of being what I could be for a time" (500–501). The key here is the changed meaning of *being*. The final phrase refers not just to existing, as in "love of being," but to making something of existence, finding a viable role. Cass's acceptance of "being" what he "could be" is a recognition of limitations, both of life itself and of the kinds of responsibilities he can take on. Looking back with Peter, he has shed the unrealistic side of his idealism and can examine events in a more detached, even amused way; hence he describes his now-happy marriage as "harmonious disharmony" (249). Content with the potential of what he has—part-time job, painting class, family—he no longer neglects them to shoulder responsibilities beyond him. His existential acceptance of what "plain *is*" (52) allows him some inner harmony.

In Peter's view, Cass has resolved his "paralyzing death of the soul" (8) and found some contentment prior to the narrative's start. It is

8. David D. Galloway, *The Absurd Hero in American Fiction* (London, 1981), 93. Samuel Coale sees both Peter and Culver as "clear-eyed witnesses" (*William Styron Revisited* [Boston, 1991], 57). Ihab Hassan sees Peter and Styron as one, arguing that the novel is morally "flawed" because it brings us near the "facts of violence" but "ends by evading them" ("The Novel of Outrage: A Minority Voice in Postwar American Fiction," *American Scholar*, XXXIV [1965], 244). Gray thinks the novel "does not so much find a solution as impose one" (*The Literature of Memory*, 290). On Cass as the narrator and central consciousness of the second half, see especially Philip W. Leon, "Styron's Fiction: Narrative as Idea," in *The Achievement of William Styron*, ed. Robert K. Morris and Irving Malin (Athens, Ga., 1981), 134. On Peter's role, see especially John Kenny Crane, who calls the novel a "third person story in which the first person narrator can never seem to find a role for himself" (*The Root of All Evil: The Thematic Unity of William Styron's Fiction* [Columbia, S.C., 1984], 161).

therefore Peter's progress toward harmony—with the help of Cass's story—that we witness. Inattention to this has led to confusion over Peter's role and contributed to the negative reaction to the novel.

Most critics also see Cass as narrator of the second half, or at any rate as the key figure in a joint narration. Philip W. Leon rightly argues that "the narrative structure is the meaning of this novel." He then quotes Styron's comment that he tried to create a "narrator who, beginning in the first person, could convincingly end up in the third person, the story so merging and mingling that one might accept without hesitation the fact that the narrator himself knew the uttermost nuances of another man's thought." Leon then claims, as if that supports his view, that the second half, "largely composed of Cass' talking to Peter," continues "at such length that Cass effectively becomes the narrator."[9] But Styron's and Leon's assertions are in conflict. For Styron, the "narrator himself" is always Peter. There are sections, longer in the second half, where Cass's voice seems to dominate, but the point is that his voice is always filtered through Peter.

The conflict arises because the label *narrator* is poorly defined. Peter is always the primary narrator, and so the orchestrator. It is he who presents us with the illusion of Cass's verbatim narrative, selects extracts from Cass's journal, and summarizes Cass's thoughts, just as he appears to enter the mind of Luigi when, in Chapter 10, he summarizes what Luigi has told Cass. At most, Cass is a secondary narrator. Far from taking over Peter's narration, he is part of it, and his voice is subordinate to it. The only difference between Peter's narration in the first and second halves is that, at times, the devices that signal him as recorder and editor of Cass's words all but disappear.

A quick textual overview shows that even in the second half Peter directly narrates the vast majority of the pages. The broad breakdown looks like this:

> 245–49 Peter narrating
> 249–78 Cass talking, with Peter's interruptions
> 279–91 Peter narrating

9. Leon, "Styron's Fiction," in *The Achievement of William Styron*, ed. Morris and Malin, 133. Styron's comment is in William Styron to *Publishers Weekly*, in *Publishers Weekly*, May 30, 1960, p. 55.

291–96 Cass's journal
296–361 Peter narrating
361–64 Cass's journal
365–80 Peter narrating
380–402 Cass talking, with Peter's interruptions
403–39 Peter narrating
439–47 Cass talking, with Peter's directions
448–88 Peter narrating
488–501 Cass, uninterrupted
505–507 Letters to Peter

Not only does Peter speak directly for much of the second half but even when silent he is orchestrating Cass's voice. Cass may become a focus, but page distribution confirms that Peter retains control and, as we will see, shapes the narrative to fit his viewpoint. Even apart from the evidence of the division of pages, the existence of the epilogue reminds us of Peter's role as the text's unifier. Since he is the recipient of the letters, it is presumably he who places them. The idea that Cass takes over the narration is illusory.

Recognizing that Peter orchestrates the telling from start to finish and shapes the account to his needs helps us understand the language and structure of the novel. But awareness of the gap between Peter and the author is also important. The gap is implicit in the Italian epigraph: "L'ambizione del mio compito non mi impedì di fare molti sbagli" (The ambition of my task did not prevent me from making many mistakes), which speaks to the novel's uneasy, searching quality. For Styron, as for Cass, the movement is only *toward* a workable position, whereas Peter means us to see events as reaching a tidier conclusion.

Describing the author's position in a polyphonic novel—a novel where a character's voice retains a high degree of autonomy—Bakhtin stresses that the author is still "profoundly active" behind the textual voices, "but his activity is of a special *dialogic* sort": "It is one thing to be active in relation to a dead thing, to voiceless material that can be molded and formed as one wishes, and another thing to be active *in relation to someone else's living, autonomous consciousness*. This is a questioning, provoking, answering, agreeing, objecting activity; that is, it is dialogic activity no less active than the activity that finalizes, materializes, explains, and kills causally, that drowns out the other voice with nonsemantic arguments."[10] In *Lie Down in Darkness*, Styron as author and narrator manipulates our view of Helen so that he "drowns out" her full discourse to fulfill the novel's pattern. But in *Set This House on Fire*, Peter as narrator is neither on a level with the author nor drowned out but is an independent voice implicitly questioned by Styron, the ventriloquizing author whose intentions are "refracted" in the text.[11] Styron as author shifts from his centripetal role—now filled by the artist-composer Peter—to a more centrifugal one. Even as Peter organizes Cass's story, Styron is actively showing that Peter ideologically rationalizes and shapes elements of the story that contradict his conviction that by the end stability has been achieved, answers found. Styron's ventriloquizing presence is always apparent behind Peter's voice. The narration is the first of Styron's to be truly double voiced. But this quality reflects the relationship not between Peter and Cass but between Peter and the author.

The gap between Peter and the author is made plain by the specific characteristics and personal history Styron ascribes to Peter, and in the way textual events leak out of the movement toward harmony that Peter engineers. There are several clues to Peter's disposition. He looks at both his law job and his wish to be a composer as pursuing the centripetal. Styron lets his narrator's profession not only testify to Peter's propensity for order but also, we will see, undermine Peter's claims of solutions in his composition. Peter's wish to be a composer permits a musical motif for his orchestration toward harmony, a development from first-half discord—a "grotesque fantasia of events lacking sequence or order" (30)—toward musical, verbal, and mental concord. This development, linking the halves into a single movement, shows Peter—plainly the dominating control of the first half—at work throughout.

Peter selects and edits the whole account, and it is his whether he chooses high- or low-profile narration. Given his disquietude before

10. Mikhail M. Bakhtin, "Prefatory Comments on 'Toward a Reworking of the Dostoyevsky Book,'" in *Critical Essays on Dostoyevsky*, trans. Caryl Emerson, ed. Robert F. Miller (Boston, 1986), 248.

11. Mikhail M. Bakhtin, *The Dialogic Imagination: Four Essays*, trans. Michael Holquist and Caryl Emerson, ed. Michael Holquist (Austin, Tex., 1981), 299–300.

seeking Cass, we can assume that what he shows us and what interests him link with his own plight and the recovery he relates. The several narrative devices—Cass's diary, Luigi's viewpoint, the letters—merely veil his hand in the composition. Most important, the movement reflects both his position in society and his emotional needs. Like Culver, he serves well for bringing ostensible closure, since his liberal goodwill allows (almost) all voices to be heard. But more definably than in *The Long March*, Styron works to thwart the effort at harmonizing the voices.

Peter, in beginning his composition, parallels his role in the Marshall Plan for postwar European recovery—itself an attempt to rebuild a shattered whole—by reconstructing the unease his fragmentary knowledge of the events in Sambuco has caused him. In the second half of the novel he then conducts the conflicting voices of the piece toward harmony. In the first half we learn of the anxiety that leads him to visit Cass in South Carolina to try to find out what really happened and—since he tells Cass his story first—of the extreme exhaustion he suffered as he witnessed the events of two years before. Peter has the reader share his initial confusion by experiencing events as he did. Only later his conversations with Cass reward us with what he hopes is an integrative understanding of the order and meaning of the events.

Throughout, however, Peter's role inspires doubts, in virtue both of the elements Styron has Peter use in his composing, and of the position Peter holds in the story. Peter deploys three specific pointers toward harmony: pastoral scenery, which looms gradually larger in the course of the story, and Poppy and Luigi, two of his important secondary characters. But as will become evident, each of these impedes as much as advances the effect his composition aims for. Peter's way of resolving the problems the narrative raises becomes transparently an arrangement to fit his ideological and emotional interests rather than to answer to what the events themselves require.

From the opening, Peter is keen, perhaps too keen, to establish his credentials as a responsible, trustworthy narrator. To borrow a phrase of Saul Bellow's, "to want his credentials known" is "his one immediately apparent weakness."[12] But the qualifications he lays out are not

12. Saul Bellow, *Mr. Sammler's Planet* (New York, 1970), 224.

entirely reassuring. He tells us that, having once hoped to be a "composer," he has settled—like Culver—for being a lawyer. Unlike with Culver, Styron here makes the shift in professional goals an intimation of deepest personal nature. Peter presents the law as authoritative discourse capable of ordering a chaotic world. Unable to be a composer, he links composing and the law in his role as narrator, creating an account of events that implies that justice is done and order restored. Having renounced composing because law is far more "lucrative" and because "in America no one listens to composers," he tenuously melds the two fields to which he has been drawn by arguing that the law "works its own music" on "the minds of men" (5).

Such rationalization is characteristic of Peter in the novel that evolves, but the first point is the ambiguity of the word *compose*. On the one hand, Peter is an artist, composing an account of what happened. Thereby, he is the creator and organizer, as much as the recorder, of events. But the word *compose* is double-edged, meaning not only to create but to becalm. Peter, like many writers of a realist or modernist aesthetic, is intent not only on opening up dialogue and examining conventional assumptions but ultimately on stilling the tumult that exposed contradictions spawn. In that, he parallels the earlier Styron, who unleashed diverse voices but also tried to harmonize them and hence create meaning. Styron's choice here to harmonize only through the highly ambivalent figure of Peter attests to what was a growing uneasiness over the limitations of the ordering function of art.

As a lawyer, Peter implicitly believes in a need for rules to master chaos. Far from being either ambitious or radical, he is a "square," content to remain "mediocre" (5), and consequently more likely to uphold than to question the status quo. Nor is he willing to take responsibility for his own actions, or those done in his name. His reaction to di Lieto's mother's accusations—pleading that it was not he who bombed her house (35)—is later matched by his insistence that he "wasn't the boss" in reply to Cass's complaint that relief aid did not spread far south (206). Peter's career suggests he not only seeks order but also hopes to avoid responsibility by appeal to something larger than himself. Unwilling to acknowledge complicity in the activities of his own society, he has nevertheless snuggled himself into that society's apparatus like a bug in a crevice.

His opening two paragraphs set the tone. We barely hear his voice at all, because he introduces Sambuco by way of Nagel's guidebook. That captures his belief in the possibilities of an ordered life—where guidebooks, Nagel or legal, can be relied on—and suggests, as his emphasis on credentials does, that if possible, he will resort to authority in creating a sense of order. (Even his extensive use of Cass's words in the second half can be seen as a retreat from personal answerability.) The events in Sambuco have disoriented Peter, and one reaction is to refamiliarize the place by finding it on a tourist map. The extracts from the guidebook, like the letters in the epilogue, are among the many "scraps and snippets" (67) he pastes together in his attempt to contrive harmony.

That Peter is a lawyer, a would-be composer, and a guidebook user, is consistent with his organizing role. Part materialist like Mason, part artist like Cass, he sees himself as a mediator. Having shown us his qualifications—which leave him marked rather than convince us—he tells of the uneasiness and dislocation that have led him to compose his account. The first half of the novel is thus a depictive amalgam of spiritual, linguistic, imagistic discord, enveloped by a musical trope, all anticipatory to the eventual composition toward harmony. Spiritual uneasiness, Peter tells us early on, is what leads him to visit Cass just over two years after the events troubling him, and what lies behind his composition of the narrative. In Styron's play, *In the Clap Shack*, Wallace Magruder tells Schwartz that Wallace Stevens "writes pure music."[13] As a would-be composer, Peter embodies Stevens' preoccupations. Like the female protagonist in "Sunday Morning," who "feels the dark / Encroachment of that old catastrophe,"[14] he sees Sundays as a time haunted by "those old questions '*What am I doing? Where am I going?*'" as a "churchbell lets fall its chimes upon the quiet, hopelessly and sadly" (7). Through linguistic and musical analogies, Peter gives voice to his spiritual disarray throughout the first half.

He tells us how his distress increases when, on his way to see Cass in South Carolina, he visits his father in Virginia. The destruction of his boyhood haunts leaves him even more rootless and restless, as do his father's forebodings of "moral and spiritual anarchy" (12). Peter

13. William Styron, *In the Clap Shack* (New York, 1973), 32.
14. Stevens, "Sunday Morning," in *The Collected Poems*, 67.

feels "as if my identity had slipped away, leaving me without knowledge of where I had been and where I was going" (16). His spiritual disorder, mingled here with chronotopic dislocation, leads to moral unease about Sambuco and what to him is the unfinished business there.

Visiting Cass, Peter relates to us what he disclosed to Cass of his own experiences leading up to the murders. He re-creates the sense of dislocation and exhaustion that colored his arrival and night in Sambuco hours before the killings occurred. His "composure hopelessly unmoored" (26), his exhaustion reaching "lunatic dimensions" (76), he had driven all night from Rome, finding little on his car radio but a "faint windy snatch of Beethoven," an American program called *Hill-billy Gasthaus,* and the "chill comfort" of bilingual phrases like "Un po' di allegria negli Spikes Jones" (26). Far from giving him the "bit of happiness" the Italian phrase promises, the "liaison of tongues" left him "gripped with anxiety" (26).

His exhaustion and anxiety, he tells us, were compounded with shock the next morning, when his car collided with di Lieto's motor scooter. At the scene of the accident he was subjected to a grotesquely mismanaged attempt by the Italian police to discover the order of events, and he saw di Lieto carried away in an ambulance that was "trumpeting senselessly," like "some Gabriel's horn blowing flat ruptured notes of glory" (35). He then coaxed his dented, overheating Austin up to Sambuco, its radio sputtering "deafening crackles and peeps" (29). All this, and the sight of Emilio Narduzzo's gaudy villa offending the serenity of the surrounding countryside, left him in a dismal state of mind. The mood of utter discord is established.

In retelling the story, Peter is seeking both to compose and to regain composure, and he has begun by rehearsing the sounds and voices that destroyed his composure in the first place. The musical motif, evident early on in the quasi-operatic sounds of wailing voices, mistuned radios, and clanging bells, was only one constituent of his discomposure. The night's events brought other kinds of disorder: linguistic, in his "abortive parley with madwomen" (67) when the lines were crossed while he was trying to discover di Lieto's condition; mental, in the greeting spoken by the retarded Saverio's "demented voice" (69); and social, in the violent row he witnessed between Mason and Rosemarie, whose voices rose up "in frenzied contest" with the generator (69).

The confusion he felt was exacerbated when Cass, whom he had met on the road to Sambuco, reappeared that evening. Blind drunk, Cass collapsed on a piano—a continuation of Peter's musical motif—with a "thunderous uproar of sharps and flats" (119) and roiled the party by playing a record of Mozart's *Don Giovanni* alternately with one of a doom-laden hillbilly song, at various distorting volumes, before strangling the music "with the jagged uproar of a phonograph needle scraping like a raw blade across the evening" (122). Punctuating all this were disconnected cries, wails, and laughter that, says Peter, "washed around us in waves on senseless wave" (187). Connected with the musical and psychological discord, the first half of the novel reflects structurelessness, dissemblance, and conflict, and throughout it genres are mingled, in particular in the disconcerting oscillation between the realism of Peter's early descriptions and the cartoonlike quality of subsequent characters and events: the crash with the one-eyed di Lieto; Fausto Windgasser, "flatulent as his name" (70); the drunken Cass, whose eyes make "comic-strip X's behind his glasses" (183). The overall effect is to leave the reader not only off balance with regard to what happens but unsure whether to read the account as tragedy, comedy, or farce.

If voices and sounds are constantly clashing in the first half, the discord Peter portrays is also apparent in chronotopic terms, both within the operatic world of Italy, where hillbilly competes not only with Mozart but with the Sambuco bells' "discordant requiem" (121), and between the Italian and New York scenes, the latter fraught with "jazz, the music not of fusion but fission" (154). The appearance in Sambuco of Mason and his ilk has not only brought the two worlds together but increased the already existing contrast between Sambuco, "aloof upon its precipice" (4), and valleys like Tramonti, hardly changed for centuries. Thus not only does spatial and cultural dissonance reign but time, too, becomes subject to conflict and disorder. Peter's daydreamed memories of Virginia intermingle with his feverish sleep in Sambuco and Rosemarie's calls for him to awaken. During these reveries, the chimes in Mason's house are a "clashing, outlandish centerpoint of tortured clockwork" (86), while the presence of Peter, Mason, and Wendy, with their beer cans and jazz, in the eighteenth-century library, is "anachronistic" (82). In both the Sambuco and Virginia scenes, Peter weaves an uneasy mixture. All kinds of discord—

musical, discursive, mental, spiritual, chronotopic—seem to unite in a great blur.

Peter has found himself "on the periphery" of events of which Cass is the "dead center" (19). But Peter's sense of being on the edge of events, unsure of the extent of his responsibility, is, for Styron, not a peripheral matter. Peter's questions are limited to the specific events, but Styron implicitly points us toward wider questions of responsibility. What responsibility, for example, lies with the likes of Peter, and maybe many a reader, happy to make the "pleasant best" of situations (5), to seek coherence, and so perhaps evade potential conflicts and give the Masons of this world a chance to thrive?

Peter, restricting attention to specific events, is already preparing to harmonize the discord he recounts. The link between musical and literary composition is strong. Like a composer, his mind full of unrelated musical notes he hopes to arrange coherently, Peter is pasting together the "scraps and snippets" of information and intuition that constitute his sense of what happened. When Mason throws away Cass's message—his written note—Peter pockets it for later use. His specific aim is to "learn about Sambuco—about Mason and my part in the matter" (19). Cass is the key to the possibility of composing meaning out of the off-pitch notes and melodic fragments he collects, and so of quelling his doubts.

But Styron continues to undercut Peter's shaping of his account. Peter's pursuit of personal and social harmony has a price. This is most evident in his friendship with Mason. In Sambuco, he saw Mason's brutal treatment of Rosemarie but did nothing. The doubts this inaction raises over his character are confirmed by his memories of still earlier days. The worst of Mason's sycophants in youth, he admits that before leaving for Europe he was the "crown prince among his freeloaders" (149). He sporadically insists that all that is past, but in fact the "tainted" relationship (130) between the two remains. His reaction to Mason's ugly comment on how pleasant Sambuco is with its cheap servants who "out-yassuh any coon" was to head straight there, since Mason made "it all seem lazy enough" (21). His declarations, moreover, that he hoped Mason had changed are unconvincing. Mason's letters belie this. Peter remains a sycophant, happy to settle for an easy life that does not confront injustice or difficulties. If his earlier disgust at Mason's treatment of Celia dissolved when "old Daddy" Mason filled his cabin with goodies (166), in Sambuco he was ensconced in a room paid for by Mason, willing to ignore Mason's continued abuse of women and hoping to extenuate his own inaction by mentioning exhaustion.

If in part Peter's composition aims at excusing his links with Mason, it at the same time implicates him both in Mason's deeds and in ills of wider scope. One reason he remained uneasy was that when he first met Cass on the hill up to Sambuco, Cass downplayed Peter's worry over the cost of the accident by reminding him of the local poverty. Peter felt "betrayed" because Cass's comments did not "harmonize" with his own resentment (42). He damped his annoyance, but Styron's implicit criticism resonates, for Peter was displaying a self-centered arrogance toward the Italians that was also evident not only in Sambuco, where he shouted at the film crew, "Do I look like an Italian? I've as much right to this square as you" (57), but also in his halfhearted attempts to "extend a democratic hand" in his job. Of his work we learn only that he was "embarrassingly" well paid but hoped the Italians would be happier to have given of their hospitality and resources than for the little they received from his "grotesque attempts" to help (21). His sense of "self-implication," here as elsewhere, is characteristically short-lived (177), and he was happy to tuck into his share of Mason's "tons of provisions" while the peasants of Tramonti went hungry (95).

It is arguable that Peter's retrospective composition is a step he takes toward accepting some of the responsibility he shunned prior to the murder. His examination of his role is at least evidence of reflection, of a learning process, and in the second half of the novel he does tell how he entered Michele's cabin and how Cass "opened" his eyes "to a lot of things" (246). Still, his disposition to harmonize leaves fissures in his self-presentation that Styron subtly exposes.

In the second half of the novel, Styron ensures that Peter's attempts to harmonize his account undermine themselves. So far Peter has told us his experience of the events in Sambuco and has set up a mood of discordant confusion. Always concerned to find the answer, he turns his aim to showing how he and Cass, on their Carolina riverbank, resolve the questions raised. He intends to compose the clashing voices and jumbled memories he has related in the first half into an unproblematic, harmonious whole that will let him "get on with the job" of living his "decent, mediocre" life (19). Although Cass's voice comes to be heard at length, the dialogic tension remains between Peter's narration and the ventriloquizing author.

The second half contains much of the violence presaged earlier, but Peter portrays it as less shocking than cathartic, since it provides answers to the questions he raises. But his answers do not address other questions Styron implicitly broaches in connection with Peter's composition, questions that have to do especially with cultural domination and exploitation. As the second half traces Cass's journey to Sambuco and his recovery there, Peter's overriding need to find the answer leads him to compose an account capable of freeing him from any sense of complicity either in the deaths of Mason and Francesca or in the wider question of American activities abroad.

Both the new tone of the second half and Styron's questioning of Peter's discourse toward harmony are adumbrated by the epigraph from "The Waking" between the two parts. Roethke's title sounds a positive note after the dissonant voices and disjointed events of the first half. Cass and Peter apparently experience a mental and moral waking as a result of Sambuco. Peter says that Cass "opened" his eyes, and Cass refers to how he was "wakened up in many different ways" by events in Sambuco (369). The line "I learn by going where I have to go" voices the deterministic aspect of Cass's journey to Sambuco, as well as Peter's compulsion to find answers by seeking out Cass and composing this account. Both the line and the title also express Styron's own awakening to a less solipsistic, less purely aesthetic vision of the novel form.[15]

The contrast between the end of the first half and the start of the second is indicative that Peter's composition is moving toward harmony. The first half ends in the Kinsolvings' chaotic apartment. Having killed Mason, Cass returns, his face "aged a dozen years" in a day, but he staggers off again, leaving Poppy "swooning, in a crumpled

---

15. Theodore Roethke, "The Waking," in *Words for the Wind* (Bloomington, Ind., 1964), 124.

heap" (241). If the tone is comic melodrama, the discord remains unexplained. Cass and Poppy seem lost to each other, and Peter as bewildered as when he entered Sambuco. The second half, by contrast, starts with a return to the Carolina riverbank and the easy dialogue between Peter and Cass as they reminisce. It is patterned, moveover, by an increasing displacement of the jangling bells and vying voices of earlier by the sounds and voices of accord. The second half returns us to Europe and the story of how Cass fell into Mason's hands, but Peter's editing, shaping, and diction ensure a movement toward harmony. Even when we learn of the equally melodramatic Sambucan climax, where Cass chased Mason to the cliff edge, Cass, in Peter's words, heard a ship's "sonorous" horn "floating up faint but clear through light like a pearl" (463).

Through the pointers Peter has set out in the first half toward the harmony he is composing, we can see both how he attempts to dispel dissonance and how Styron subverts his attempt. Peter's first pointer, his wealth of pastoral motifs, is tied to the riverbank conversations. If in the first half the dichotomy between Italian scenery and American materialism is part of the discord, in the second half pastoral scenes, especially Cass's "bucolic glade" of Tramonti (340), promise concord. But even in the first half, Peter's references to his conversations with Cass in South Carolina at least assure the reader that answers will be found—that Cass and Peter have escaped, physically at least, from the confusion Peter is unfolding. In contrast to Peter's portrayal of spiritual tumult, the tranquillity of fishing beneath the "Carolina sun," far from the clang of the Sambuco bells, anticipates the harmony that Peter will steer the narrative toward: "The . . . shores were immensities of shade," says Peter, "the heat and stillness like a narcotic" (48). Cass, whom Peter first shows benevolent but drunk in Sambuco, is here serious and sober. Though Peter observes occasional signs of "remembered pain" (49), the progress toward harmony is heralded. Peter tells us of their shared "love for music" (53) and explains that they develop "understanding and harmony" because "just as I thought he could clear up my oppressive mysteries, so he saw in me the key to his own" (51).

Peter's second pointer is his portrayal of Poppy, whom he links to pastoral harmony. Ostensibly she is a mess; from the first she misunderstood his explanation of the crash. But hints of a more even-flowing potential exist in "her sweet face" and "huge blue eyes" (39), in her concern for di Lieto, and in the pastoral imagery that surrounds her and her children. Near Sambuco, Peter saw them hitching a lift after they had gathered "wild flowers," and his eye was caught by the "cornflowers, poppies and wild roses" that sprouted around him "in the enveloping steam" (38). Peter suggests that Poppy was part of Cass's problem but also stable enough to support Cass in his rehabilitation. Like her floral namesake, she has a dual nature. Just as poppies yield heroin, so at worst she is another drug for Cass, since her forgiving temperament enables him to continue his self-pitying debauchery. Yet her weaknesses are also her strengths. Like the pastoral imagery, which becomes stronger in the novel's second half, so Poppy is there to the end, as resilient as the poppies after World War I. She withstands Cass's drinking and adultery and is glad simply that he has "come back" (500).

The third pointer, introduced near the end of the first half, is Peter's depiction of Luigi Migliore. If Poppy, in Peter's composition, becomes a major reason for Cass's choice of "being," the opportunity to choose might not have existed without Luigi's willingness to cover up. Congruent with the tensions of the first half, much of Luigi's thought harbors paradox. A "Fascist Humanist" (198) and an "intellectual policeman" (194), he has no religion but warns Cass of the "dark whiteness" (197) of the "horrible vista of eternity" (195). Full of compassion, he sees the peasants as helpless animals who should be put out of their suffering. Yet he also believes that "the single good is respect for the force of life" and that "the primary moral sin is self destruction" (195). Despite his unintegrated convictions, he is a catalyst for Cass's turnaround. His castigation of Cass for self-destructiveness helps get the American to sober up and start his recovery. The justification for Luigi's fluid logic—which does not preclude an orderliness reflected in his "neatly barbered" presence (195) and "formal, meticulous" speech (329)—becomes clear when he explains that Italians "are the most expedient people on earth" (337–38) and that he is using other people's frames of reference to get by in practical terms.

As the second half progresses, ostensible harmony gains. Peter's pastoralism becomes more pronounced, Poppy wins Cass back, and Luigi helps Cass secure his mental and physical freedom. But all three pointers are infused with contradictions and force questions that jeopardize Peter's movement toward genuine harmony.

Peter's pastoral motif lends itself to Styron's dialogizing, which is evident both in the diction he gives Peter and in Peter's treatment of events. Peter's description of the scenery as like a "narcotic" suggests that pastoral harmony is not for him a way to reality. Moreover, much of the pastoral imagery of the second half is associated with Cass's involvement with Francesca Ricci's family in Tramonti. So while the pastoralism brings calm, it brings as well problems for Peter's composition, and an unsettledness regarding his own "part in the matter." Cass's regeneration through his love for Francesca and his attempts to save her father, Michele, are in conflict with the reemergence of Poppy. The way Peter disposes of the conflict, especially by sidelining the Italian family, shows both his manipulation of events and an ideologically contestable viewpoint.

The "enchanted" valley of Tramonti seems to suggest both a more idyllic setting and worthier goals for Cass (206). When Cass begins to break away from Mason, the chronotope shifts. The palace chronotope has its ironic counterpoint in the peasants' hut, where Cass appears to find a sense of purpose. Hence, toward the end of the first half, Peter shows Cass—for the first time in the narrative—leaving the precipice of Sambuco and descending into Tramonti, "escaping at last that palace-hemmed chicanery" (206). The space and the timeless quality of the valley seem to mirror the freeing of Cass's mind from the self-centeredness that has kept him in bondage. At the same time, though, any vision of a developing pastoral harmony is obstructed by the misery of the peasant family's home, by the cruel lives of the old women, and by the eventual deaths of Michele and Francesca, both partly a result of the callous indifference of the commerce-centered, materialist world of Mason.

The supposed escape into pastoral harmony, implicit in Peter's and Cass's conversations on their riverbank, is thus controverted by sociohistorical realities touched upon in the narrative but marginalized by Peter. The fact is that the "enchanted" valley is really at the mercy of the rich American in Sambuco. Cass can have the drug for Michele only if he bargains with Mason; nothing is given without return in Mason's world. Everything Mason does is concerned with acquisition, either through sexual conquest or in his attempts to buy friendship and control. His lust for power is the indirect cause of Cass's worsening condition and Francesca's death. The chronotope of the palace thus sets the fate of the valley of Tramonti and of the seemingly remote Ricci family in their hut. Cass's experience there may help him gain both perspective and a sense of self-worth, but in Peter's account the peasants' suffering is merely instrumental to Cass's redemption. At the end, Peter makes no mention of the peasant family's having been destroyed, presumably because that would shake his impression of satisfactory closure.

Although the apparent idyll of Tramonti seems to advance the movement toward harmony, it sparks questions about Mason, cultural imperialism, and Peter's exact reasons for being in Italy. Alongside Peter's focus on specific events, the novel portrays the Marshall Plan he is part of as enabling a cultural imperialism through economic coercion. Mason tells Cass that General Marshall is a "fountainhead, or fathead, of goodwill" and that, since "everything political can be reduced to human terms, a microcosm," Francesca's thievery is the "*reductio ad absurdum* of what's going on" (410). But instead of accepting Mason's view that the Marshall Plan let Italy, or Europe, steal from a foolishly benevolent America, it is possible to see Cass, Mason, and Peter as representing in satiric microcosm a political situation in which the American rather than the European role is ethically dubious. Mason, whose name makes both nationalistic and divisional allusions—to the national flag and the Mason-Dixon Line—incarnates a view of postwar foreign-policy objectives, and perhaps of northern economic objectives in the South, as essentially acquisitive. On that reading, Cass tries to combat the coercion of Mason through direct action, such as by helping Francesca steal. Peter allows the story to unfold but never makes the connections between his own role as an apathetic cog in a machine that gains power by granting economic aid, his sycophantic support of Mason, and the struggle between Mason and Cass. Peter is as sarcastic and indignant as Mason about Italian petty thievery—as when the watch and razor were stolen from him in Rome—but he is also content to milk enjoyment and comfort from Mason, the system, and the country.

There are occasional echoes in the novel of comments that C. Vann

Woodward makes about postwar American foreign policy in *The Burden of Southern History*. Peter's despair at urban encroachment in Virginia brings to mind Woodward's discussion of the "bulldozer revolution."[16] But Styron, in using the southern voice of Woodward, seems to include a broader national and international subject matter. Woodward's brief query whether the Marshall Plan sprang from benevolence or was at least as much concerned to ensure that "America must be strong enough to carry her way by economic coercion or by force" takes on pivotal importance in the play between Mason's coercive generosity, Cass's struggle against that, and Peter's ambivalence. Certainly, here the aid does not seep down to the peasants but is instead manipulated by Mason to secure his power over Cass. Mason exploits poverty at least as much as he relieves it, and Peter is his passive accomplice. This seems to concern Styron but not Peter, who is unwilling to make the connections.

Styron's doubts about Peter's composition are also evident in Peter's portrayal of Poppy and Francesca. A conflict clearly exists between the pastoral innocence Peter associates with Francesca and the continuing marriage of Poppy and Cass. Francesca's death may settle the course events take, but Peter's reductive description of her raises further questions about the way he shapes his account. For Peter, Poppy represents stability. After all, she and Cass are married, so legally partners. He shows how Poppy offers the focus that Cass has lacked. Cass tells him that "you can't work without faith" (250), and Peter presents Poppy as a paradigm of faith, not only the faith of Catholicism but also faith in her husband. He shows Cass growing aware of the selflessness that is her great attribute—of the way "she gives & loves" while Cass takes (295). Peter is thus suggesting that with regard to the worth of Poppy, Cass simply, in Roethke's words, takes his "waking slow."

There are two problems for Peter: the manner of Francesca's death, which impedes his search for meaning, and her position as a rival to Poppy, which further disturbs his sense of order. His depiction tells us less about Francesca than about him. He allows her love for Cass to be seen as important to Cass's regeneration, conveying the atmosphere of Edenic innocence around them in their "marvelous little secluded

16. C. Vann Woodward, *The Burden of Southern History* (New York, 1960), 6, 185.

grove" (440). But ultimately he tries to discount her importance, intimating that she could never have become more than a passing interest for Cass. He links her, as he does Poppy, to the pastoral harmony, but ensures that she never attains the same hold on our emotions as Poppy. Francesca remains one-dimensional, less a person than a symbol. Cass says he was shattered by her death, but Peter's selective account of Cass's revitalization and return to Poppy vitiates the declaration. Alive and in death, Francesca is described in symbolic terms. For all the good she did Cass as a temporary illusion of harmony, Cass still, we are assured, is not facing up to reality. He admits that their romance, spiritual and unconsummated, "became a kind of daydream" (439) that existed as if "under a spell" (440). Of her death we hear merely Cass's abstract comment that Mason "tore that meaning limb from limb" (444). As far as Peter is concerned, that is better than having the meaning he is constructing torn to pieces by what has happened to an Italian peasant.

The real evasion, then, is not Cass's love for Francesca but Peter's—and to an extent Cass's—elision of the implications of Francesca's life and death. She is reduced from a person to a "meaning" that Cass has found on his path to regeneration—something useful for allowing Peter and Cass to move toward harmony. Peter prompts the reader to accept Francesca's death as part of the movement toward harmony, and Poppy as the true reason for Cass's salvation. The logic of Peter's composition, however, ricochets upon itself, for if the pastoral scenes with Francesca are, as Peter implies, an evasion by Cass, equally an evasion are the pastoral scenes between Peter and Cass where, seeking harmony and meaning, they avert their eyes from anything discrepant with what they want to believe.

For Peter, Francesca, despite her utility, is finally an expendable part of the composition. But Styron has Peter's treatment of her make inroads upon his discourse toward harmony. When he saw her distress after Mason raped her, he was "torn both by a futile, gallant desire to help and by the beast inside, which drew [his] eyes down to that delectable, troubled bosom" (123). Reducing Francesca's rape and death to the loss of a "meaning" all but constitutes a second, this time textual, rape. Peter does his best to make Poppy, rather than Francesca, the vessel of potential harmony and realistic stability. His elevation of

Poppy to the decisive role in the recovery may be in line with his need for order, but larger questions are inescapable about his artistic sense of justice, particularly with regard to the foreign other.

Given that one of the structures that uphold Peter's sense of order and justice is the law, the character of Luigi similarly vexes Peter's composition. At first glance, he appears to enhance it; he not only helps Cass but is linked to Peter's unifying musical trope, which includes plot and character parallels with *Don Giovanni*.[17] With hindsight, Cass tells Peter that "a man cannot live properly . . . without music" but that "when abused," music "is a form of corruption." In Paris and Sambuco, Cass did abuse it, playing it "loud as hell" on a "scratchy hoarse" record player in an "endless circle of self-loathing, and venom and meanness" (255). Luigi helped Cass's recovery by cautioning him and taking steps toward correction. Turning off the record Cass had left on the turntable, he said that that was the way to "ruin *Don Giovanni*" (194).

Luigi's lessons were obviously about more than making the most of music. He taught Cass to regain belief in his own worth—to put his sense of responsibility into perspective. That leads to Cass's later admission to Peter that his sickness stemmed from "despair and self loathing and greed and selfishness and spite" (269–70). Poppy's selflessness, as Peter portrays it, was equaled by Luigi's. Warning Cass against abusing alcohol, and putting himself at risk in Cass's behalf, Luigi showed Cass how responsibility can manifest itself not in self-destructive, metaphysical guilt but in achievable goals, like that of looking after his family—who, among other things, are Cass's *legal* responsibility.

Yet Luigi also helps unsettle Peter's composition. To save Cass, Luigi subverted the law, one of Peter's mainstays against chaos. Since

17. Such parallels are only suggestive. Cass might be seen as a Don Giovanni figure, chasing the ideal, with Luigi as Leporello. But the darker side of Giovanni, pursuing love through force, is closer to Mason. Peter then becomes the onlooking Leporello figure. Parallels are also evident between Luigi and Leopold, Mozart's father, whom Cass names his nagging ulcer after. Harold C. Schonberg calls Leopold a "pedantic, well-organized, cautious, prudent" man, "constantly bombarding his son with sage advice" (*Lives of the Great Composers* [1970; rpr. London, 1980], 70). See also Kenneth A. Robb, "William Styron's Don Juan," *Critique*, VIII (1965–66), 34–46.

in the circumstances a legal solution may have been a moral injustice, harmony was possible only by hiding the truth, but Luigi's molding of the evidence to keep the facts from the Italian legal authorities—an interference that damaged Francesca's reputation—has its counterpart in Peter's own narrative manipulations as he assesses his part in the events of Sambuco. Peter's condoning of Luigi's illegal measures may reflect his awareness of Mason's nihilistic character, or his own friendship with Cass, but it also once again shows the hypocritical lengths to which he is willing to go to live a life of equanimity. An upholder of social and legal order, he is unwilling to face troublesome facts and defend troublesome interests.

Peter is a centripetal figure, an artist who composes events and, as we will see shortly, concludes the novel as if solutions have been found and a degree of social and personal harmony restored. But Styron reacts centrifugally, constantly dialogizing Peter's discourse toward harmony. He repeatedly draws our attention to questions that subvert Peter's attempts to reconcile voices and impose a desired meaning on events. He gives us the means to see that harmony of the sort Peter seeks is not just unattainable but undesirable.

The whole novel, even when Cass speaks, is shaped by Peter's conservative, self-interested viewpoint. Luigi provides the opportunity to probe the limits of responsibility, which Peter, burdened by a concern over his own guilt through complicity, does only with an apologist motive. When Peter begins to speak of his encounter with the recently raped Francesca by saying that "a really rather distressing thing occurred" (122), the limitations of his outlook are patent. Although he often records Cass's words, he is rarely aware of their full implications. When Cass questions whether the discovery of meaning might not be worse than the search for it, or when Luigi reminds Cass that the idea of a discoverable harmony is merely "middle class romanticism" (197), there is no sign that he understands how such views threaten the very structure of his narrative.

One figure, whom, along with the Ricci family, Peter will ignore in his summing-up, tears Peter's discourse toward harmony "limb from limb." That Francesca's killer turns out to be not Mason but Saverio, a "blank, mindless space, beyond reach of pain or punishment" (472), destroys the coherence Peter seeks. He has sought, after all, "to find the answer," but that answer, Saverio, is a centerlessness, beyond morality, rationality, or anything that will fit Peter's need for meaning and pattern. Cass seems to see this; he has found no definitive "belief" or "rock" (500). But Peter, using Cass's words, doggedly ends his account in the same conviction with which he has shaped it, the conviction that the events lend themselves to a harmonious ordering.

Peter completes the main narrative by stepping down from his earlier high profile, leaving Cass's quasi-Sartrean summing-up without comment. At the end—as an epilogue—he places a letter from Cass, and a letter from Sister Marie-Joseph about di Lieto. He presumably means this as a gesture of his contentment with Cass's views and with his discovery of harmony in their conclusions about the boundaries of responsibility. Peter wants us to see that during the narrative he too has felt guilt over the possible murder of di Lieto. As Butor notes, clear parallels exist with Cass's murder of Mason, for Peter describes his heart as having been "full of murder" and "revenge" just prior to the accident (28).[18] Cass's concern, similarly, is about whether his only motive for Mason's murder was "revenge" (445). Di Lieto recovers, but he ends up back in the hospital after another accident. Thus, with respect to di Lieto but also implicitly more broadly, Peter appears exonerated. His epilogue lets us see that he is ready to suppose that the questions raised have all been answered, with the letters as the final documentary evidence. He is grateful to have his case closed, stamped Not Guilty.

By channeling attention to his innocence regarding di Lieto's misadventures, he evades questions about his complicity in other wrongs: the degradation of Cass, whom Poppy asks him to save but whom he merely watches until he follows Cripps's lead and helps rescue him; the suffering of Francesca, whom he fails to help, caught between pity for her distress and lust for her "troubled bosom"; and the predations of Mason, whom, with sycophantic support, he helps thrive. In the case of each, his resolve to act, hampered by a morally crippling self-interest, is too weak and too late.

18. Butor, "Oedipus Americanus," in *Critical Essays on William Styron*, ed. Casciato and West, 136.

By bringing this to the reader's awareness, the novel transcends the idea of the creative process as merely a way to order a seemingly random world. Peter, like Culver and the narrator of *Lie Down in Darkness*, orchestrates a movement toward harmony; by composing a narrative that builds on the affinities between his and Cass's predicaments, he yokes the two stories in a seemingly harmonious whole. Having laid out his own take on the events in the first half, in the second half he bends Cass's account to fill in the gaps and bring the story to coherence. Really, though, he has little desire to discover his true "part in the matter." He refers to himself as Coleridge's Wedding Guest (478). But if he is "stunned" by a purgatorial tale, he is not, ultimately, a "wiser man."[19] Unlike the Wedding Guest, he remains the central consciousness—Styron's "narrator himself"—fashioning our view of events to suit his own interests. Reconstructing the events through his experiences and the memories he steers the helpfully amnesic Cass to dredge up, he fulfills his earlier hope of being a composer by leading discordant voices and events toward harmony so that the "pressure on his brain," like di Lieto's, is lifted (506). But his act of composing falsifies the conflicts inherent in life. As Styron himself asserts, this narrative device "gives to the book whatever power and tension it has."[20]

Cass in effect wrests life out of "nothingness." He chooses "being" and so survives, doing battle, in Ibsen's definition of life, "with trolls in the vaults of the heart and the brain."[21] But it is Peter who wrests a kind of art from nothingness. What he produces, however, is not a work resulting from aesthetic distance but one tailored to the personality he unwittingly exposes in the narrative.

Peter's composition amounts to a detective story purportedly designed to discover—but really adapted to cover—the extent of his own guilt as an evader of responsibility and as an expedient exploiter and apathetic sycophant of the people and situations he encounters. His gathering of evidence combines music and law: it is a composition and

19. Samuel Taylor Coleridge, "The Rime of the Ancient Mariner," in *Lyrical Ballads*, ed. Edward Dowden (1798; rpr. London, 1890), 51.

20. Styron to *Publishers Weekly*, in *Publishers Weekly*, May 30, 1960, p. 55.

21. Henrik Ibsen to Ludwig Passarge, June 16, 1880, in *Henrik Ibsen: A Critical Anthology*, ed. and trans. James McFarlane (Harmondsworth, Eng., 1970), 91.

a trial, with Peter as sole attorney, codefendant, and key witness. Practiced in the art of law, of which rhetoric and interpretation—as Gray reveals in *The Confessions of Nat Turner*—are a key part, Peter affects to judge whether he is implicated in the events of Sambuco. Reaching the unsurprising verdict of Not Guilty, he trusts that, as "the law works it own music on the minds of men," so his conducting of language will work musically on the reader's mind and inspire assent. But attuned to Styron's dialogic demur, the reader may not be willing to clear him so easily; issues of broader sociohistorical culpability seep through Peter's composition. His self-professed "mediocrity" produces an arrangement in which his proclaimed closure fails to chime with the events we witness.

Styron's ventriloquizing presence is successful in casting moral and aesthetic doubt on Peter's idea that art is a way of ordering conflicting voices. In this, Styron meets Ibsen's definition of writing by sitting "in judgment" also on himself and on his own inherited narrative pattern. The obvious shortcomings of Peter's narrative all amount to limitations in the artistic conventions Styron himself had been accepting. Peter's early anxiety in New York—"*Where am I going? What am I doing?*"—gives expression to Styron's own questioning exploration of the direction of his writing.

The idea that *Set This House on Fire* includes an explorative search for direction draws the authorial level of discourse under the lens. In this novel, the authorial level becomes less the seat of an anxiety over influences than of an anxiety to work out a new literary course. Nowhere is this more apparent than at the end. Perhaps the book's most quoted, and some say contrived, passage is the one there in which, choosing being over nothingness, Cass is propped up by Sartre at one elbow and Faulkner at the other.[22] But apart from the letters of the epilogue, the very end of the narrative is a short paragraph that critics almost always ignore: "As for the rest, I had come back," says Cass. "And that for a

22. Gray calls it "pure bombast" (*The Literature of Memory*, 290). The ending is reminiscent of that of the penultimate chapter of William Faulkner's *The Wild Palms* (London, 1939). Wilbourne thinks that, "between grief and nothingness," he "will take grief" (p. 200). On Faulkner's passage, see also William Styron, *This Quiet Dust and Other Writings* (Rev. ed.; New York, 1993), 284.

while would do. That would suffice" (501). Perhaps this comes across as a rather redundant authorial flourish and that is why critics so often slice it off their quotation.[23] But in connection with the authorial level, it is of some interest, because it harks back to Wallace Stevens' description, at the start of "Of Modern Poetry," of the writing process as exploration (see p. 69 above):

(see p. 69 above)

> The poem of the mind in the act of finding
> What will suffice. It has not always had
> To find: the scene was set; it repeated what
> Was in the script.[24]

If the novel not only shows us Cass's and Peter's search but also the author's "mind in the act of finding," then for Styron, as for Stevens, the search is for "what will suffice." So the ending can be seen not only as Cass's final statement but as Styron's own comment on the novel as a questioning exploration.

Stevens' poem, moreover, seems to hold an apt description of Styron's career to the point of *Set This House on Fire*. It is not true that this novel, as one critic puts it, shows "no significant advance on *Lie Down in Darkness*."[25] If, despite limited reaccentuation, Styron's first novel largely "repeated what was in the script," *Set This House on Fire* explores the script more critically. Styron's interest, albeit tangential, in political and cultural domination led him in the later novel to question the narrative pattern of his early work. His struggle in this novel was still to find his own voice, but it was also to come to terms with the implications of an urge to harmonize once a preoccupation with personal angst and pure arts has been dislodged by concerns of a political and historical nature.

An anxiety about influences remains. Traces of other writers abound. The novel, as Foster has said, can be read as a "bundle of apparent influences." Although, as he remarks, "there are only touches of Faulkner," certainly Fitzgerald can be heard again, and especially

23. See, for example, Gray, *The Literature of Memory*, 290; and Shaun V. O'Connell, "Expense of Spirit: The Vision of William Styron," *Critique*, VIII (1965–66), 32.

24. Stevens, "Of Modern Poetry," in *The Collected Poems*, 239.

25. Gray, *The Literature of Memory*, 290.

Malcolm Lowry's *Under the Volcano*.[26] Mark Twain and J. D. Salinger, too, are evident in Cass's Huckleberry Caulfield–like experiences with Vernelle Satterfield. When Cass described the "goddamdest gallery of Jesuses you ever saw" and, asked what he thought of Vernelle's pictures, "allowed as how they seemed to me long enough on religion but powerfully short on art" (263), he switched from Holden to Huck. He reverted to Holden in describing her "clickety-clack godawful phony voice" (264).

But two important shifts are apparent in Styron's relationship with other writers. One is that, whereas in *Lie Down in Darkness* there were attempts to emulate and to tear free from influences, here there is also a conscious use of other texts to inform the work. That may be so in the philosophical discourses, discussed by some critics, although even the references to existentialism, at least Sartre's version, are at times superficial. Cass's views on being and nothingness are not Sartre's on Being and Nothingness. Sartre describes consciousness as a flight from brute Being, but Styron marks the more conventional contrast between life and death, making of being merely an affirmation of life.[27] The references in the novel to other philosophers are less than serious. They come mostly from Luigi, who refers with comic ponderosity to the "great German philosopher Nietzsche," the "famous Frenchman Descartes," and the "esteemed Spanish-Dutch philoso-

26. Foster, "An Orgy of Commerce," 63–64. Echoes of Malcolm Lowry's *Under the Volcano* (1947; rpr. Harmondsworth, Eng., 1986) are numerous. Like Cass, Geoffrey Firmin struggles against alcohol addiction, a "tyranny of the self" (p. 331) and a "sickness" of "soul" and "body" (p. 245). There is also the Bella Vista bar (p. 189) and the comment, on Yvonne, that "it was not herself that was on fire. It was the house of her spirit" (p. 367).

27. Sartre argues that "consciousness is a being, the nature of which is to be conscious of the nothingness of its own being" (*Being and Nothingness: An Essay in Phenomenological Ontology*, trans. Hazel E. Barnes [London, 1957], 47). He thus draws a distinction between "Being-in-Itself" and "Being-for-Itself." The former is brute Being, identical with itself. Being-for-Itself is consciousness, which can only define itself through awareness of the being that it is not. Hence, Being, Sartre argues, is solid and unthinking. Consciousness, or Being-for-Itself, is a perpetual wrenching-away from Being. So Nothingness is not the result of annihilation, because Being and Nothingness depend on each other for definition. The choice Styron posits between being and nothingness is between existing and not existing, so only superficially resembles Sartre. Galloway sees Cass's choice as the one "between suicide and life" posed by Camus in *The Myth of Sisyphus*. See Galloway, *The Absurd Hero in American Fiction*, 103.

pher, Spinoza" (339–40). But Styron does make conscious use not only of *Don Giovanni* but of Sophocles' *Oedipus at Colonus* and, Lewis Lawson argues, Kierkegaard, adumbrating a more purposeful use of other works in his later novels.[28]

Styron's second clear shift is away from the South. Critics have detected parallels between southern Italy and the American South, which the references to Woodward may enhance.[29] But as those references equally suggest, the European setting also symbolically and psychologically removes Styron from Faulkner and the South even as the influence of the southern environment and literary tradition remains evident. Styron's turn away from the South is one face of his anxiety concerning direction. When Peter, referring to his southern roots, feels as if his identity has "slipped away, leaving me without knowledge of where I had been and where I was going" (16), this is surely not just Peter's anxiety but Styron's too as he muses over the direction of his work and partly distances himself from his identity as a southern writer.

The struggle between Cass, Mason, and Peter, besides operating as a reductio ad absurdum of the conflicts in America's immediate postwar foreign policy, exemplifies the conflict in Styron himself. In the dreams of Peter and Cass, the motif of the divided self emerges clearly. Peter has a nightmare in which the monster turns out to be "that self-same friend" (6); Cass, in his journal, speculates that the figures haunting dreams are "one's own self" (364). In a like vein, Cass comments to Peter that when you kill a man, "you have removed a part of yourself" (446), and after the murder he wonders how it is "understood" that a murdered man has "killed himself" (480).

The "act of finding" on view in the novel relates to the artist's search for direction. Cass says that Mason made him "as helpless as

---

28. On Styron and Greek myth, see Butor, "Oedipus Americanus," in *Critical Essays on William Styron*, ed. Casciato and West, 135–45; and Hugh L. Moore, "Robert Penn Warren, William Styron, and the Use of Greek Myth," *Critique*, VIII (1965–66), 75–87. On Styron and Kierkegaard, see especially Lewis Lawson, "Cass Kinsolving: Kierkegaardian Man of Despair," in *Critical Essays on William Styron*, ed. Casciato and West, 98–109.

29. See, for example, Louise Y. Gossett, *Violence in Recent Southern Fiction* (Durham, N.C., 1965), 128.

Romulus, sucking on the fat tit of a wolf" (402). Mason represents all in America that is inimical to an artist's growth; he is pretentious, hip, and faddish, and he follows superficial trends in order to impress others. Unable to create anything much himself, he declares that "art is dead" (145). Cass, on the other hand, is the rudderless, self-destructive artist who finishes little but finds a partial answer by leaving the "remote" precipice of Sambuco (4)—a kind of ivory tower where artists, actors, and writers live in a make-believe world—and directly trying to help the Ricci family. Peter's staid doggedness at least suggests the practical effectiveness necessary to finish a product; unimaginative alone, he weds his composer side with Cass's undisciplined, driven side to create an artistic work. But if the resulting creation takes its outer form from Peter, it is suffused by Cass's—and the author's—less finalized, more questioning personality. Still, any wholly negative agency, illustrated by Mason, must be destroyed.

On this level, *Set This House on Fire* plumbs a novelist's responsibility when the idea of harmony can translate—as the fascist leanings of some modernists and Erik H. Erikson's portrayal of Hitler in *Young Man Luther* suggest—into ordering the sociohistorical world by dominating or silencing competing voices or by evasion.

Having symbolically broken from the South by moving to Connecticut and writing a novel set elsewhere, Styron was to reimmerse himself in it with *The Confessions of Nat Turner*. It is as if, having come of age, he had become confident enough to take on the southern tradition on his own terms. His return to a southern setting and theme confirms that he had found a subject or style that could dispel his fears of languishing as a Faulkner epigone. But in fact there is a tension in this next novel between his specific subject matter and his broader concerns, leading to a superimposition of national and contemporary preoccupations upon an antebellum southern setting.

4

Bonds of Discourse: *The Confessions of Nat Turner*

Five years ago, even the most audacious visionary would not have dared pre-dict the slashing do or die desperation and the sizzling up-tempo beat which has exploded into our nightmares and dreams.
—*Eldridge Cleaver,* Soul on Ice

Do you ever have the feeling that contemporary events are outstripping your own insights?
—*Styron, comment to James Jones, 1963*

White people live with the nigger they've invented. They don't see the per-son. It's easy to blame what you are not. But you could be that person. In some ways you are that person.
—*James Baldwin, comment to Mavis Nicholson, 1987*

At first, *The Confessions of Nat Turner* appears both less and more complex than *Set This House on Fire*. It seems to present a straightfor-ward narrative yet bites deep into extremely controversial subjects. Prior to this novel, Styron had written about a girl's suicide, the death of eight soldiers, and the gothic catastrophes of Sambuco. Here he tackled a documented massacre of fifty-five people that brought many more deaths in its wake. His subject not only led him into issues of slavery and race but, because it involved a historical figure, also re-quired him to engage questions he previously did not have to regarding the relation of history to fiction, and the artist's responsibility to his-torical truth. Moreover, his direct entry into the sociohistorical field made more urgent the struggle in his writing between his radical op-position to hierarchical institutions—religious, military, legal, govern-mental—and his more conservative disposition either to enclose the subversive voices or to bring about equal dialogue, enabling a move-ment toward personal, spiritual, and social harmony. As a result, if *The*

Confessions seems in its technique to forgo the narrative complexity of *Set This House on Fire* and *Lie Down in Darkness*, its "obvious simplicity . . . of plot," as one critic describes it, masks a highly complex substructure.[1]

With *The Confessions*, close reading is imperative, not least to avoid focusing on strands that have scant import for the whole, thereby creating a mound of criticism against the novel by eliding details and collating voices. In any case, *The Confessions* defuses much of that criticism, for it is built around a language trope that—aside from helping to undercut the novel's discourse toward harmony—accentuates misunderstanding through linguistic multivalence. Misreadings are thus encompassed by, and reinforce, its main theme.

Equally, the novel cannot be fully examined without reference to its contexts. John Kenny Crane clears space for his ahistorical reading by maintaining that "too much has been made of Nat Turner as a Negro slave *qua* Negro slave." The novel is, of course, about more than slavery, but what Crane envisions as a step forward to an ahistorical study is really a side step that lets him pass by the controversy raised by the ten black writers who at once took Styron to task.[2] The controversy is an unambiguous marker in Styron's abandonment of ivory-tower attitudes, pointing to the eventual unseating of his urge to harmonize. Moreover, it reminds us that literature, without necessarily being highly partisan, has a place in political dialogues. There are at least three relevant contexts for the novel: the years leading up to 1831, the 1960s, and the present, or in other words, the period the novel purports to be about, the years of writing and publication, and the times in which we now read it. But the contexts cannot be adequately appreciated without recognizing the reach of the dialogues figuring in the novel.

Much of the present chapter is thus a close examination of both

1. Robert Coles, "Blacklash," in *Critical Essays on William Styron*, ed. Arthur D. Casciato and James L. W. West III (Boston, 1982), 182.

2. John Kenny Crane, *The Root of All Evil: The Thematic Unity of William Styron's Fiction* (Columbia, S.C., 1984), 43. For the ten black writers, see *William Styron's Nat Turner: Ten Black Writers Respond*, ed. John H. Clarke (Boston, 1968). On the question of contexts, see also Shaun V. O'Connell, "The Contexts of William Styron's Nat Turner" (Ph.D. dissertation, University of Massachusetts, 1970).

the dialogic nature of Nat's narrative voice and the clash of voices out of which his story arises. The penultimate section looks at some of the many external discourses evident on the authorial level. All kinds of writers and critics seem to infiltrate the novel, among them Stanley Elkins, Erik H. Erikson, Albert Camus, W. E. B. Du Bois, Feodor Dostoyevsky, Ralph Ellison, James Baldwin, Frederick Douglass, and Booker T. Washington.[3] But those chosen for attention here—Erikson, in *Young Man Luther;* Douglass, in *Narrative of the Life of Frederick Douglass;* and James Baldwin, in his essays—not only offer insight into the novels' concerns but are also of special importance in connection with either the novel's shape or the controversy it inspired. The often-discussed reactions of the ten black writers of 1968 themselves will initially come under scrutiny only so far as the writers mounted aesthetic rather than sociological criticisms. The controversy they precipitated will be canvassed only in the final section, since my reading of the novel as preoccupied with language, together with my concentration upon the movement toward harmony, will put their arguments in a different light.

Like *Set This House on Fire*, Styron's fourth novel consists of a retrospective first-person account in which the narrator, disturbed by events that have upset his world view, reexamines the events in the hope of attaining personal harmony. The story, as Styron puts it, is "of man's quest for faith and certitude in a pandemonious world."[4] But, unlike Peter—or the focalizer Culver—the narrator here is the protagonist of the events reviewed. Samuel Coale's remark that Styron's novels are told by "remarkably unscathed witnesses" is clearly not true in the case of Nat Turner.[5] Indeed, one of the common judgments about *The*

---

3. For Styron's comments on Elkins and Erikson, see his *This Quiet Dust and Other Writings* (Rev. ed.; New York, 1993), 9–30. On Camus' influence, see David D. Galloway, *The Absurd Hero in American Fiction* (London, 1981), 110–15. On Baldwin, Douglass, and Du Bois, see appendix conversations, 218–19.

4. Douglas Barzelay and Robert Sussman, "William Styron and *The Confessions of Nat Turner: A Yale Lit* Interview," in *Conversations with William Styron,* ed. James L. W. West III (Jackson, Miss., 1985), 96.

5. Samuel Coale, "Styron's Disguises: A Provisional Rebel in Christian Masquerade," *Critique,* XXVI (1985), 57.

Confessions—that Styron should not have used Nat as the narrator—hits precisely, if unwittingly, upon the change of emphasis in Styron's fiction.[6]

Styron's choice of Nat as narrator has a double significance. It is, first of all, indicative of the writer's changing interests—of his direct engagement with a historical and political subject. He had to defend his novel as the direct result of attempting to join the central debates in American society. With *Set This House on Fire*, the authorial theme of American power abroad was formative but subsidiary. In *The Confessions*, the greater authorial involvement—the attempt to get inside a controversial issue—is symbolized by trying to become the protagonist: to "be that person."

Second, the choice of Nat as narrator bespeaks the novel's concern with language. Much of the conflict portrayed relates to Nat's use of language and his inability to communicate effectively with even sympathetic whites. The attention paid him by Judge Cobb and Margaret Whitehead only elicits a heightened anger and frustration. Part of what Styron is showing, Eugene D. Genovese and others see, is that the perversity of slavery and the racism at its root imprison oppressor and oppressed, with human communication breaking down under the tyranny of the system.[7] Hence, a white narrator, even one who, like Cobb, is sympathetic, would not exhibit what Styron wants us to perceive. What is more, given the use of language for deceit—a strategy of survival for the blacks and of rationalization for the whites—a white narrator of the time could not be privy to Nat's thoughts.

A close analysis of the novel's language trope reveals just how important it is to Styron's purpose that Nat narrate. First and foremost, Nat's tragedy is that he is a slave, so he needs no other justification for revolt. Despite what Crane says, one cannot ignore this; it is the main

6. See, for example, John O. Killens, "The Confessions of Willie Styron," in *William Styron's Nat Turner*, ed. Clarke, 36; Frederick R. Karl, *American Fictions, 1940–1980: A Comprehensive History and Critical Evaluation* (New York, 1983), 341; and Richard Gilman, "Nat Turner Revisited," in *The Nat Turner Rebellion: The Historical Event and the Modern Controversy*, ed. John B. Duff and Peter M. Mitchell (New York, 1971), 232.

7. See Eugene D. Genovese, "William Styron in the People's Court," in *Critical Essays on William Styron*, ed. Casciato and West, 201–12.

extenuation of the murders. This, and the record of American Negro slavery in general, are the unsaid accompaniment of white judgment on him after his capture, and they should not become the unsaid accompaniment of critical writing on the novel.[8] But the language trope ultimately connects the novel as text with the novel as political utterance, thus leading into the controversy with the ten black writers. The connection between the novel's concern with language and its concern with slavery and black-white relations is illuminated by a comment of Baldwin's. Baldwin, whose voice pervades the work, observes in *Notes of a Native Son* that the Negro "is always acting." He "learns to gauge precisely what reaction the alien person facing him desires, and he produces it with disarming artlessness."[9] Nat, having learned that skill, proffers a narration that is not so simple as it may appear. The novel sets in sharp relief the use of language in a power struggle that is of central importance to Nat's life. We learn from his relations with others that he is an expert manipulator of language who uses its ambiguity to the full. That should alert us to the likelihood he is also performing and manipulating in his narration.

Nat's language, especially its split nature, has been the subject of frequent critical discussion. Several critics, including Mike Thelwell and most recently Coale, see Nat as having two languages, and Melvin J. Friedman and Edward Weeks see him as having three.[10] But only Carlos Fuentes, in a letter to the *Times Literary Supplement*, has suggested that language is not merely a theme of the novel but the theme. Argu-

8. Aside from Crane, according to whom "Styron is only secondarily examining the struggles of a black slave" (*The Root of All Evil*, 42), see Philip Fisher, who thinks Styron tries to give an "air of reasonableness to a single act of insane violence" (*Hard Facts: Setting and Form in the American Novel* [New York, 1985], 97). Fisher links the novel to Norman Mailer's *The Executioner's Song* and Truman Capote's *In Cold Blood.*

9. James Baldwin, *Notes of a Native Son* (1955; rpr. London, 1964), 69. As Baldwin says, he is echoing Richard Wright.

10. Mike Thelwell, "Back with the Wind," in *William Styron's Nat Turner*, ed. Clarke, 80; Samuel Coale, *William Styron Revisited* (Boston, 1991), 89. See also especially Richard Gray, *The Literature of Memory: Modern Writers of the American South* (London, 1977), 293, 297–98; and George Core, "*The Confessions of Nat Turner* and the Burden of the Past," in *The Achievement of William Styron*, ed. Robert K. Morris and Irving Malin (Athens, Ga., 1981), 216. Melvin J. Friedman cites, and agrees with, Weeks. See Friedman, *William Styron: An Interim Appraisal* (Bowling Green, Ohio, 1974), 17; and Edward Weeks, Review, *Atlantic Monthly*, November, 1967, p. 130.

ing that the "first of all master-slave relationships" is linguistic, Fuentes writes that "Nat is caught in a schizophrenia of language. More than in the bonds of slavery, he is caught in the chains of aping two linguistic models: the openly servile pickaninny slang that the masters expect of him, or the secretly servile rhetoric of status, or prestigious language of Reason-Bible-Elegance-Puritanism and Optimism tempered by Apocalypse." Fuentes' own rhetoric may cloud his point here. The "prestigious language" is the "rhetoric of status," and not a third language; it is "secretly servile" since it imitates the masters' language. His chief point is that not only is Nat's "first rebellion"—against the masters through imitation of their language—his "most radical failure" but his linguistic "schizophrenia" is a key to the novel.[11]

In fact, if Fuentes sees Nat as caught between two languages, and Friedman three—"the one of his thoughts; the one of his conversation with most white men; and the one of his conversation with fellow slaves"—it is possible to see his use of language as even more complex. Nat can be seen as employing at least four modes of speech: "nigger gabble," which he uses, as Friedman says, with most whites, as well as Negro dialect, his narrative idiom, and his preacher rhetoric. Friedman might consider the final two to be of a single linguistic style, but Nat's narrative voice differs from the biblical rhetoric of his preaching even if, as Friedman holds, the narrative voice dominates.[12]

But even Nat's narrative voice is far from unitary. Not only is there a dialogic dynamic between narrator and author—a point we will return to—but Nat's narration is itself dialogic. His story looks back—in the way of much autobiography—at the changing attitude of his former self. As in *Sophie's Choice*, there is a significant mental and temporal gap between the voices of the present and former selves. In this, *The Confessions* is unlike *Set This House on Fire*, where the disparity is only between narrator and author. Much of the time the narration in *The Confessions* includes two contrasting views of events. Both the narrating Nat and Nat as a figure in the narrative have a strong affinity

11. Carlos Fuentes, "Unslavish Fidelity," *Times Literary Supplement*, May 16, 1968, p. 505.

12. Friedman, *William Styron*, 17, 18. *Nigger gabble* is Styron's term. See *The Confessions of Nat Turner* (New York, 1967), 214, cited in the present chapter by page number, without title.

with language, but their attitudes toward it differ. The Nat within the narrative feels a proud certitude in his ability with language and the promise it holds for him. His pride in his linguistic proficiency is linked with his desire to be white and his disdain for fellow blacks. In contrast, Nat as narrator has lost his certitude about both language and his destiny. He has learned that the slipperiness of language can work against as much as for him. Like most of Styron's narrators, he starts the novel in turmoil and confusion. During his narration, the now wiser but more troubled Nat constantly supplants the Nat of earlier language and world view. Narrator and narrative figure converge in the retrospective examination as Nat traces the gradual loss of his sense of destiny and turns his search to trying to understand what has happened.

The conflict of Nat's narrative voice with the voice of the Nat of before is matched by conflicts between Nat's voice and the voices of other characters in his narrative. His first dialogue is with Thomas Gray. But he also has dialogues that matter with Samuel Turner, Margaret, Cobb, Hark, and Will. The one with Samuel Turner, especially, is crucial—in its consequences both for Nat's sense of destiny and for the trauma he undergoes when he finds himself sold to Thomas Moore.

The complexity of Nat's narrative voice also increases so far as his voice mingles with that of Gray, as the recorder of the historical confessions, and that of Styron, who oscillates between being close to Nat and ironically distant.

The position of language as a major trope is apparent in the opening pages. The reader must negotiate a myriad of texts—the alpha-omega sign, the author's prefatory words, Gray's introduction to the historical confessions, and a biblical passage—before reaching Nat's narrative. The alpha-omega sign reminds us of the nature of signification. It also relates to Nat's biblical motivation, and to the passages from the Book of Revelation framing and embedded in the novel. As John Lang has appreciated, it is important for understanding what is religiously allegorical in the novel, since it is the sign denoting Christ in the New Testament.[13]

In an "author's note," Styron seeks to explain a purpose behind the

13. John Lang, "The Alpha and the Omega: Styron's *The Confessions of Nat Turner*," *American Literature*, LIII (1981), 499.

account and to impress on us the fictionalized quality of the narrative: Styron is not Nat, but the man of Styron's portrayal is not the historical Nat either, only an imaginative re-creation of him as part of a "meditation on history." The reader is cautioned about the tenuous relationship between the historical material and the author's use of it, and is told that, since 1831 is a "long time ago and only yesterday," the novel need not be read as having relevance only to its historical context and subject.

Since the Gray of the introduction to the original confessions was the lawyer to whom the actual Nat recounted his story, Gray's depiction of Nat as a "diabolical" and "gloomy fanatic" offers reason enough for Styron's re-creation—and rehumanizing—of the black rebel. The pamphlet of confession that Gray published turned out to be an amalgam of the voices of Gray and the historical Nat Turner, but since Gray had clear motives for steering the reader's attitudes about Nat, we cannot be sure, as the historian Henry I. Tragle says, "where Gray stops and Nat begins."[14] Gray assures us his document is a "faithful record" of Nat's "full and free confession"—a claim "attested" by a Southampton court "certificate." But Gray is asking us to accept—as some critics do—that what is legally stamped is the objective truth.[15]

Such a credulity, however, weakened by Styron's previous novel, is disabled by *The Confessions*. The novel supersedes Gray's purportedly official record, offering an imaginative rendition of the unspoken story immured between the lines of Gray's authoritative discourse. That Gray's claims of legality and objectivity are flimsy is evident from the omissions in his introduction. His description of Nat's rebellion— "Men, women and children, from hoary old age to helpless infancy, were involved in the same cruel fate"—might equally summarize the evils of slavery, which dwarf the gruesome horrors of Nat's lunge for freedom. In addition, Gray chose his language so as to reduce the in-

14. Henry I. Tragle, *The Southampton Slave Revolt of 1831: A Compilation of Source Material* (Amherst, Mass., 1971), 409. Tragle is criticizing Styron, but Styron is aware of the dubiety of the pamphlet. In reply to Herbert Aptheker's charges of inaccuracy, based mainly on it, he raises his own question about the "*accuracy* of the Confessions" ("From Herbert Aptheker and William Styron, Truth and Nat Turner: An Exchange," in *The Nat Turner Rebellion*, ed. Duff and Mitchell, 198).

15. See, for example, Lerone Bennett, Jr., "Nat's Last White Man," in *William Styron's Nat Turner*, ed. Clarke, 8.

surrection's importance as anything other than carnage: the rebellion was "entirely local," the band were "shot down" in a "few days," Nat was "grappling" with ideas beyond him, the confession was to "give general satisfaction." Like Peter's composition, Gray's presentation of events is meant to alleviate fears and fit preconceptions of what is acceptable. His picture of Nat is consequently a mere interpretation, configuring a new Nat, separate from the historical person. We must realize that the historical document on which Styron's novel is based is of unascertainable truth and that, even when Styron uses the earlier confessions in the novel, Nat's words have probably been lent a "dignity of style" (30) that has altered the voice and meaning of the historical Nat. That history is text has to be recognized from the start.

Like the first, the fourth preliminary text is biblical: it is from Rev. 21:4. Being a prophecy, it, like the others—the alpha-omega sign, Styron's note, which he wrote near the novel's completion, and Gray's introduction—is phrased with certitude.[16] Through its insistence that final judgment is yet to occur, it challenges whatever judgment whites have passed on Nat.

Nat's own narrative is very different. It comes from a man whose certitude has evaporated and who now seeks meaning, not least in the dream he begins by describing. Condemned to die, he faces in life as in his dream a "confusion of choppy waves where the river merges with the sea" (3). Borne inevitably toward the sea—an age-old symbol of eternity—he faces the mystery of existence after the vision he has lived by has failed him. He must come to terms with his actions above all to bridge the gulf that has opened between him and his God.

His dream is mostly characterized through negations. There is no definite season: it may be "spring or perhaps the end of summer." Even "the air is almost seasonless—benign and neutral, windless, devoid of heat or cold." The scene is "forever unchanged," the sun "motionless" (3), and the building that he describes nameless, maybe a temple where none worship or a monument to something "without a name" (4). It has "no columns or windows" and no evident door (6). The opening paragraphs of the narration stress "great silence" (4), preparing the ground for the gradual introduction of the language trope by way of sounds and voices that build into a "babble" (13).

16. Appendix conversations, 220.

What does exist, in the "half dream, half waking vision" at the start of the narrative is a sense of a lost destiny that Nat ties to his childhood, when he "would hear white people talk of Norfolk and of 'going to the seaside'" (5). That the destiny is a lost one becomes evident when we realize that the river of the vision is the James, symbol of slavery, the source of Nat's undoing. The vision dissolves and Nat is wrenched back to the present when he tries to move but feels "the metal bite deep" as the irons "reach the limit of their slack" (6). A vision of freedom in youth thus poses itself against his entrapment now in a "web of chain," condensing the tension throughout the novel between Nat's early sense of destiny and his subsequent enmeshment in doubt and despair. At the same time that we witness his entanglement, noises begin to punctuate the silence: a "distant drumming noise" grows, "louder and louder," into an "uproar of hooves and squealing timber" (6–7). Finally, voices—portending the entanglements of language—are heard: the petrified, sporadic stutters of Kitchen, then the entrance of Gray, led by the jailer, and the first words of Gray's verbal contest with Nat.

From the novel's beginning, language is in the foreground, as is the sense of emptiness and discord from which Nat will mentally strive to move forward. The highlighting of language drives home that between the real Nat and the voice Styron re-creates for him lie all manner of corruptive pressures, and that Styron's Nat Turner is really an amalgam of other voices, especially those of Gray, Styron himself, and the Bible—the one text Styron and his narrator certainly share—but also those in Styron's mind at the time of writing. Choppy with diversity, the multivoiced opening of the novel is bound up with the work's linguistic themes, not least with linguistic multivalence. It compasses the problems of communication that Nat must deal with in his quest for mental harmony in the face of imminent execution and that Styron must do justice to in the novel's exploration of disturbing and disparate discourses.

Both Nat and Gray see language as a tool by which to manipulate. In conversation in Nat's cell, surrounded by the "babble of hundreds of distant voices" (13), they test each other by deploying linguistic stratagems calculated to deceive or coerce rather than communicate. "The idea of misunderstanding," said Styron during the writing of the novel, "is at the center of all human relationships which go awry."[17] The comment prophetically anticipated the novel's reception but also bears on Nat's first dialogue with Gray and on the various interactions their talks frame. The story Nat goes on to tell reveals how early misunderstanding sealed his fate. But as the novel opens, he has become fully aware of his need to play the language games that are part and parcel of his relationship with white society. The misunderstanding at this point is Gray's alone. The success of Nat's verbal artifice is an ironic counterpoint both to Gray's physical power over Nat and to the lawyer's misguided confidence in his own eloquence.

If Gray's naïve belief in his linguistic mastery matches the earlier Nat's, the narrating Nat has far better knowledge of the power and the pitfalls of language. "Sundered from the divine spirit" (10), he is spiritually bereft and uses the time between interviews with Gray to trace the roots of his predicament. For all the verbal facility he displays, he recognizes how the trust he used to have in language has contributed to his plight. Only in the final section, after the voice of narrator and of the figure in the narrative merge, does he, to appearances at least, move toward some form of spiritual harmony. The narrating Nat's first dialogue with Gray shows the sensitivity to language with which he will reminisce about his early belief in language, about what he sees as his betrayal, and about his subsequent reappraisal of the effects of verbal ambiguity. Distraught, he is nevertheless acutely aware of the potentials discourse has—of the power of language to obfuscate as well as enlighten, and to entangle as well as draw people closer. Talking with Gray, he is at the peak of his verbal proficiency and uses his awareness of language's capabilities as fully as the situation allows him. He is indeed a "preacher of the Word" (173), but less the religious Word than the spoken. If both Nat and Gray possess a special dexterity in verbal manipulation, Nat's hard-earned awareness of the snares of language guarantees that he always wins at least verbally—and the text's important battleground is verbal—to the degree of showing up the hypocrisy of the lawyer and the system he represents.

When Gray arrives, his "hearty voice" and "overpowering perfume"

17. Jack Griffin, Jerry Homsy, and Gene Stelig, "A Conversation with William Styron," in *Conversations with William Styron*, ed. West, 60.

sicken Nat (11). His appearance and scent—dirty pink gloves, stained waistcoat, blotches, belly, and apple-blossom aura—give warning of the form his verbal prowess takes, in its sickly, overbearing embellishment and its sleazy corruption beneath an eloquent veneer. Nat has learned to be circumspect, whereas Gray speaks with the blasé arrogance of someone confident of his social status. In the early pages, Gray strives to manipulate, deceive, and goad Nat in order to drive him into verbal defeat. Gray's problem is that he cannot stop talking: his sentences runs away from him. Instead of capitalizing on Nat's silence, he just festoons his own speech, threatening Nat with further discomfort "over and above and *in addition*" to what he already feels (14) and even adding "emphasis" to Nat's confession (40).

But if Gray at times appears comic, a latent violence comes out in his prolixity, straining the pleasant intimacy he seeks to establish. His cynicism and malice show up in these early episodes in the way he develops his definition of *"in-an-imate"* as opposed to *"an-i-mate"* chattel. A wagon, says Gray, is an inanimate chattel, whereas a slave is an animate chattel. Hence, he claims, an owner is responsible if his runaway wagon crushes a young girl but is not responsible for the unlawful actions of a slave. The argument is obviously specious, but in it Gray reveals a sadistic streak not only in the choice of example but even more so by enlarging on how "the poor little girl is mashed to death beneath the wagon wheels right before her stricken mother's eyes" (19–20). The threat of violence behind Gray's pose also surfaces when Nat questions what constitutes a "fair trial": "I want to advise you not to get *impudent* with me. I still say it proves we run a fair series of trials, and I don't need none of your lip to show me the contrary. You set here givin' me a line of your black lip like that and you'll wind up draggin' more iron ruther than less" (24). Like Templeton's, Gray's form of dialogue is ingenuine: Nat's "black lip" is not welcome unless it says what Gray wants to hear.

Gray at this point—like the other whites—represents authoritative discourse. Nat's confession takes place in Styron's novel beneath and despite their talks. When Gray says to Nat, "I'm a man of my word, Reverend" (21), the truth is that he is indeed a man of *his* word; Nat's views do not much interest him. Few whites here—except Margaret and Cobb, who, given the institution of slavery, are threatening—

really want to listen to blacks. Daydreaming in court, Nat thinks of Richard Whitehead's sermons. Composed "for annual dispensation," they do "not vary" or "even belong to the one who speaks them" (97). Like the lectures in *The Long March*, they follow a set pattern, leaving nothing unscripted.

In contrast to Gray's loquaciousness is Nat's early silence, and then his minimal responsiveness. "White people often undo themselves by such running off at the mouth," he says, "and only God knows how many nigger triumphs have been won in total silence." Nat's strategy is less transparent than Gray's, and vastly more effective in the verbal battle. When Gray misinterprets his silence, thinking only "small favors" will get results, Nat gains a "private initial victory." During the silence, a form of textual dialogue exists, but beyond Gray's range. Gray has "misjudged everything," and Nat's mocking thoughts deflect the points Gray thinks he is scoring (14). He dislikes Gray's "trickery" and sees no reason not to "blab" now that he has nothing to lose, but he uses his silence to gain what little he can (12).

In talking with Gray and as a prisoner in court, Nat appears fully aware of how he is entrapped as much by language as by the institution and society the courtroom represents. His awareness itself brings small victories. Baldwin writes in *Nobody Knows My Name* that Negroes are nearly always dissembling "before a white audience—which is quite incapable of judging their performance."[18] To avoid being part of the audience taken in, we must be ever alert to Nat's "performance." The cell has become a microcosm of the text's linguistic palaestra, and the first engagement is Nat's.

When Nat does speak, he responds to Gray with enough mild "nigger gabble" to satisfy him and keep him in a mood favorable enough for the prisoner to exploit: "Now sir, I'm a tired man, but I'm ready to confess, because the Lord has given this nigger a sign." That Gray fails to spot the falsity of Nat's words signals that Gray's verbal proficiency is less than he thinks. Eager for the confession, and gulled by Nat's use of the word *sir* (15), he feels superior and safe and agrees to have Nat's manacles removed. Nat's true confession—the confession constituting

18. James Baldwin, *Nobody Knows My Name: More Notes of a Native Son* (1961; rpr. London, 1964), 167.

Styron's novel—then flows freely, beyond the shackles of the surface dialogue.

Eventually Nat will ignore Gray's voice and those in the jail and courtroom, and override the white voices textually, reciprocal to the way the white voices in the court and the society ignore his. Much of the time, Gray's words make only a "dim, grotesque impression," since they are the "quintessence of white folks' talk" such as Nat has "heard incessantly" his whole life (22). But he lets Gray have his say in the narration, permitting him to inflict injury on himself. Gray's limited interest in what Nat has to say allows Nat to gain further verbal victories. The subtlety of Nat's tactic is evident when he responds to Gray's assertion that he should now see the "plain ordinary *evil*" of his "dad-burned Bible" (111):

Gray leaned forward, slapping his knee. "Well, *Jehoshaphat,* Reverend, look at the record! Jes' look at it. Look at your own words! The words you rattled off to me for three days runnin'! *The divine spirit!* Seek ye the kingdom of Heaven! My wisdom comes from God! All that hogwash, what I mean. And what's that line you told me the heavenly spirit said to you when you were about to embark on this bloody course of your'n? *For he who knows—* What?"

"*For he who knoweth his Master's will,*" I said, "*and doeth it not, shall be beaten with many stripes, and thus have I chastened you.*"

"Yeah, hogwash like that, what I mean." (112)

What Nat quotes are lines others might use to support slavery, the kind of biblical excerpt favored by Richard Whitehead and Maria Pope. But Gray is so intent on telling Nat that all his biblical impetus is hogwash that he misses Nat's irony and sneers at words that support the system he is part of. Nat plays with Gray, inverting his argument without his catching on. In this case, Styron adds a further layer of irony: Nat's quotation is the same one used by Douglass in his *Narrative* to illustrate how his master "found religious sanctuary for his cruelty."[19]

Much of the time, however, Gray is allowed to hobble his own line of thought, not least in what he fails to say in goading Nat. His silences stand out like his facial blotches and the grease stains on his waistcoat,

19. Frederick Douglass, *Narrative of the Life of Frederick Douglass, an Americ Slave,* ed. Houston A. Baker, Jr. (1845; rpr. Harmondsworth, Eng., 1986), 98–99.

telltale signs of his careless sleaze. The words he speaks in accusation underscore—as they do in the historical document—just what he would suppress. He describes the revolt as "not a nightmare" but an "actual happening" whose "toll in human ruin and heartbreak and bereavement can be measured to this very day" (83). Because that description could serve for slavery itself, it is at cross-purposes with an insistence on Nat's guilt. The effect is similar when he accuses Nat's band of committing "crimes unprecedented in the annals of this nation" (21), for its crimes are dwarfed by the forms of exploitation that incited them. At such points the novel fulfills its claim to be a "meditation on history," reverberating with the contradictions in American history.

Gray also fails when he attempts to assert authority by using words he assumes Nat will not grasp. He erroneously defines a "contradiction" as "two things that mean one and the same thing at the same time" (21). Moreover, he goes on, without realizing it, to illustrate the correct meaning with an inconsistent statement: "You're goin' to be tried next sattidy," he says, "and hung by the neck until dead" (22). The trial, in other words, is no trial at all, since the decision is predetermined; the logical contradiction reveals the inherent contradiction within the system, its laws, and the Constitution itself. Repeatedly Gray's statements, accusations, and strategies turn on themselves, reminding us of the inconsistencies not only of his position but of all he represents concerning American society in the antebellum South and after, and the law he upholds. Nat concedes Gray plenty of space in the narration, but mostly to Nat's gain in the larger battle. Gray upholds order—grammatical, social, and legal—but that sense of order and eloquence deconstructs its own discourse. Like the colonnades of a plantation mansion, his eloquence crumbles amid the Spanish moss of its own metaphors.

Gray reverts at different times to legal and scientific authority. He calls on legal authority in cell and courtroom, changing his voice to suit the context. In court his voice is full of "eloquence and authority, free of the sloppy, patronizing half-literate white-man-to-nigger tones he had used in jail" (92), and armored with the Latinate diction of officialdom. Terms like *ameliorate* and *videlicet* put his remarks in respectable verbal dress while removing them from the crude reality: "I have been authorized by the court to, within reason, ameliorate any such continuation of present misery that might obtain, providin' you co-operate to a degree as would make such amelioration, uh, mutually advantageous" (16). As the *uh* suggests, he delights in finding phrases to clothe his racist discourse in a felicitous style. His broaching of the "advantageous" is a delicate admission that what really matters is self-interest. There is a constant warring, though, between Gray's official language, scientific and legal, and his colloquial turns of phrase revealing subjectivity: "I am, uh, delegate of the court, empowered to take down the confession. Which I've gone and done. But your goose is cooked already" (29).

In the courtroom, Gray draws on quasi-scientific concepts like that of the "gnathic index" in trying to demonstrate that, far from being like the Caucasian, the Negro is "closer to the skulking baboon of the dark continent from which he springs" (101). But Gray compromises the appearance of scientific objectivity by venting personal emotion: he is not content to liken Negroes to baboons but has to portray them as "skulking." His scientific discourse is thus shown up as a facade for prejudice. Nat sits back in his manacles and watches Gray's eloquent embellishment tie the lawyer in verbal knots. Nat is sentenced to be hanged, but the judgment the novel reaches occurs in the cell, where Nat as narrator tries Gray and his system, listens to the evidence, and lets him hang himself and the system he represents with his own discourse.

In the opening dialogue, then, Nat reveals his verbal mastery and helps the unwitting Gray dismantle official discourse. But for all the prisoner's cleverness, his activities achieve nothing positive for him. Since the whole episode is one of miscommunication, his victory is hollow; his brilliance only makes his fettered and bereft state more unbearable. In addition, for all Gray's limitations, he is a skillful needler who skewers Nat with remarks that, like the ladies' hatpins on the way to jail, may leave him only smarting but do pierce the skin. Coupled with Nat's uneasy doubts, the dialogues with Gray push Nat toward reflection. It hardly matters that Gray again distorts the evidence, claiming that Nat's Christianity has brought only "senseless butchery" of "black and white" and the "horror of lawless retaliation" (113), because Gray is right about what is bothering Nat most, his sense of emptiness and guilt.

In the opening section, neither man has been anything as

"frank and level" as Gray pretends concerning himself and assumes concerning Nat (17). But neither is blind to the benefits that better communication would bring. If Nat is enmeshed in chains, he is also the "key" to Gray's need to be sure of the revolt's limited scope (18); Gray is not merely needling but trying to pick a lock. His attitude has to alter from the usual indifference regarding miscommunication between blacks and whites, for to find out more about the rebellion he must understand Nat's motivation, and that entails understanding him as a man. Within the seemingly aborted dialogue, then, there are pointers toward a more genuine communication between the two men, and so in the direction of harmony.

Gray's saving quality, ironically, may be his semiawareness of how he manipulates words in behalf of the status quo. His phrasing in court—"the blood of helpless innocence, babies and so on" (81)—suggests weariness of his own clichés. His capacity to see the hypocrisy of the society he represents augurs the change in him between his first and last talks with Nat. His first step in acknowledging Nat comes by way of emotional involvement. He is genuinely appalled by some incidents and puzzled that "darkies" should rise in liberal Virginia and Nat rebel against a master like Travis (17). He is thus moved to consider the situation of a slave and, like Nat, to make reevaluations. His attempt to get Nat a Bible shows further potential for understanding. However halfhearted his attempt, he is not acting from self-interest— he is not trying to save his own soul—but only out of the recognition that Nat has beliefs, even if they are a "delusion" (114). There is a hint, too, that Nat's antipathy toward Gray eases when he notices the blotches on Gray that suggest cirrhosis and a death perhaps almost as imminent as his own. The apparent mellowing may, in light of our next section, be merely the outward face of Nat's sarcasm, but it may also mean that Nat comes to see Gray as a man with his own death sentence, in his own prison. In the opening section, however, Nat and Gray remain at odds, locked into their roles and their linguistic power struggle.

The cell—a microcosm of the world of the novel and a macrocosm of Nat's mind—is a battleground for power through language. Nat, wholly aware of the verbal battle he faces and of the gap between word ₁ intent, begins a journey toward a better understanding of society, himself, and relations between blacks and whites. His renunciation of dialogue for rebellion reflects his conclusion that dialogue is not possible in slavery. Styron suggests, however, that, beyond Nat's specific situation, the attempt at dialogue that acknowledges a common humanity is the only option. As Baldwin hoped when the book came out, if it started a "tremendous fight," people might at least "learn what they really think about each other."[20]

As a Negro and a slave, Nat has learned to speak indirectly. His opening dialogue with Gray, indeed his whole narration, reveals that. Like other narrators in Styron's fiction, he is trying to reconcile his actions with their consequences. Behind his inner conflicts and verbal subtlety is his hatred of Samuel Turner. It is his one real hatred, but radiates to all whites. Such hatred, he says, must be "exquisitely sharpened" (257), "intelligent and unrepenting" (258). A close reading of his narration in Parts II and III of the novel suggests that his hatred is exactly that. A Negro, he says, must "like a dog" forever "interpret the *tone*" of a voice (61). In reading his words, we must do likewise, keeping in mind his hatred, verbal acuity, and ongoing inner dialogue, and the comparable bitter, ironic tone of Dostoyevsky's *Notes from Underground* or Ellison's *Invisible Man*.[21] His despairing narrative voice slowly converges with the voice of his former self, which possessed a faith in language and in whites. Only then, in Part IV of the novel, can he approach personal, spiritual, and social harmony.

Judgments about the tone of a narrative voice may seem baseless, since we cannot literally hear the voice. But Bakhtin's form of close analysis of the "double-voicedness" of seemingly unitary discourse shows how tone can disclose itself in sentence structures, and by the friction of voices within the discourse.[22] Nat, especially, has several

20. Raymond A. Sokolov, "Into the Mind of Nat Turner," *Newsweek*, October 16, 1967, p. 67.

21. Harry B. Henderson III discusses Dostoyevsky and Ellison. The invisible man, he observes, uses "two voices": that of the "trusting, innocent . . . Southern black boy," and that of an "ironic, disillusioned, and detached intellectual" (*Versions of the Past: The Historical Imagination in American Fiction* [New York, 1974], 288).

22. Mikhail M. Bakhtin, *The Dialogic Imagination: Four Essays*, trans. Michael Holquist and Caryl Emerson, ed. Michael Holquist (Austin, Tex., 1981), 354.

means available to convey meanings that go against his apparent intentions. One, already seen in his dialogue with the unwitting Gray, is his use of metaphor and gratuitous detail to invert the surface meaning of what is said. This is also evident when he talks of Sarah Travis' death:

I do not wish easily to malign her by declaring that the affection she bore toward me resembled the warm impulsive tenderness which might be lavished carelessly upon a dog. I even came to be fond of the woman in a distant way (but largely with attentive, houndlike awareness of her occasional favors) and I intend no sarcasm when I say that much later, when she became almost the very first victim of my retribution, I felt an honest wrench of regret at the sight of the blood gushing like a red sluiceway from her headless neck. (273)

What at first sounds like a voice of regret that intends "no sarcasm" is really a voice of hatred. Nat's nuances alter the apparent meaning. The word *easily* is the first signal, intimating that he may well be content to malign the woman, but subtly. His comparison of himself with a dog clarifies the sarcasm. That he does intend sarcasm is confirmed by the vividness of his description of the "blood gushing like a red sluiceway from her headless neck," which is at odds with the regret he affects.

A second means Nat avails himself of for imparting hidden meanings is what Bakhtin calls "parodic stylization." This device is at work when Nat describes Judge Cobb's misfortunes: "Shortly afterward his stable, a brand-new structure on the outskirts of Jerusalem, burned to the ground in one horrid and almost instantaneous holocaust, incinerating all therein including two or three prize Morgan hunters and many valuable English saddles and harnesses, not to mention a young Negro groom" (58). A shift into "parodic stylization," says Bakhtin, "is prepared for by the sentence's construction."[23] Nat here adapts his sentence's structure to make his point. Once again, he pretends a degree of sympathy, but his sentence structure belies this by parodying white values when it lists Negroes last, behind not only horses but "saddles and harnesses." Nat heightens the effect by employing terms—*brand-new, prize, valuable*—from the white value system, thereby exhibiting the scale on which stable, horses, and saddles matter more than the groom. Cobb's loss is juxtaposed against the plight of slaves, and Nat's

23. *Ibid.*, 303.

voice in commiseration with Cobb holds a bitter sarcasm beneath its placid magnanimity.

A third device is Nat's juxtaposition of seemingly innocuous senti-ments with feelings he expresses elsewhere. Witness what at first seems an oddly objective summation of slavery: "It may have been seen by now," he says, "how different each owner might be by way of severity or benevolence" (299). At least one critic takes this at face value, criticizing Styron for it.[24] But there are different voices here; the words *severity* and *benevolence* belong to the young Nat; they name qualities he—not the narrating Nat—would ascribe to Moore and Turner respectively. The author's voice may also be present, since Nat's words might be read as ventriloquizing the authorial observation that not all slave owners were monsters. Yet the caustic tone of the narrating Nat cannot be doubted in the next remark, that the owners run "from the saintly (Samuel Turner)" to the "monstrous." Nat, we know, hates Turner; he is the worst of masters because he offers hope, then betrays his promise for money, establishing that he sees Nat above all as a commodity. Nat thus communicates his attitude by jux-taposing a declared feeling not only against other of his current feelings but also against feelings he realizes stemmed from a misperception of their object. His parodic juxtaposition of earlier views is equally effec-tive in his description of Turner's "splendid vision" of freeing him (239).

The tone of Nat's narrative voice sounds most clearly in his sen-tence structures and in the voice's inner tensions. His voice is really a combination of voices that he uses to make his true sentiments under-stood. His indirect communication continues the strategy he has had to resort to throughout his life to protect himself against whites. Once aware of this, we can see that his narrative voice is far more acerbic with disillusion than it first seems.

For all his cleverness, he remains desolate and guilt-ridden. Intent on coming to terms with what his revolt has wrought, he continues to reflect. The language trope remains central as he traces his rise and fall. He reviews how his early faith in a destiny derived from his verbal

24. See Charles V. Hamilton, "Our Nat Turner and William Styron's Creation," in *William Styron's Nat Turner*, ed. Clarke, 74.

ability, how each event seemed to point toward the fulfillment of the destiny, and how he was kept from achieving the destiny when Turner broke his promise. Nat's journey, in the story he narrates, began with a growing sense of a clear narrative prospect that, however, clashing as it did with what language inflicted upon him, eventually dissolved. He traces the way events confronted and ultimately undermined his faith in people, in language, and in his sense of destiny. As narrator, he is thus in the process of trying to find personal and spiritual harmony by reexamining the apparent collapse of his earlier world view.

Nat's initial development of a sense of destiny, he reflects, sprang from his mother's predictions of his "great purpose" (31). His family's prophecies and his friends' belief in his "divine inspiration" (32) seemed to lead naturally to the apparent benevolence of Turner that made Nat the "beneficiary"—or the "victim"—of Turner's experiments (154). Nat's recognition that he may have been the victim of Turner's attention is articulated in Nat's reinterpretory voice—the voice that, against the young Nat's sense of destiny, asks where he has been deluded. Even as we witness Nat's rise through language, we witness as well his recomposition of events in a retrospective attempt to understand his experience.

Nat recalls how his verbal abilities fed his delusion of having a destiny. He came to Turner's attention for stealing a book, and his ability to read gained him a favored position within the limits that being a slave allowed. Hearing a conversation between Turner and a salesman, the young Nat felt a "voluptuous stirring" as he echoed the "traveling man's words—*Full springtide, spring, spring*"—and was "filled with" feelings of "tantalizing promise" (123). Language seemed at first to work for him, since he had command over it. It let him interpret anything that did not fit his sense of destiny in ways that did, since he believed Turner's promise of freedom because he believed in the promise of the word.

As the narrating Nat portrays the rise he owes to language, he continues to cast doubt on the sense of destiny felt by his earlier self. Since his favored position in the system depended at first on Turner's benevolence, he revered his white master and learned to read, write, and speak the language of the master class. He identified with whites because they shaped his formal education. He remembers how Miss Nell, in her lessons, corrected his colloquial "I forgets" with "*Forget, Nat, not forgets. No darky talk!*" (157). But his education hid a contradiction, teaching him the language and values of a society that was to block his path. With verbal access to both black and white worlds, he was at home in neither. Alienated from blacks, he felt no closer to whites. He had absorbed white language "daily" (141), yet felt he would "vomit" (153) when they circled him to see if he could read the stolen book. Nat's education would draw him away from his own race but leave him in a no-man's-land between cultures. His resulting naïve disdain for blacks was bolstered by his mother's house-slave snobbery.

In maturity, Nat views this early disdain of others of his race with ironic distance. But the early white influence continues a source of conflict even in his narration, which quarters a confusion of allegiances. The emotional and practical source of his failure lies in the way he is bound up with the values of the white culture he rebels against. The books available to him—the Bible, Bunyan, Scott—were works retailing white world views and, as Fuentes notes, white morality.[25] Nat struggled to translate such voices to speak to uncustomary goals; in his visions of angels, he reversed the religious iconography so that black, standing for righteous indestructibility, vanquished white (291). He appropriated white models of rebellion and created a "nigger Napoleon," the "scourge of all white creation," and a "Joshua and David (turned also into Negro heroes by my artful tongue)" (331). But his inventions were vain, not only because his followers could not fully understand the freedom they sought but because Nat remained tied to cultural aspirations that frustrated him. Hark's geographical confusion in trying to escape replays Nat's disorientation by the reference map of white culture.

Nat's most fully developed narrative voice cannot escape the ideals of the American culture that enslaves him. His awareness of his conceptual thralldom is useless. He feels close to the grandmother he never knew, but his Africa is mythical, the reality being as far beyond

25. Fuentes, "Unslavish Fidelity," 505.

his mental horizons as beyond the horizon of the ocean he dreams of. His education ties him to white culture even as he seeks to evade or redefine it. He is aware of the irony that by setting July 4 as the first date for the revolt he demonstrated an American mind-set. Everything he appropriates underlines just how bound up he is with all he seeks to reject. The white culture is embedded in his vocabulary. He sees himself as "manifestly called to by God and by destiny" (323). Of his early learning, he describes the "vainglory of a black boy" who was probably the only one "among his race in bondage" to have read Scott and known the "name of the President" and the "capital of the State of New Jersey" (171). Abandoned by Turner and about to be groped by Eppes, the unsuspecting Nat was "excited by the promise of a new world, liberty, the fruition of all those dreams" of himself "as a freed-man" (229). His diction—*manifest, destiny, new world, liberty*—shows that his bondage is more than physical. His employment of such words may be partly sarcastic, but if so, he himself is one focus of his irony, which acknowledges how tied he is to white language and ideology.

Only occasionally, talking of blacks, is he able to make language work for him, without irony or sarcasm: "I couldn't make out their words, but in the cold air their voices were shrill and bright. Black hands and feet and faces, bobbing, swooping, dancing shapes silhouet-ted like lively birds against the white purity of the forest and the morn-ing" (40). At these points, Nat casts out white rhetoric to catch a con-trasting ideological position, where the blacks are seen as full of energy, their voices bright against the cold, struggling against an envel-oping whiteness. But even here, where they are set apart, Nat cannot "make out their words."

The various modes of speech of the Nat within the narrative are all subject to the same cultural schizophrenia. Having risen by harnessing the "power of the Word" (225)—through storytelling, reading, and spelling *columbine*—he can nonetheless manipulate whites through "nigger gabble." Since all slaves know this to be a contrivance for fool-ing masters, it functions as a private bond—in a positive sense—with fellow blacks. But speaking it is for Nat no less playing a role than speaking any of his other three languages is. It sets up a screen between black and white that, fool whites as it may, also leaves indubitable the gap between the world Nat has been led to strive for and the one that must remain his lot.

Nat's two modes of speech besides this and the narrative mode are Negro dialect and preacher rhetoric. He employs Negro dialect with other blacks to be understood and accepted rather than because it is natural for him. Since he is a partly educated house slave, it is no more his than "nigger gabble." It is only a half-learned English, an uneasy hybrid, one more aspect of his cultural schizophrenia. Of his Bible-based preacher rhetoric he says, with considerable unconscious irony, that "my language was theirs, I spoke it as if it were a second tongue" (308). But that is the point: it is a second tongue, not a first. As a mode of speech, Nat's preacher rhetoric stretches from Negro dialect to the King James Version. If at times Nat uses direct black speech in his preachings—"Them Jews was just like black folk. They had to sweat their fool asses off fo' ole Pharaoh" (308)—there are also biblical undertones and vocabulary. "When white men in they hate an' wrath an' meanness fetches blood from that beautiful black skin then, oh *then*, my brothers," Nat tells the crowd, "it is time not fo' laughing but fo' weeping an' rage an' lamentation!" (311).

Aware during his narration of how torn he is between cultures, he, for the most part, describes his early naïve faith and certainty with conscious irony, juxtaposing details that gainsay the optimism he felt at the time. The very moment Turner makes his promise, Nat describes the slave chain heading south to be resold, signaling the depression beginning to afflict Virginia. The young Nat was blind to this, and he felt merely a "trace of disillusionment" (212) when Turner sold Willis and three others, despite the clear indication there that Turner's promise was far from certain to be fulfilled. In contrast, the narrating Nat makes us see that however good his masters may appear, economics are always their first concern.

Language again comes to the fore at the moment Nat realizes his betrayal. Right up to Eppes's sale of Nat to Moore, at the end of Part II, Nat retains faith in Samuel Turner's verbal promise. Even as he is sold he shouts about the "written agreement" (246). But the wheel has come full circle; Nat's sense of his mastery of language has been shattered not only by Turner's betrayal but by Moore's assertion of power, first through the whip and then through language:

"Say *master!*" Moore roared.
  "Mastah!" I cried in terror. "Mastah! Mastah! *Mastah!*"
  "That's better," said Moore. "Now shut up." (252)

This crisis reduces the space between Nat as narrator and as figure in the narrative. Nat experiences two rebirths. The second occurs after he has completed his reflections, but the first he narrates here. He remembers that his heart "disappeared, and rage like a new born child exploded there to fill the void" (306). Sold by Eppes and having to cope with the shift in his destiny, he redirected his thinking toward the hatred and mistrust of whites that his experiences had aroused and that are so evident in his narrative voice.

His original faith in language was tied up with religious belief: the word fused with the Word. On the eve of Turner's first sign of breaking his promise, Nat compared his master's word to the Word of God: "And God said Let there be light: and there was light" (210). Nat's personal Genesis was Turner's promise. Having had faith in Turner like that usually reserved for "the Divinity" (126), Nat dealt with his betrayal by transferring his faith to the Word of God as found in the Old Testament prophets, and so to vengeance. Owned by Moore, he retained his sense of destiny—and indeed his belief in his *command* of language— by altering his vision to his new circumstances. The "trace of disillusionment" Nat felt when Willis was sold turned to a hatred for Turner that allowed Nat a kind of rebirth. Still, the very sensitivity that led to his verbal proficiency, and then his faith in Turner, ill equipped him for the violence he decided on. That is so not least because he had a close association with whites. His "sharpened hatred" stemmed from having lived in "intimacy with the white man" (257). But that intimacy, given Nat's basic decency, was the chink in his hatred, allowing it to begin to break down.

At the same time, though, that we witness such a change in the Nat of the narrative, the narrating Nat is further attenuating his faith in language by recognizing how he has all along been caught in the fetters of linguistic ambivalence. Whereas he once saw events as conforming to his plan, he now can let us perceive the flimsy structure on which the revolt was based, and thus, in ironic contrast, he foreshadows its failure before he tells of it. Illustrating his former subjection to language as much as his command of it, he displays the limited understanding he had of the narrative in which he once clothed his existence. Torn between "two worlds" (322) even as he reflects, the narrating Nat reveals the way the Nat of the narrative remained bound to the white culture he was rejecting.

From then on, Nat identified with the Old Testament prophets. His sense of destiny, inspired by both his mother and his master, became a sense of a "bloody mission" (48). With Ezekiel as his guide, he was readier than ever to see natural phenomena as "auguries" and "portents" of his role as the "instrument of God's wrath" (52). Unable to carry off the revolt on the day he first planned it for, he rationalized that that augured the "beginnings of an even more propitious design" (315) and saw only ambivalence and deceit in the language of whites. At this point the only difference between Nat as narrator and as figure in the narrative is that the latter retains a sense of destiny, albeit drastically realigned, whereas the narrating Nat is in uncertainty and despair.

By the end of Part III, Nat has reflected on the preparations for the revolt and on its failure yet is still faced with Gray's dismissal of it as "total futility" (112). Spiritually bereft, he is at his lowest ebb. His sense of destiny shattered, he mocks his former naïveté, spits out his hatred of whites, but seems to have no basis to build on: "I know nothing any longer," he says (417). The voices of narrator and figure within the narrative meet in bitter despair. Nat, entwined in the culture he rebels against, feels both disdain and love for his own people. Like earlier narrators of Styron's, he will try to reconcile his contradictory impulses. But if his story, like theirs', is a "quest for faith and certitude," he, unlike them, faces imminent death. He acknowledges the naïve certitude that propelled him before, but the "sharpened hatred" evident in his narration is useless now and may even be contributing to his spiritual crisis. Caught in the bonds of discourse, he is desperate to reconcile his two worlds: the white one of his aspirations, and the slave world he is consigned to. Integral to his reevaluation, however, are not only his inner dialogue and his thoughts on Turner but also his reexamination of his meetings with those he met before the rebellion but after his first rebirth, his rebirth into hatred.

If the promise of Samuel Turner dominated Nat's early life, once Nat's discourse within the narrative has shifted from destiny through trust to destiny through hatred, he has encounters with Cobb and Margaret, and a friendship with Hark, each affecting his journey toward harmony through reflection. Since all three interactions occur between his two rebirths, all of them are colored by his recognition of the gap between word and intent and of his ambivalent position between two worlds, and all of them have an effect on the second rebirth, presaged by Nat's final meeting with Gray.

When Nat meets Cobb and Margaret, he is set on mistrust and revenge. True dialogue between black and white seems irretrievable. Nevertheless, there is something in the way Cobb and Margaret speak to Nat—Cobb in drunken candor, Margaret in innocence—that hints that each is a hope as well as a threat. Nat's meetings with them capture not only the chasm between the races but also the potential for racial reconciliation rather than prisonlike separation. Whereas Nat's relationship with Turner gives rise to a generalized hatred of whites after Turner has gone, his meetings with Cobb and Margaret to some extent shake that result.

Throughout Nat's meeting with Cobb, he and Hark assume the "posture of respect" necessary "whenever a strange white" appears (54). Thus they erect the usual barrier between black and white. Nat is angry with Hark for assuming an overly servile air and rebukes him for feeling sympathy toward Cobb: "Feel sorry for a white man and you wastin' your sorrow" (58). For Nat, Cobb's voice is "touched with threat" (60). Unlike Gray, the judge is aware of black stratagems and consequently approaches Nat by focusing on the failings rather than the advantages of slavery. He asks Nat to say with "honesty"—knowing that he cannot speak his mind—whether "the handwriting [is] on the wall" for the "old dominion" (64). Nat's reply, "That sure is true," garnished with an idiotic chuckle, does not fool Cobb (65). "Oversensitive (as always) to the peculiar shading of a white man's tone," Nat fears a trap. His unease worsens when Cobb tries to make him spell *cat*. Again Nat parries with gabble: "Kindly please, Mastah. Don't mock me" (67). As in the encounter with Margaret, potential understanding turns toward violence, with Nat feeling he might have to "try to kill" Cobb (68).

This scene is in ironic counterpoint to the earlier episode in which Nat spelled *columbine* and began his apparent rise. Where once language was Nat's great hope, it is now at best a cover, at worst a threat. Knowing that Cobb may genuinely be trying to communicate, Nat despairs. "Even when they are somehow on your side," he says, "they cannot help but taunt and torment you" (68). But if both he and Cobb retreat from a meaningful exchange—Nat into gabble and Cobb into a resigned repetition of "yah" (73)—Nat at least remembers the "thrill of hope" Cobb gave him, and vows that the judge will be spared (69). That Cobb turns out to preside over Nat's trial adds to the irony and underscores the corrupting power of the system.

The pattern is similar between Nat and Margaret. In her innocence, she talks unguardedly to Nat and expects him to do the same to her. She too is thus a threat but also, as Nat later realizes, a hope. While Gray reads him the confession, Nat reminisces over a conversation with her. Margaret's "clear" voice accords with the way she says what she feels without thought of disguise or deceit. Her naïveté both irritates and attracts Nat, who is only too aware of living in the shadow of a society that mutilates any possibility of direct communication. As with Cobb, he must veil his feelings with gabble. She reads her romantic ode, and Nat tells "missy" what a "very beautiful poem" it is, all the while "eyeing her" with a "cautious, evasive glance" that is in tandem with his evasive language. But, as in the exchange with Cobb, Nat is thrown by Margaret's attempt at direct communication, and he is "confused" and "embarrassed" when she gazes straight at him (89).

Contrary to the view of some commentators that Nat stereotypically lusts after a white woman here, the attraction—obscured for him by anger at her dangerous naïveté—is, as Genovese says, mutual.[26] Margaret is drawn by Nat's intelligence and biblical knowledge. "Oh, you're not like Mama or Richard," she says, "you've been the only one

26. Genovese, "William Styron in the People's Court," in *Critical Essays on William Styron*, ed. Casciato and West, 209.

I could talk to" (90). For Nat, her "closeness" is "oppressive," since he cannot afford the feelings she arouses, which offer a glimpse of what he cannot have. As she "chirrups" on about a Christian love, he feels a "reasonless hatred" (91–92). All the same, he is aware that she is the only white with whom he has experienced even a moment's "confluence of sympathy" (92). It is the very glint of potential harmony between people, regardless of color, that widens the chasm between the two of them.

The closest Nat comes to genuine dialogue once he has shed his ingenuous faith in the word of the whites is with Hark. As Cobb and Margaret to some extent moderate the result of Nat's relationship with Turner, Hark reverses Nat's disdain for fellow blacks. The narrating Nat is aware of his foolish aloofness in youth. He tells of the incident with Raymond and the slave chattel at a time when his trust in Turner was at its height. Proud in his saddle and "still listening to Marse Samuel," the young Nat tried to ignore Raymond's voice (199). Finally replying that Turner would set him "free in Richmond," he was deaf to Raymond's warnings and rode off to his master. The narrating Nat, however, says Raymond was "prophetic" (200–201). Nat has learned, between the experience and the recollection, that he cannot ignore his blackness, indeed, that it was central to his master's interest in him. Hark assists in that recognition.

At first, Nat's relationship with Hark merely replays Samuel Turner's relationship with Nat and gives new life to Nat's early attitudes toward blacks. Turner admitted that Nat was an "experiment" (124), as much so, Nat sees in retrospect, as a "new type of manure" (155). Nat sees Hark as a "crucial experiment" (57). In this respect, Nat uses Hark as much as Turner used Nat. Like Turner with Nat, and Nat in his earlier friendship with Willis, Nat sees Hark as someone he has to "teach." During the incident with Cobb, he tells him, "You just got to *learn*, man" (57). It has been argued that Styron emasculates Nat, but really the emasculated one—at first—is Hark, since despite his noble bearing he lacks "dignity," as Nat calls it, in front of whites (57).[27] His face, "fearless, scary, resplendent in its bold symmetry," reminds Nat of an "African chieftain." Yet "something" is "wrong with the eyes,"

27. See Bennett, "Nat's Last White Man," in *William Styron's Nat Turner*, ed. Clarke, 5; and Alvin F. Poussaint, "*The Confessions of Nat Turner* and the Dilemma of William Styron," *ibid.*, 21.

suggesting a "malleable docility" (56). Nat counteracts Hark's emasculation by reminding him of his family, goading him to an inner "fury" so that, revitalized like a "hawk burst free from a snare" (99), he threatens Putnam.

Ultimately, though, the teacher is not Nat but Hark. He shows Nat that violence and hatred are not the only ways to transcend oppression. One reaction to oppression which he exhibits is humor, or what we might see as Camusian scorn. "Free of spiritual rules," Hark can "laugh with abandon" at each "new absurdity" (63). If Nat realizes the limits of this response—he tells Cobb that "outside" Hark is "cheery, but inside he's just all torn up" (72)—a clearer lesson Nat draws from Hark concerns the contours of dignity. The form of dignity Hark in the end achieves, moreover, pinpoints a contradiction in Nat's own outlook.

Almost to the last—perhaps even then—Nat is unaware of the inconsistency between being disappointed that his "Christian teachings" have made little imprint on Hark and being himself converted to pre-Christian vengeance (53). Before the revolt, Nat sees Hark as his potential "right arm" but frets over how to teach him "to behave with dignity." He means that Hark must not just stop cowering but learn to "gut a white and gut him without a blink or qualm" (57). The Nat within the narrative does not yet know that he himself will be unable to do what he asks of Hark. The one black who delights in murder is Will, whom Nat credits less with dignity than with madness. But if Nat at that stage is not aware of his own nature or the values he pursues, the narrating Nat sees a different side of dignity in Hark's final attitude.

In a long drawn out breath, Hark's wails die away. Now I hear a hurried sound of snapping ropes as they tie him into the chair. Then the white men whisper and grunt whilst they strain beneath the weight of their burden and lift Hark out into the hallway. Shadows leap up and quiver in the lantern's brassy radiance. The white men shuffle in furious labor, gasping with the effort. Hark's bound and seated shape, like the silhouette of some marvelous black potentate borne in stately procession toward his throne, passes slowly by my door. (427)

Hark transcends his fate, in Nat's eyes, through a dignity that comes not from the ability to butcher but from inner strength.

Nat's recognition here that dignity can exist apart from vengeance becomes a key to his other discoveries. Hark's dignity and humor on his way to death, "no longer a servant of servants" but one who has asserted his humanity (391), bring him the nearest either of them can come to peace of mind. That is consistent with Nelson's sentiment that it "mought make a nigger worth somethin' to hisself, tryin' to git free, even if he don't." Nat says of Nelson, however, that, "like Hark, he has little religion" (100). Nat's perplexity has more complex roots, for it is not just words but the Word in which there is ambiguity. The conflicting messages he finds in the Bible itself lie behind much of his anguished reflection. Nat's final attempt to reconcile his aims with their consequences and make sense of events is connected to both the word and the Word.

Many critics have pointed out the religious theme, and Styron, as Lang notes, has described Nat's "relationship with God" as important in his own "conception of the man."[28] There is plenty of textual evidence that this is so. The conflict between Nat's teleological discourse and Gray's atheism, for instance, comes to a head when Gray argues that Nat's beliefs have produced "evil" (111), thus prodding Nat into reexamining his understanding of God's Word. Biblical discourse is at work not only in the conflicts of the novel but also in the movement toward Nat's harmony and the harmony between Nat and others that constitutes the novel's structure. It informs Nat's ultimate sense of having reconciled conflicting voices on a personal and social level, but it also works against Nat's final sense of harmony.

Although the Bible is a fundamental source for Nat's sense of destiny, its message inherently equivocates. From its heteroglossia, passages can be selected to validate contrary viewpoints. Nat looks to the Prophets for comfort and inspiration, but the white master class claims biblical justification for slavery. Cobb is exploiting the lack of a single biblical voice when, drawing from Isaiah, he asks Nat whether the writing is "on the wall" for the South but also mimics apologist arguments against his own questioning: "Theology must answer theology. Speak you of liberty? Speak you of the yoke of bondage? How then country magistrate, do you answer this? Ephesians Six, Five: *Servants,*

28. Lang, "The Alpha and the Omega," 500.

be obedient to them that are your masters according to the flesh, with fear and trembling, in singleness of your heart, as unto Christ" (64). Similarly, Maria Pope's favorite passages include 1 Tim. 6:1: *"Let as many servants as are under the yoke count their own masters as worthy of all honour, that the name of God and his doctrine be not blasphemed"* (43). These words contradict those of Paul of Tarsus quoted by Cobb, that one should stand fast in Christ-given liberty *"and be not entangled again with the yoke of bondage"* (63). Nat can preach the Word to exalt his fellow slaves, but Richard Whitehead can lard his sermons with biblical verses that instill fear and obedience.

Nevertheless, the Bible—for all the problems Styron points to—remains crucial for Nat's eventual passage toward social, personal, and spiritual harmony. At the start there is the question whether Nat can have a Bible. Gray's efforts to help him acquire one are minimal; he says that he stressed "in the strongest possible terms" that any condemned man "should have the fullest spiritual comfort" (110), but given his thinking about "animate chattel," this is unconvincing. At the end, however, it is clear that not only Nat has spent the night in reflection. With the contest over, there are suggestions of a harmony between Nat and Gray that transcends their social positions. Gray brings the Bible. It stays shut, but it attests to his recognition of Nat's needs and his human dignity. On this last morning, Gray speaks in a "soft voice" and is "composed," as if "another man." He quietly declares that it was his personal decision to bring a Bible. "It is," he says, "my risk." In contrast to what happened at the first meeting, when neither spoke candidly, the two now "gaze at each other" until Gray "reaches through the bars and grasps" Nat's hand, the "first black hand he has ever shaken."

Equally, Nat feels "pity for Gray" and "his mortal years to come." Reaching through the bars, Gray could almost be behind them, as in a sense he is, since he must go on living with slavery. Gray, earlier a chatterer, is now "subdued," and the final words between the two men contrast sharply with their earlier linguistic vying:

"Goodbye, Reverend," he says.
"Goodbye, Mr. Gray," I reply. (425)

The dialogue is now without sarcasm and pretense. There is just the recognition that both are caught in a structure that has generated conflict between them. But if Nat's relations with Cobb and Gray suggest the potential for harmony between all people regardless of race, what Douglass called the "brutalizing effects of slavery upon both slave and slaveholder" bring it about that it is only near the end that any honest communication appears.[29] The tragedy is that it has taken murderous destruction to get Gray to this point.

With Margaret, the tension Nat feels is, in biblical terms, between Old Testament revenge and New Testament love. He feels ambivalent toward her because she disturbs his belief that his destiny is to avenge. Although Nat is irritated by her naïveté, her adolescent pretentiousness hides a commitment to good that remains unsullied by the realities weighing on Nat, Gray, Cobb, and Hark. Nat resents her idealism but feels "*not* hatred" but "something else" (92). What he really resents is that she reminds him of his own lost innocence—of the trust long destroyed by slavery and betrayal. Occupying Nat's mind, along with hatred and the wish for revenge, are memories of innocent trust and a desire for harmony, love, and companionship. Margaret awakens his former disposition, distorted now by hatred. She recalls to him his early sense of destiny and his faith in both language and people. Hence, when he kills her, he finds himself thinking of "moments of childhood" (415), and his final fantasy of her stirs in him a "longing" as unbearable as "memories of time past and long-ago voices" (426).

The war that Nat's love and his hate of others wage within him is apparent in his description of the massacre. Throughout, he equates murder with love and sex. Even witnessing Will's ferocity, he sees "the tar-black man and the woman, bone-white, bone-rigid with fear beyond telling, pressed urgently together against the door in a simulacrum of shattered oneness and heartsick farewell—the porch seemed washed for an instant in light that flowed from the dawn of my own beginning." Then he sees "Will draw back as if from a kiss and with a swift sideways motion nearly decapitate Mrs. Whitehead with a single stroke" (412). This is not a rape scene but Nat's view of events. "Nearly torn apart" and in shock, he sees things in a way that is true to his inner conflict (410). That conflict is apparent as well in the—maybe too blatant—sexual and love imagery of Margaret's murder. Their "last

29. Douglass, *Narrative of the Life of Frederick Douglass*, 90.

encounter" seems to Nat perhaps the "quietest that there ever was." Margaret utters "no word" (413). At the novel's end, Nat remembers her biblical quotation: *"Beloved let us love one another: for love is of God; and everyone that loveth is born of God, and knoweth God"* (426). Thus he takes a step toward recognizing that his reaction to the wrongs he has suffered and witnessed, however justified the reaction is, runs fatally contrary to his yearning for harmony rather than hatred.

Nat at least approaches peace of mind with his vision of unity through love. He imagines Margaret arch against him so that "the twain—black and white—are one" (426). He does not repent the revolt but does repent her death, for she has helped him hear a message of love. The morning star is a symbol less of transcendent harmony, then, than of the possibilities for black and white social unity. For Nat, it symbolizes the example of Jesus, who in Rev. 22:16 is called "the bright and morning star." Seeing Venus in the morning sky, Nat undergoes a rebirth that is based on a mediation by language of what is before his eyes. He understands the message of "Him whose presence I had not fathomed" (428), experiences his second rebirth, and seems to find a state of spiritual, and so personal, harmony. Like the "black potentate" Hark, he attains a sense of identity and dignity, but he also seems to gain a greater understanding. His last words—"Surely I come quickly. Amen. / Even so, come, Lord Jesus. / Oh how bright and fair the morning star" (428)—are taken directly and indirectly from the final chapter of Revelation. His words, that is, are at one with the Bible's.

Styron, however, descries problems in Nat's movement toward harmony, as he did in Peter Leverett's. Nat gains spiritual harmony, but only by papering over personal, and biblical, conflicts—by using language to give the impression of reconciling voices that remain in contradiction. Made conscious of the ambiguity of language, he avails himself of it to come to terms with events. But the resulting "serenity" (427) is largely superficial. Nat's repetition of the biblical phrase *come quickly*, aside from its sexual overtones, repeats the words of Samuel Turner that Nat earlier obeyed (200–201). The conflicts of Nat's life persist in that simple sentence. Equally, Nat's own viewpoint is contradictory: *"I would have done it all again,"* he says, confirming his belief in violent revenge, but *"would have spared her that showed me*

Him" (428). Jesus is invoked even as Nat affirms his vengeance; the multiple voices in the Bible, in Nat—perhaps in Styron too as he seeks not to muffle opposing outlooks and yet to find some semblance of harmony—remain. The hope of transcendence is the only one Nat has left. But for the reader who continues in earthly husk, the hope must be in the identification with Nat that Gray arrives at through the prison bars, and the pity that Nat has for one victim.

Once more, Styron has questioned the discourse toward harmony. Nat's final vision is by its nature illusory, with little relation to Margaret herself. More real are his chains, the harsh voices of the jailers, and the violation of his corpse. The contrast here reminds us, as does the whole novel—as well as, ironically, the subsequent attack on Styron's attempt at empathy—that the difference between vision and reality is important. The movement toward harmony is at one level a political plea for cooperation and dialogue, so as to harness our ability to love against our ability to hate, but at the same time Styron's underlying centrifugal voice acknowledges the clash between dream and actuality, and Nat's contradictory embrace of both Old Testament vengeance and New Testament love.

If *The Confessions* quarters a clash of discourses internal to Nat and between characters, a novel, especially when dealing with history, is also a meeting place for voices otherwise separated by place and historical time. Styron not only weds his own voice to Nat Turner's but incorporates other textual voices from outside the cast of characters the novel names. The voices of Erikson, Douglass, and Baldwin are all heard contributing to the presentation of what is at issue.

Traces of *Young Man Luther*, Erikson's psychoanalytic study of Martin Luther, are myriad. Styron mentions the work in his essay "This Quiet Dust," calling it a "brilliant study of the development of the revolutionary impulse in a young man." He observes that both Luther and Turner were thirty-one at the "moment of their insurgency." Wary of "heavy psychoanalytical emphasis," he nonetheless finds it hard not to see Nat's relationship with his "surrogate father," Samuel Turner, as "tormented and complicated, like Luther's" with his father.[30] Bernhard Reitz has suggested in passing that Erikson's influ-

30. Styron, *This Quiet Dust and Other Writings*, 16.

ence appears "in the ardor with which Nat embraces his divine vision, in the anxiety he feels about losing his special relationship with God, and in the radical way" that "he transmutes his belief into a historical mission."[31]

Erikson's theories shed light on the younger Nat's sense of destiny and contribute to the novel's structure. Erikson defines *ideology* for the purposes of his book as the gifted young man's unconscious tendency "to make facts amenable to ideas, and ideas to fact," so as "to create a world image" to support his "sense of identity." This is equally a description of what Styron's Nat does early in life, accepting others' comments as prophecies so as to mold a sense of destiny, and what he goes on to do in remolding his original vision when sold to Moore. Erikson mentions the need young Luther had to interpret natural phenomena in ways that bolstered his sense of identity or gave him a sign that allowed him to act. He suggests that since an "anxious wish to be ready for the judgment" was part of Luther's frame of reference "long before" the storm that made him vow to enter a monastery, his expectancy may have "made that storm what it became."[32] Visions play the role of the storm for Nat.

Much in Nat's psychological makeup seems to have been suggested by Erikson. Nat's repressed sexuality connects with Erikson's idea that Luther's early sexual repression found an outlet in masturbatory fantasies. Nat's youthful disdain for fellow blacks and his yearning for whiteness match Erikson's portrayal of the "young great man" as suffering an identity crisis that "alters between extreme self-repudiation and a snobbish disdain for all groups—except, perhaps, for memberships whose true root and obligations are completely outside his reach."[33]

Erikson's study also influences the novel's structure. Nat has two rebirths. Sold to Moore, he discovers rage and hatred, which rise in him "like a newborn child" (306). Then, in his last redemptive moments,

31. Bernhard Reitz,"Fearful Ambiguities of Time and History: *The Confessions of Nat Turner* and the Delineation of the Past in Postmodern Historical Narrative," *Papers on Language and Literature*, XXIII (1987), 477.

32. Erik H. Erikson, *Young Man Luther: A Study in Psychoanalysis and History* (London, 1958), 20, 56.

33. *Ibid.*, 97, 98.

he shudders in the world's "newborn beauty" (428). Each rebirth is prompted by a crisis corresponding to one explored by Erikson: the first to what Erikson labels the "Identity Crisis" and the second to what he calls the "Crisis of Generativity." Nat's first crisis is sparked by Turner's broken promise, which leads to "disbelief," a sense of "betrayal," "fury," and "hatred" (246). Styron's image of rebirth fits Erikson's view of the Identity Crisis as a "kind of 'second birth' apt to be aggravated by widespread neuroticisms or by ideological unrest." Equally, the contradictory feelings Nat has for Turner, and for others, dramatize Erikson's view that "whatever ends in divorce . . . loses all retrospective clarity" so that "every item which once spelled love must now be pronounced hate."[34]

The second crisis is even more fundamental to the novel's structure. Nat's retrospective narrative plays out the Crisis of Generativity, the kind of crisis that occurs, says Erikson,

> when a man looks at what he has generated, or helped to generate, and finds it good or wanting, when his life work as part of the productivity of his time gives him some sense of being on the side of a few angels or makes him feel stagnant. All this in turn, offers him either promise of an old age that can be faced with a sense of integrity, and of which he can say, 'All in all, I would do this over again,' or confronts him with a sense of waste, of despair.[35]

Nat, faced with his loss of God, with Gray's needling, and with the failure of the insurrection, reflects on "what he has generated." Accordingly, at the start of his narrative he feels "stagnant." Gray's taunts almost seem palpable hits. Doomed to die, Nat must find the question of justification urgent. He must strive to discover whether his despair stems from the revolt itself or from something else. He ends reaffirming his belief in the revolt: "*I would have done it all again*" is a paraphrase of Erikson. A rebirth into spiritual harmony, accompanied by a vision of union with Margaret, appears to resolve his Crisis of Generativity.

Erikson's study may also lie behind the language trope. Erikson argues that the Reformation was partly the result of a successful deployment of the German vernacular against Latin. To that degree, Luther's

---

34. *Ibid.*, 12, 141.
35. *Ibid.*, 236–37.

success was in gaining mastery over what Nat—to use Fuentes' description—fails to dominate: "a new language, and a new culture."[36] Since Nat is "adrift between two worlds" and, being educated, finds even the hybrid vernacular of his people only indirectly available, he lacks Luther's advantage. Unlike Douglass, who by escaping slavery was able to make the most of his verbal skills—though his way with words did not shake off white culture—Nat remains enslaved literally, and hence verbally. The "theme of the Voice and the Word," linguistic and biblical, is as intrinsic to Nat's story as to Luther's.[37] But unlike Luther, Nat fails to make a language his own.

The way Erikson's study is formative for Styron's novel disables the argument that the characterization of Nat was meant to emasculate him. Styron tried to create a psychologically complex character, which entailed shaving off the implausibly heroic edge of the mythic figure that some black writers would have preferred.[38] But, like Camus' influence on *The Long March*, Erikson's here introduces a discrepancy between subject and portrayal. Erikson's preoccupation with the constructive and destructive impulses in the individual deflects attention from the issue of slavery. Erikson writes of an "eerie balance between destructiveness and constructiveness" and discusses that by reference to Hitler, who as a failed artist and architect carried his frustrations into politics and made an attempt at "re-designing" Europe to suit his vision. "Maybe," ventures Erikson, had Hitler "been permitted to build, he would not have destroyed."[39] Styron's portrayal also shows creativity—Nat's preaching and carpentry—that has been frustrated into destructiveness. Nat's change from someone who constructs into a destroyer may flow ineluctably from his enslavement and thereby constitute an indictment of even benevolent forms of the system. But the psychoanalytic discourse inspired by Erikson also invites the conclusion that minor systemic adjustments allowing Nat a constructive

36. Fuentes, "Unslavish Fidelity," 505.

37. Erikson, *Young Man Luther*, 44.

38. See Bennett, "Nat's Last White Man," in *William Styron's Nat Turner*, ed. Clarke, 5; Vincent Harding, "You've Taken My Nat and Gone," *ibid.*, 25; and Vincent Harding, *There Is a River: The Black Struggle for Freedom in America* (New York, 1981), 77–85, 94–100.

39. Erikson, *Young Man Luther*, 103, 104.

future—say, promise keeping by masters—could have obviated the need to rebel. Thus, the novel at times elevates Nat's personal concerns in a way at odds with its alertness to the repugnance of the system of slavery as a whole. In this there is also a clash of historical contexts, since the psychoanalytic discourse chimes more easily with the 1960s than with a story about a nineteenth-century revolt from slavery.

The voice of Douglass' *Narrative* is heard as well in Styron's novel and enables us to recognize other clashes between contexts. The novel takes after Douglass' account in diction, incidents, and incidental detail. Douglass addresses the destitution of freed slaves and the peculiar loyalty slaves can have for masters, and like Nat he comments on the "stupidity" of many fellow slaves. The sarcasm in Nat's at first blush benign prose is reminiscent at times of Douglass' narrative style. Douglass' reference to the vicious Master Thomas as "one of the many pious slaveholders who hold slaves for the very charitable purpose of taking care of them" compares with Nat's ranking of owners from the "saintly" to the "monstrous."[40]

But Douglass' firsthand account of slavery and Styron's novel portray the violence in slavery differently despite the similar situations that Douglass and Styron's version of Nat face. Both Douglass and Nat are talented and literate, and most of the time they are slaves to masters no worse than the norm. During the same period that Nat was a slave, Douglass, in comparatively liberal Maryland, belonged to a small slaveholder. But for all Douglass' recounting of the ease of his life in comparison with others' experiences, his matter-of-fact voice does not keep a variety of outrages from peppering his account. Douglass and his fellow slaves—women included—endured constant, often prolonged, whipping; he had an old aunt his master "used to tie up" and whip "till she was literally covered in blood." Douglass' description of violence shows that it was a routine part of even the best life a slave might expect:

I suffered more anxiety than most of my fellow slaves. I had known what it was to be kindly treated; they had known nothing of the kind. They had seen

---

40. Gray's references to "chattel" recalls Douglass, in *Narrative of the Life of Frederick Douglass*, 81. Douglass also refers to fellow slaves' "stupidity" (p. 84), tells of their arguments "about the relative goodness of their masters" (p. 62), and is sarcastic about Master Thomas (p. 99).

little or nothing of the world. They were in very deed men and women of sorrow, and acquainted with grief. Their backs had been made familiar with the bloody lash, so that they had become callous; mine was yet tender; for while at Baltimore I got few whippings, and few slaves could boast of a kinder master and mistress than myself; and the thought of passing out of their hands into those of Master Andrew—a man who, but a few days before, to give me a sample of his bloody disposition, took my brother by the throat, threw him on the ground, and with the heel of his boot stamped upon his head till the blood gushed from his nose and ears—was well calculated to make me anxious as to my fate.[41]

The current of violence and degradation running through Douglass' *Narrative* renders the cozy atmosphere Styron sometimes conjures implausible. The violent moments Douglass tells of are proffered almost as asides. He simply takes this aspect of slavery for granted. He can describe without rancor the "few whippings" his "kinder" master gave him. Yet, between dashes Master Andrew's violence stands out the more starkly.

Outrages occur in Styron's novel too, but he presents them less baldly. A common practice of his is to give the description secondhand, lessening the impact:

Hark had risen to his feet to gawk and I told him that he had better go find out what was happening; he moved off slowly.

After a minute or so Hark came back to the gallery, and the sheepish half-smile on his face—I will never forget that expression, its mixed quality of humor and gentle bewilderment—filled me with a sad foreboding, as if I had known, sensed what he was going to say the instant before his mouth opened to say it.

"Ole Francis he puttin' on a show fo' dem white trash," he proclaimed loud enough for most all of the other Negroes to hear. "He drunker dan a scritch owl and he makin' dem two niggers Will and Sam fight each other. Don't neither of 'em want to fight, but ev'y time one of 'em draw back an *don't* whop de other, old Francis he give dat nigger a stroke wid his whip." (305–306)

Nat himself rarely witnesses severe physical abuse from a master and is hit only once. What Nat "will never forget" is not the owner's behavior—which figures so large in Douglass' account—but Hark's ex-

---

41. *Ibid.*, 51, 90–91.

pression of humorous bewilderment. We see plenty of violence by Nat's band, and we see blacks kick Hark and decapitate whites, but we witness no white abuse of blacks except for Moore's hitting Nat and the rape of Nat's mother, the latter violation one that—in the novel's least sensitive passage—the victim ends enjoying.

Styron may have wanted to portray Nat's experience of slavery as a good deal better than most in order to reinforce Douglass' point about the "brutalizing effects" of even the best of slavery on master and slave alike. But the absence here of the indignant rage found in Douglass and the secondhand reporting enfeeble the effect even though no less violence is mentioned in the novel than in Douglass' *Narrative.* Since a movement toward harmony, although dialogized, remains a part of Styron's novel, it may be that Styron felt the need to mute the violence of slavery to allow scope for limited reconciliation. But if so, there is again a clash of nineteenth- and twentieth-century contexts.

James L. W. West III and Arthur D. Casciato may not be right that the adjudication of the claims of "historical 'fact'" and of "imaginative 'fiction'" is a "tired debate," but the amount of commentary devoted to it in connection with *The Confessions* is at the least daunting.[42] Bernhard Reitz and Dawn Trouard have written on the novel's postmodernist sense of history, and Albert E. Stone has suggested that the novel had an "initiating role in redirecting attention to the actual and symbolic function of history within our multicultured culture."[43]

What is a tired question is whether Styron was right or wrong about

42. James L. W. West III and Arthur D. Casciato, "William Styron and *The Southampton Insurrection,*" in *Critical Essays on William Styron,* ed. Casciato and West, 213.

43. Albert E. Stone, "The Return of Nat Turner in Sixties America," *Prospects,* XII (1987), 252. See also Reitz, "Fearful Ambiguities," 465–79; and Dawn Trouard, "Styron's Historical Pre-Text: Nat Turner, Sophie, and the Beginnings of a Postmodern Career," *Papers on Language and Literature,* XXIII (1987), 489–97. Stone has revised this article, and the quoted remark, in *The Return of Nat Turner: History, Literature, and Cultural Politics in Sixties America* (Athens, Ga., 1992). Like Tragle years earlier (see 105n14 above), Stone criticizes Styron for what he perceives as a carelessness with the historical sources. Stone's own casual attitudes—including a readiness to attend more assiduously to opinions about the novels than to the novels themselves—rather compromise his argument; for instance, he repeatedly misspells Emmeline Turner as *Emmaline* (pp. 61–62, 92–93), and states, oddly, that Styron's earlier novels are all "in significant respects southern historical fictions" (p. 72).

the historical facts. Not only is there a surfeit of material on this but the degree to which the historians who seek to refute Styron—like Vincent Harding, Henry I. Tragle, Stephen B. Oates and Herbert Aptheker—contradict each other, reminds us that they no less than Styron select, grade, and interpret the evidence.[44] No doubt Styron departs from certain known facts—he says as much in the Author's Note—but the net result of the historians' animadversions is less to refute Styron than to confirm E. L. Doctorow's assertion that there is no nonfiction or fiction "as we commonly understand the distinction" but "only narrative."[45] In the words of Robert Anchor, a historian "is an artist in spite of himself."[46] A further point, of course, is that the Author's Note makes it clear that the work is a novel and that Styron is exercising the "utmost freedom of imagination" even if he "rarely" deviates from what is known to be the case.

More easily challenged is Styron's remark in the Author's Note that "the relativity of time allows us elastic definitions: the year 1831 was, simultaneously, a long time ago and only yesterday." John Searle has clarified the distinction between fiction and "assertion." He holds that an "assertion," unlike fiction, is bound "to certain quite specific semantic and pragmatic rules." One is that "the maker of an assertion commits himself to the truth" of what he says. Another is that he must be able to give "evidence or reasons for the truth of the expressed

---

44. Because Herbert Aptheker ("A Note on the History," in *The Nat Turner Rebellion*, ed. Duff and Mitchell, 191–95) and Stephen B. Oates (*The Fires of Jubilee: Nat Turner's Fierce Rebellion* [New York, 1976], 140) see Gray's text as in the main reliable, they attack Styron for departing from it. But Tragle attacks him because every aspect of Nat "seems to depend upon, or to be conditioned by, Gray's account" (*The Southampton Slave Revolt*, 403). And whereas Oates ("Styron and the Blacks—Another View," *Nation*, May 31, 1975, p. 663), Harding (*There Is a River*, 78), and others see Nat as a talented artisan, according to Tragle the evidence "does not support Styron's portrayal of him as a talented artisan" (*The Southampton Slave Revolt*, 401). For retrospective comments on artistic license, see William Styron, "Nat Turner Revisited," *American Heritage*, XLIII (October, 1992), 64–73. This is reprinted as an afterword to the 1993 Vintage edition of the novel, which has the same pagination as the standard edition.

45. Richard Trenner, ed., *E. L. Doctorow: Essays and Conversations* (Princeton, 1983), 26.

46. Robert Anchor, "Narrativity and the Transformation of Historical Consciousness," *Clio*, XVI (1987), 127.

proposition."[47] The Author's Note is the "assertion" by which Styron proceeds into his fictional discourse. In contrast to how he conducts the subsequent narrative, he is there speaking, as Bakhtin would put it, in a "direct authorial" discourse, rather than through other voices.[48] Thus the Author's Note—unlike, say, Twain's parodic preface to *Huckleberry Finn*—commits him to the truth of what he says.

Not surprisingly, given this and the language trope, the note is phrased carefully and elusively. Styron talks of the "only effective, sustained revolt in the annals of American Negro slavery," using qualifiers that render challenge futile; *sustained* and *effective* allow room for opinion. When he states that he has "rarely departed from the *known* facts," *rarely* covers minor or disputable details like Nat's earlier escape and his having a "wife."[49] For the most part, the note releases Styron into his fictional discourse, from where, as he says, the reader is offered a "contract" to accept or reject.[50] But both reader and writer know it is a contract and thus that the main narrative is what Searle would call a "nondeceptive pseudo-performance."[51]

In contrast, Styron's assertion that "the relativity of time allows us elastic definitions" seems to evince a commitment to more than contextualized historical truth. That is open to objection at least to the extent that aspects of the novel seem to belie the relativity Styron proclaims. In many ways the novel is rooted in the historical context of its subject in a way that Lukács, whom Styron has often invoked in defense, would have approved, but Styron made it clear that he was also concerned with the sixties, and so, in a sense, was modernizing Nat.[52] This is not least so in Nat's very twentieth-century existentialist

47. John R. Searle, "The Logical Status of Fictional Discourse," *New Literary History*, VI (1975), 322.

48. Bakhtin, *The Dialogic Imagination*, 262.

49. On Nat's earlier escape, see especially Bennett, "Nat's Last White Man," in *William Styron's Nat Turner*, ed. Clarke, 12. On Nat's "wife," see Oates, "Styron and the Blacks," 662.

50. Appendix conversations, 218.

51. Searle, "The Logical Status of Fictional Discourse," 325.

52. Styron has said a number of times that he read Lukács only after writing the novel, but for his comments on Lukács, see his "Nat Turner Revisited," 68–69; and Ralph Ellison, William Styron, Robert Penn Warren, and C. Vann Woodward, "The Uses

angst, as David D. Galloway has noted, but it is also clear in the novel's opening, where time and space are indeterminate.[53] The interviews Styron gave during the writing confirm the intention. In 1965, he spoke of how "the seeds of the revolt are in the *promise*. This—of course, without belaboring the thing—is what's going on right now."[54] Styron thus stood historical periods together in order to make a comment, however tangential, about the later one, the sixties, even as he tried to "recreate a man and his era."

Here, as in Styron's handling of what he took from Erikson and Douglass, the collision of contexts occurs because of the discourse toward harmony. A call for dialogue may have been appropriate for the sixties, but it did not offer a remedy for slavery. Nat ends up a slave looking for and in a limited way achieving dialogue with a representative of his white oppressors, when dialogue—seeming to imply that the problem is on both sides—fails to fit the reality of slavery. Styron's taming of slavery's horrors, through his structuring, may have been necessary in order to achieve the movement he wanted, but it serves goals at variance with the historical context of the story.

Perhaps the main black influence on Styron's novel was his friend James Baldwin. Baldwin lived in Styron's guest cottage in Connecticut from the autumn of 1960 until early the following summer and, according to Styron, worked on *Another Country* and *The Fire Next Time* there. Baldwin, writes Styron, "told me more about the frustrations and anguish of being a black man in America than I had known until then, or perhaps wanted to know." The two writers spent nights drinking together, each drawn to the other by Styron's being the "grandson of a slave owner" and Baldwin's being the "grandson of a slave."[55]

Baldwin's essays manifest sentiments that Styron accords Nat. The

of History in Fiction," in *Conversations with William Styron*, ed. West, 122–24, 131–32.

53. See Galloway, *The Absurd Hero in American Fiction*, 105–17.

54. Robert Canzoneri and Page Stegner, "An Interview with William Styron," in *Conversations with William Styron*, ed. West, 74.

55. William Styron, "Social Animal of Manic Gusto," *Observer*, December 6, 1987, p. 10; Styron, "Nat Turner Revisited," 66.

sense of alienation from black and white, the schizophrenic theme, and the love-hate dichotomy all appear in Baldwin, as—crucially for Styron's novel—does a sense of inseparability. For Baldwin, black and white Americans "are bound together forever," so the "walls" that "have been up so long to protect us from something we fear—must come down." He stresses the shared destiny of the two races since "the one thing that all Americans have in common is that they have no other identity apart from the identity that is being achieved on this continent."[56] This means that the thrust of Styron's narrative toward reconciliation has affinities with the views Baldwin has expressed. In *Nobody Knows My Name*, Baldwin muses whether a white man he is talking to "had ever really *looked* at a Negro and wondered about the life, the aspirations, the universal humanity hidden behind that dark skin."[57] Styron tries to look inside, to be Nat Turner, to wed his own voice and Nat's in an exploration of their "universal humanity." He strives to know something of the experience of Baldwin and other blacks, and so to find out about himself, and about white values in relation to blacks. As Baldwin says, whites must identify with blacks "as people like themselves" because they "will not, otherwise, be able to see themselves as they are." For this reason he was able to affirm, in contrast to many black commentators, that Styron had "begun the common history—ours."[58]

The presence of Baldwin's voice in *The Confessions* makes plain that it, like *Set This House on Fire*, is about the mind in the act of finding. As Styron says of *The Confessions* and *Sophie's Choice*, both are "self-exploration."[59] Baldwin's allegiance to "reconciliation" and "fusion" is a clear note within the novel.[60] Baldwin hence contributes to the tension between obedience to the imperative of historical fi-

56. Baldwin, *Nobody Knows My Name*, 115. See also Styron, "Nat Turner Revisited." Styron ends with Baldwin's "brave and lovely words" that each of us "contains the other—male in female, female in male, white in black, black in white. We are part of each other" (p. 73).

57. Baldwin, *Nobody Knows My Name*, 85.

58. Sokolov, "Into the Mind of Nat Turner," 69.

59. Robert K. Morris, "Interviews with William Styron," in *The Achievement of William Styron*, ed. Morris and Malin, 62.

60. Baldwin, *Nobody Knows My Name*, 176.

delity and commitment to that of ameliorating the sixties. Styron tries to show that even in the gentlest forms of slavery the degradation was appalling, and the sight of freedom the more embittering. But aligned as he is with Baldwin's call for harmony, he also needs to show Nat's relationship with whites to shelter at least the *will* for reconciliation. He consequently marginalizes the worst of slavery—talking about it rather than showing it—not for an apologist's reasons but in an attempt to draw analogies between Nat's revolt and the sixties.

Nat's narration mixes not two or three voices but many: the voices he uses to narrate, to preach, and to fool, but also Styron's voice, melding with Erikson's, Douglass', Baldwin's, and others'. The clash of voices in the story echoes a clash at the authorial level. Moreover, if the voices of Douglass and Baldwin—one discoursing on slavery, the other on the fifties—were tangled with the author's, the controversy surrounding the novel resulted partly from the way Baldwin himself proved at odds with the prevailing mood of radical blacks by the time the novel appeared. The work of Baldwin and Douglass and the sixties work of Malcolm X and Eldridge Cleaver meet in the consistent stress on black *self*-definition. Even Baldwin talks of the "necessity" for Negroes "to remake" their "own image" so as no longer to "be controlled by white America's image" of them.[61] But if Baldwin combined black self-assertion with reconciliation, in the sixties his call for assertion rather than his call for reconciliation was more in tune with the mood.

Baldwin's earlier desire to appropriate white culture—as Nat tried to do—was condemned by the radical Cleaver, writing near the novel's publication date. Cleaver seems to be writing unaware of the novel, yet he anticipates objections of the ten black writers who rose up in opposition to it. In *Soul on Ice*, he lets us see how appalled he is by Baldwin's "hatred of blacks." Baldwin, he says, "is frank to confess" in *Notes of a Native Son* that "since his own heritage" is inaccessible to him, "he would appropriate the white man's heritage." For Cleaver, this is anathema, for "those truly concerned" with helping black Americans "have had eternally to deal with black intellectuals" who take on "all the behavior patterns of their enemy" and "aspire to alien standards." He scorns the "intellectual sycophant" who "hates what

61. *Ibid.*, 35, 73.

he is and seeks to redefine himself" in the image of "white idols," becoming a "white man in a black body." He sees such integration as the best "white tool in oppressing other blacks."[62]

The controversy surrounding the novel was itself a heteroglossia, spawning book after book: document collections, casebooks of opinions, and biographical histories of the rebellion that capitalized on the renewed interest.[63] Add Stone's claim that the novel played an "initiating role" in a wider dialogue on the "function of history," and there is strong evidence for—whatever else—the vitality of the novel form if it sets crucial voices from an arena of social dispute against one another. As for the controversy itself, there can, perhaps should, be no final verdict. On the one hand, Genovese has refuted most of the ten black writers' specific claims, and as we have seen in connection with Douglass and Baldwin, some of the criticized themes also appear in black writing. Nat's aspiration toward whiteness, for instance, whether a question of class, as Genovese says, or of race, harks back to the writing of Du Bois, Douglass, Baldwin, Malcolm X, Richard Wright, and others.[64] More recently the theme has appeared in the work of Maya Angelou and Toni Morrison. In Morrison's *The Bluest Eye*, Pecola Breedlove's sense that beauty depends on blue eyes and white skin is comparable to Nat's own childhood confusion.

On the other hand, it can be argued that in appropriating a black historical figure, Styron perpetuated a pattern of white definition of black culture and history that blacks still struggle against. Styron's novel can be seen as at once an attempt at advancing black-white unity (racial harmony) and a perpetuation of white hegemony—not perhaps a "deliberate attempt to steal the meaning of a man's life," as one critic

62. Eldridge Cleaver, *Soul on Ice* (New York, 1968), 99, 102–103.

63. Aside from Tragle, *The Southampton Slave Revolt*, Duff and Mitchell, eds., *The Nat Turner Rebellion*, and Oates, *The Fires of Jubilee*, see also Melvin J. Friedman and Irving Malin, eds., *William Styron's "The Confessions of Nat Turner": A Critical Handbook* (Belmont, Calif., 1970), and Eric Foner, ed., *Nat Turner* (Englewood Cliffs, N.J., 1971).

64. See Genovese, "William Styron in the People's Court," in *Critical Essays on William Styron*, ed. Casciato and West, 207.

claims, but certainly another white version of events that, especially in the climate of the late sixties, worked against black self-definition.[65] Styron, as much as his character, was caught up in the ambiguities of language. Though he portrays Nat through and with the voices of black writers, he is trapped in the ineradicable ambiguities of his approach, which possesses a schizophrenic quality because of the way he tries to become Nat at the same time that he usurps Nat's voice. His teeter between identification and usurpation replicates the schizophrenic life of the Nat he portrays.

To try to resolve the controversy might be to try to harmonize the irreconcilable. It may be better to see how the arguments of the ten black writers are not so much a disagreement over the novel's themes as an act of black self-assertion directed against Styron largely because of the accident of the timing of the novel. The black critics, like their white counterparts, recognized aspects of both the language trope and the movement toward harmony, but in line with the mood of the late sixties, their reactions differed from Styron's and Baldwin's.

It is a large irony that Styron's work got the negative response from black critics that it did, since the response itself illustrates the themes of miscommunication and linguistic ambiguity. But several critics in the collection of essays by the ten black writers, like some of their white counterparts, acknowledge the impact miscommunication has had on black life. Thelwell especially—apparently accepting Elkins' thesis—argues that slaves had to deal with loss of language and so of culture: "When black people were brought to America, they were deprived of their language and of the underpinnings in cultural experience out of which a language comes. It is clear that they developed two languages, one for themselves and another for the white masters." Thelwell believes part of the slaves' problem was their need to create an identity through language. Styron, we have seen, portrays this. Because Nat lacks black role models and an African culture, his language and goals are white; thus his goals, given that he is a slave, are unattainable. Styron's modification of some of the minor details of the story underlines the sense of a man between cultures—of Styron writing the

65. Bennett, "Nat's Last White Man," in *William Styron's Nat Turner*, ed. Clarke, 5.

novel, and of Nat as a white-educated slave. Thelwell may see this, but he puts it negatively. Can a "white Southern gentleman," he asks, "tune in on the impulses, beliefs, emotions, and thought patterns of a black slave? This miracle of empathy entails an imaginative leap not only into history but across cultures. It necessitates the writer divorcing himself from that vast mythic tradition about slavery, black people, and history which is so integral a part of his background. Then he has to devise a literary idiom, since the gentleman and the slave lack a common language and experience."[66] Thelwell rightly concludes that it is not possible. The novel is at best a meeting of voices: Styron's, Gray's, Baldwin's, and others. But Thelwell should also acknowledge that this limitation is made clear at the start, and that it, rather than the inclination to denigrate Nat, may explain why Styron placed Nat between cultures.

When Thelwell argues that Styron's version of Nat has "a 'white' language and a white consciousness," and so white "values and desires," his reading converges with what we have remarked. He maintains that what Styron did is illegitimate. But that he would not, in 1968, have seen *whatever* Styron did as legitimate is also clear: "Conspicuously intelligent—in their terms—Nat aspires hopelessly to the culture and stature of his white masters. Naturally . . . he holds in contempt the society of his own people whom he considers dumb, mindless, unsalvageable brutes unfitted either for freedom or salvation. Hating the blackness which limits the possibilities which he feels should be his by right of intelligence and accomplishment, he becomes a schizoid nigger-baiter."[67] On the one hand, Thelwell agrees with less hostile readings of Styron's Nat as a slave whose intelligence gets him noticed despite the dehumanization of slavery but who, with access only to white-oriented education, falls between the unattainable world of the master class and the world of his own people, limited by oppression. But Thelwell tacks on to this understanding a generaliza-

66. Thelwell, "Back with the Wind," in *William Styron's Nat Turner*, ed. Clarke, 80. See Stanley M. Elkins, *Slavery: A Problem in American Institutional and Intellectual Life* (London, 1959).

67. Thelwell, "Back with the Wind," in *William Styron's Nat Turner*, ed. Clarke, 80.

tion about Styron's portrayal of Negroes and ends with the unsupportable verdict that Nat becomes a "schizoid nigger-baiter." He thereby proves little beyond his determination to read the theme in a certain way.

Thelwell recognizes the language trope, just as Fuentes and Robert Coles do. But whereas they see the union of voices as a positive attempt to form a common bond, he sees it as a slight and a threat. Fuentes praises Styron's "risk" taking in "creating a meeting place," and Coles acclaims Styron for wedding "his voice, his personal experiences, his generous heart to Nat's yearning, suffering, gifted life."[68] Thelwell, however, on the basis of a similar observation, condemns.

Thelwell is not alone among the ten critics in that sort of thinking. Lerone Bennett argues that the book "tells us little about the historical Nat and a great deal about William Styron"—a negative way of saying that the book is a "self-exploration" in which Styron has "wedded his voice" with Nat's to create a "meeting place."[69] Harding criticizes Styron for making "only one major attempt at a sermon," though Styron's restraint might equally be seen as a realistic awareness that he can go only so far in wedding his voice with that of a black slave.[70] John A. Williams, too, discussing the language of the novel, is impressed with the prose but complains that Styron gave the basest swearwords only to blacks and that these words were unlikely to have been in common use at the time. His objection also differs from more favorable reactions only in the tongue clicking. Others might see the same thing as a "necessary anachronism," in Lukács' phrase. If Styron gave the characters nineteenth-century swearwords (of which Williams offers no examples), they would sound ridiculous.[71] Anyway, to give the oppressed

68. Fuentes, "Unslavish Fidelity," 505; Coles, "Blacklash," in *Critical Essays on William Styron*, ed. Casciato and West, 182–183.

69. Bennett, "Nat's Last White Man," in *William Styron's Nat Turner*, ed. Clarke, 4.

70. Harding, "You've Taken My Nat and Gone," in *William Styron's Nat Turner*, ed. Clarke, 29.

71. John A. Williams, "The Manipulation of History and of Fact: An Ex-Southerner's Apologist Tract for Slavery and the Life of Nat Turner; or, William Styron's Faked Confessions," in *William Styron's Nat Turner*, ed. Clarke, 48–49; George Lukács, *The Historical Novel*, trans. Hannah Mitchell and Stanley Mitchell (1962; rpr. Harmondsworth, Eng., 1981), 235.

the swearwords is in line with the idea of the subversive potential of language. When Will punctuates a sermon by Whitehead with his own "demented litany" of "*Ole white cunt*" (102), he brings to mind Mannix at the military lectures. John O. Killens similarly combines neutral insight with negative appraisal when he writes of the "contradiction of Nat, himself, sometimes thinking and speaking in biblical or Victorian English, and at other times lapsing into an Amos and Andy dialect." Styron, he says, "misses entirely . . . the unique-to-our-blackness methods of expression; the Afro-American psyche."[72]

The ten black writers are as intent on attacking as some white critics are on praising, but the features of the novel that come in for blame and commendation are essentially the same. The emotivity of the collection is evident not only in the contradictions within essays but, as in the case of the historians who have taken the novel to task, in the range of dissension between the writers, who manage both to laud and to disparage Styron's prose; to attack him for relying on Elkins and to endorse Elkins themselves, and to accuse him of humanizing Nat and of dehumanizing him. As Genovese says, "Some critics praise Styron's writing and see it as enhancing the ideological threat; others deride it, more or less in passing."[73]

But where both black and white critics tend to err is in failing fully to take into account the novel's multiplicity of voices, its "combination of styles." Partial readings lie behind much of the disagreement in interpreting similar themes. There is little sense of Nat's changing viewpoint as he shifts from faith in whites to hatred and finally toward reconciliation. Partial readings of the welter of voices are inevitably unbalanced. Several black critics, for example, are troubled that Styron gives Nat a mild adolescent homosexual experience, but no black—or white—critic has pointed out that two white boys, Putnam and Joel Westbrook, are also caught in a "carnal union" by Hark (62). A novel should be judged not by individual threads but by the overall pattern.

The black writers also see elements of the movement toward harmony but as a perpetuation of white hegemony, not an expression of

72. Killens, "The Confessions of Willie Styron," in *William Styron's Nat Turner,* ed. Clarke, 43.

73. Genovese, "William Styron in the People's Court," in *Critical Essays on William Styron,* ed. Casciato and West, 202.

common humanity. Styron, working from Camus' view that "if men cannot refer to common values, which they all seem separately to recognize, then man is incomprehensible to man," emphasizes the bonds between people.[74] Barriers break down as Cobb and Nat at the end seem to share "for the briefest instant some rare secret" (106) and Nat, in Travis' last moments, looks "into his eyes" and has a "glimpse of who he might truly be" (388). Most white critics see this as a gesture toward greater dialogue and integration. But the interpretation of the black writers, as Harding writes—reprising one aspect of Baldwin—is that "there can be no common history until we have first fleshed out the lineaments of our own, for no one else can speak out of the bittersweet bowels of our blackness."[75]

Given the novel's themes, the whole controversy comes to appear highly ironic. The conflict of viewpoints reproduces the novel's conflict of discourses and illustrates the kind of verbal misinterpretation the novel attends to but without, in 1968 at least, a subsequent movement toward harmony. Again and again the rejection of Styron's initiative is evident in the black writers' assertion of self-definition. Most of the critics repulse any attempt at black-white harmony because, in Charles V. Hamilton's words, "black people today cannot afford the luxury of having their leaders manipulated and toyed with."[76] If Styron fell short of black language, no one suggests how a white writer might come closer. For Killens, the "first mistake was for Styron to attempt the novel" and the second "was to pretend to tell the story from the viewpoint of Nat Turner."[77] Bennett complains that the "thrust" of Styron's writing is "to reconcile Nat Turner to an unacceptable reality by making him confess that he would have spared at least one white person."[78] Thelwell writes, "What this Nat Turner wants is to become

74. Albert Camus, *The Rebel*, trans. Anthony Bower (1953; rpr. Harmondsworth, Eng., 1986), 29.

75. Harding, "You've Taken My Nat and Gone," in *William Styron's Nat Turner*, ed. Clarke, 32.

76. Hamilton, "Our Nat Turner and William Styron's Creation," in *William Styron's Nat Turner*, ed. Clarke, 73.

77. Killens, "The Confessions of Willie Styron," in *William Styron's Nat Turner*, ed. Clarke, 36.

78. Bennett, "Nat's Last White Man," in *William Styron's Nat Turner*, ed. Clarke, 10.

white, and failing that to integrate."[79] Cleaver has said much the same: "In America, everything is owned. Everything is held as private property. Someone has a brand on everything. There is nothing left over. Until recently, the blacks themselves were counted as part of somebody's private property, along with the chickens and goats. The blacks have not forgotten this, principally because they are still treated as if they are part of someone's inventory of assets."[80]

Styron, searching for the bonds of a common humanity through language, is thus caught, like his character, in the bonds of discourse, where union and appropriation become tangled. In 1968, this led to an obturation, a stoppage created by the black commitment to asserting an identity and rejecting white images and interpretations of black history. Styron's exasperation with the obstacle was apparent in a comment of his to a black questioner that same year: "Well, then, we're at an impasse, my friend, because you say it's one way, and I say it's another."[81] The novel reached publication in a climate that had changed dramatically in the time Styron took to write the book. In Marcus Cunliffe's view, "If it had appeared a few years earlier it would probably have been acclaimed as both brilliant and sympathetic."[82] Among the facets of the novel recapitulated in the controversy was that exhibiting Nat and Margaret's, and Nat and Cobb's, inability to talk honestly. Entering the field of historical and political concerns, Styron had to deepen and decenter the movement toward harmony, but since it remains part of the novel, it also, at the time, elicited a hostile reaction. Harding's view may be closest to the truth: the power of the book may be the "power of unfulfilled desire."[83]

We now read the novel a quarter century on, black voices having

79. Thelwell, "Back with the Wind," in *William Styron's Nat Turner*, ed. Clarke, 82.

80. Cleaver, *Soul on Ice*, 134.

81. Ellison, Styron, Warren, and Woodward, "The Uses of History in Fiction," in *Conversations with William Styron*, ed. West, 139.

82. "The evident reality of the 1960s was a mounting radicalism and vehemence that . . . eventually engulfed even James Baldwin" (Marcus Cunliffe, ed., *America Since 1900* [London, 1975], 382).

83. Harding, "You've Taken My Nat and Gone," in *William Styron's Nat Turner*, ed. Clarke, 30.

found a substantial hearing and fashioned a recognizable identity in American fiction. Among the evidence for the improvement in conditions is Morrison's Pulitzer Prize for her novel of slavery, *Beloved*, exactly twenty years after Styron's Pulitzer. Traces of the controversy remain, but there are suggestions that a recognition of what Styron, in Baldwin's words, was "trying to do" may be easier now than then.[84] There are still those, such as Alice Walker, who would apparently silence the likes of Styron. Irene, in Walker's story "Source," at least, works "diligently over a decade to erase the book from memory," while another character, Anastasia, talks of "what an insult Styron's *monster* was to the memory of the real Nat Turner"—presumably meaning the Nat Turner of heroic black myth, since the real Nat Turner is unrecoverable. Refusing to accept that there can be anything legitimate in "Styron's version of your history," Walker, or her character, dismisses *The Confessions* as another "racist bestseller."[85]

But after self-definition there has to be definition in the context of others, or else there will be a continuation of attitudes as bad as those condemned. A healthier view would seem to be Morrison's. "I was very pleased with his attempt," she has said. "He went into territory that *is* his territory and I think that was admirable." According to Morrison, Styron "may have given [Nat] one or two attributes he didn't have, but that's not important." The novel was a "step in the right direction," in her judgment.[86] If the controversy was, indeed, a disagreement less on the legitimacy of the novel's themes than on Styron's right to develop them, Morrison's judgment of Styron's aims and results may suggest that in a changed climate and a new context the chasm, for some, is not so wide as the rhetoric once suggested.

Morrison's receptivity shows that the word *harmony* need not entail an acceptance of white hegemony. It is true that black writers such

84. Sokolov, "Into the Mind of Nat Turner," 67. Baldwin is quoted by Sokolov as arguing that "it's important for the black reader to see what [Styron] is trying to do and to recognize its validity" (p. 67).

85. Alice Walker, "Source," in *You Can't Keep a Good Woman Down* (1971; rpr. London, 1988), 163–65.

86. Toni Morrison, in answer to my question about Styron's novel, City Hall, Sheffield, Eng., March 2, 1988.

as Baldwin, Angelou, and Morrison can bring a special insight to themes like those in Styron's novel, but the realization is growing that Styron's confidence in the possibility, irrespective of his own color, of comprehending a good deal of Nat's viewpoint because Nat was above all a human being is not some kind of arrogant Anglo-Saxon assumption but an instance of a tenet held by writers black and white. Morrison appears to agree when she says, in an interview, that she once reproved a woman who, in writing a book on women writers, apologized in the preface for not including black writers because she did not "feel qualified to criticize their work": "I think that's dishonest scholarship. I may be wrong but I think so, and I took the trouble to tell her that. I feel perfectly qualified to discuss Emily Dickinson, anybody for that matter, because I assume that Jane Austen and all those people have to say something to do with life and being human in the world. Why she could not figure out that the preoccupation of black characters is this as well startled me, as though our lives are so exotic that the differences are incomprehensible."[87] Now that the dust has settled somewhat, we should perhaps read *The Confessions* in the same spirit— aware that, although differences of history and perspective exist between black and white, there is also common ground and that the differences themselves need not be "incomprehensible." Morrison takes that tack herself in *Playing in the Dark*, her study of the image of whiteness, and of the indispensable black presence, in American writing. There she, like Baldwin, insists on the need to acknowledge an inextricably shared history and literature between the races.[88]

Styron's novel is not beyond criticism. His incorporation of Erikson's thinking tends to personalize the rebellion in a way that steers attention from the historical importance of the revolt. Some episodes betray an insensitivity, and when the novel is set against Douglass' account, there is evidence of a continued willingness to subordinate political realities in the way Styron arranges his portrayal of slavery.

87. Claudia Tate, *Black Women Writers at Work* (Harpenden, Eng., 1985), 121.

88. Toni Morrison, *Playing in the Dark: Whiteness and the Literary Imagination* (Cambridge, Mass., 1992). Morrison makes the pertinent observation that Styron's use of the "sealed white structure" to open *The Confessions* "serves as an allegorical figuration of the defeat of the enterprise he is engaged in: penetration of the black-white barrier" (p. 69).

But the novel is an exploration that invites dialogue, a meeting of voices; it is not an authoritative discourse nor one that tries to efface other viewpoints but one that, like Baldwin's and Morrison's, sees the territory between the races as common ground, as an arena for a mutually respectful hearing and saying.

The worst aspect of the controversy, understandable in the light of historical grievances and the climate of the sixties but not to be countenanced in the long run, was the tendency—in the name of political ends—to deny Styron his right to try for dialogue. To refuse to hear a voice, to suppress it, or to wish it suppressed is to kill what is essential to the form of the novel and to a healthy society. What is needed is not the liberal acceptance of all offered viewpoints but a readiness to let voices compete, however violently. The possibility of further discussion should always remain open, since terminating it, whether in the way a white critic would like to refute all objections to Styron's novel or in the way Walker's character wishes to "erase" the memory of Styron's voice, means the suppression of one set of voices by another.

The Confessions reminds us that in reordering the canon we may marginalize kinds of voices that it is valuable to engage. Morrison says that Nat's perspective *"is* [Styron's] territory," because to deny him the right to enter it is to deny her the right to attempt the kinds of imaginative leaps without which the novel form would be the poorer. Styron must be accorded the right to have his say, just as the black writers have the right to reply, and vice versa.

As Baldwin, long after the novel's publication, remarked concerning the victim of racial prejudice, "You could be that person. In some ways you are that person."[89] Styron attempted empathy with that person. That he found himself caught in an aporia where the reading of the novel forever depends on the context and disposition of the reader produces perhaps its best legacy. For it matters less whether we think Styron right or wrong to write the novel than that it engenders dialogue and, whether by purpose or effect, helps readers understand themselves better through their responses.

Some twenty years after the Nat Turner controversy, Fuentes ad-

89. James Baldwin, in *Mavis on Four,* British television interview by Mavis Nicholson, shown as an obituary tribute, December 3, 1987.

154 / The Novels of William Styron

dressed a matter that made the earlier disagreement look like a chit-chat. Perhaps unsurprisingly, given the focus of the letter he wrote in 1967, he cited Bakhtin in discussing Salman Rushdie's predicament after Khomeini's *fatwa*. Fuentes argues that "the novel is the privileged arena where languages in conflict can meet, bringing together, in tension and dialogue, not only opposing characters, but also different historical ages, social levels, civilizations and other, dawning realities of human life. In the novel, realities that are normally separated can meet, establishing a dialogic encounter, a meeting with the other."[90] The ten black writers kept their arguments to the page, as Styron did, and so, however venomous the accusations, there was scope left for minds to be changed rather than annihilated. The notion of *personal* erasure shifts the argument up a gear.

For all the polemics, both Cleaver in *Soul on Ice* and Malcolm X in his *Autobiography* do finally advocate some idea of reconciliation. Cleaver remarks that the *Autobiography* makes clear that, unlike many Black Muslims, Malcolm X was glad "to be liberated from the doctrine of hate and racial supremacy. The onus of teaching racial supremacy and hate, which is the white man's burden, is pretty hard to bear."[91] Without the process of growth and change, the novel as a genre would not just be static but would cease to exist. Unquestioned truths belong to the world of the epic and to lesser historians, whereas in the novel all is dialogic. As Fuentes says, "In dialogue no one is absolutely right."[92] Malcolm X describes the approach he used before he changed his mind as a "technique [that] is non-stop, until what I want to get said is said."[93] This is a monoglossic style, allowing no space for dialogue. It is a weapon blacks have every justification to use, as white society has historically used it against them. Although many blacks availed themselves of it in the sixties, Cleaver and Malcolm X recognize that it is not something that can be sustained if a better society is to result. Fuentes points out that "in fiction, truth is the search for truth, nothing is pre-established and knowledge is only what both of

90. Carlos Fuentes, "Words Apart," *Guardian*, February 23, 1989, p. 29.

91. Cleaver, *Soul on Ice*, 56–57.

92. Fuentes, "Words Apart," 29.

93. Malcolm X and Alex Haley, *The Autobiography of Malcolm X* (New York, 1966), 246.

us—reader and writer—can imagine. There is no other way to freely and fruitfully explore the possibilities of our unfinished humanity."[94] If we think that Styron errs, we are free to write a counternovel. Indeed, some critics—Frederick R. Karl is one—itch to rewrite the novel; they would do better to try to write their own.[95] If Styron was attacked, it is because, using the novel as a meeting place, he chose to participate, as he would again in *Sophie's Choice*, in one of the most sensitive and important of dialogic clashes. It was his choice to capitalize on the novel form to the hilt as a genre that enables the writer not to state some authoritative truth about human beings, black or white, but to explore the "possibilities of our unfinished humanity."

94. Fuentes, "Words Apart," 29.

95. "So much is moving in *The Confessions* that 'rewriting' becomes a temptation' (Karl, *American Fictions, 1940–1980*, 342). See also Roy Swanson, who wants a "black Theseus" ("William Styron's Clown Show," in *William Styron's "The Confessions of Nat Turner,"* ed. Friedman and Malin, 161).

5

Dialogic Worlds: *Sophie's Choice*

That, surely, is the point: to discover the relations between those done to death and those alive then, and the relations of both of us; to locate, as exactly as record and imagination are able, the measure of unknowing, indifference, complicity, commission which relates the contemporary or survivor to the slain.

—*George Steiner*, Language and Silence

Up to *Sophie's Choice*, Styron's work had shown a steadily increasing awareness that his early discourse toward harmony, stemming partly from the notion of an artist's separation from society, became less adequate the more he took on political and historical concerns. He shifted from a straightforward attempt to compose aesthetic, moral, and social harmony from chaotic events toward a position that set other aims ahead of the achievement of harmony. His subject matter necessitated that, since it was impossible to do justice to the historical and political issues that had come to absorb him by refining the centripetal activity of seeking social and aesthetic harmony. In the two novels immediately prior to *Sophie's Choice*, the imposition of harmony—the kind that Peter imposes on events or that Gray and others try to impose on Nat—is seen merely to evade answers or to perpetuate an unjust political hegemony.

The key dialogue in Styron's career, between a belief in the power of art to order and a growing commitment to examining the political and historical world, might seem to connect with Lukács' theories on the novel. Lukács, after all, praised *Set This House on Fire*, and Styron cited him in defending *The Confessions*. But Styron's concern with history and his shift to experimentation in subject more than in technique were not a return to nineteenth-century realism. Rather they assimilated, and also perhaps instigated, recent explorations into historical textuality—into what Hayden White calls the "fictions of factual representation"—and into the problematics of language.[1]

Styron's shift away from the discourse toward harmony in making room for other priorities reaches its culmination in *Sophie's Choice.* With the Holocaust, Styron was writing about something in which it would, arguably, approach the brutish to seek aesthetic harmony. George Steiner and Theodor Adorno, writing of Holocaust-related art, have asked whether aesthetic harmony and pleasure are not a "barbaric" injustice to the victims of events that must never be papered over with meaning or used, even indirectly, in a text that is entertaining.[2]

Although a movement toward harmony remains in *Sophie's Choice,* it is radically decentered, that is, no longer the text's central movement but only present in one dialogized discourse among others. Everything before this novel includes a movement toward harmony at some level, but Styron has with each work stepped farther back from his narrators to examine the implications of the insistence on composing voices. In juxtaposing differing world views and experiences—a common practice in Holocaust literature—he extended that pattern in *Sophie's Choice,* not only scrutinizing but openly sidelining and satirizing the artistic vision with which he began his career.

Of the world views that compete in the story itself, the most basic, because they involve the narration, are those of Stingo and the narrator. The way they compete, within what critics have often seen as a single narrative voice, bears on the overall strategy of the novel. It bears also on how we read the friendships Stingo, overseen by the narrator, has with Sophie and Nathan. These relationships are at the novel's center, but others, like the lighter misunderstandings of Stingo with Morris Fink, Leslie Lapidus, and Mary Grimball, also have a "place in this narrative" (512).

There are also dialogues in passages where the narrator moves be-

1. Hayden White, "The Fictions of Factual Representation," in his *Tropics of Discourse: Essays in Cultural Criticism* (London, 1984), 121.

2. "To write poetry after Auschwitz is barbaric" (Theodor Adorno, *Prisms* [Cambridge, Mass., 1982], 34). He is quoted slightly differently ("No poetry after Auschwitz") by George Steiner, in *Language and Silence: Essays, 1958–1966* (London, 1967), 72. For Styron's comments, see appendix conversations, 216.

yond Stingo's discourse and in effect functions as Styron. The writers of Holocaust literature with whom Styron converses include not only Steiner but Bruno Bettelheim, Elie Wiesel, Richard L. Rubenstein, Simone Weil, and Hannah Arendt, and among those not mentioned, almost certainly Adorno, Lawrence L. Langer, and Primo Levi. Arendt clearly influenced the depiction of Höss and Dürrfeld, exemplars of the "banality of evil."[3] Nevertheless, my focus will at the very start be on Langer and Steiner. At the end, I will look again, and more closely, at Steiner, as well as at Rubenstein. All three seem to inform the novel's structure.

Styron also enters into dialogue with his earlier work.[4] His mention of Jewish writers has the purpose of making his novel explicitly—rather than implicitly, like *The Confessions*—a dialogue between his "particularized" or "distorted" Wasp views and the views of those closer to events (218). The novel is clearly in dialogue with the criticism of Styron's earlier work. What seemed weaknesses to the critics are rectified. Peter and Cass give way to a more dynamic dialogue between Stingo and Sophie, and Mason to the more engaging, intelligent Nathan. In contrast to the direct narration of *The Confessions*, both the narrative and the external voices in *Sophie's Choice* create layers between the narrator and the historical events. The memories are filtered through Sophie's unreliable voice, in newly learned English, then through Stingo, and again through the narrator's recall; they fade further through the dialogues the narrator has with other writers on the Holocaust.[5]

What most distinguishes *Sophie's Choice* from the work by Styron preceding it is a schizophrenic theme in which not just words and views

3. See Hannah Arendt, *Eichmann in Jerusalem: A Report on the Banality of Evil* (London, 1963).

4. See William Styron, *Sophie's Choice* (New York, 1979), 80. Sophie says things that link her to Peyton Loftis, creating the illusion that Stingo borrows aspects of Sophie's situation and vocabulary for his first novel. Compare, for instance, her childhood fantasy here of being *"inside* the clock," floating "on a spring," watching the "levers moving," and seeing the "rubies," with Peyton's dream of being *"inside* a clock," revolving "on the mainspring forever, drowsing, watching the jewels and the rubies" (William Styron, *Lie Down in Darkness* [New York, 1951], 335).

5. On this, see appendix conversations, 246.

clash but also worlds. That sort of theme typifies other Holocaust writing as well, not least Steiner's *Language and Silence* and Langer's *The Holocaust and the Literary Imagination*. Steiner is quoted in the novel, but Styron also let the schizophrenic theme influence the novel's form. In that he was responsive to Langer's study, a copy of which stands, like *Language and Silence*, on his bookshelves in Roxbury.

Langer deals with both the question of aesthetic harmony and the existence of a sense of dislocation in the "literature of atrocity."[6] Attending most to the writings of those with firsthand experience of the events, he sees as one of their chief concerns the portrayal of disparate worlds. In his preface, he describes his book's genesis in three personal moments of dislocation: his seeing, in 1964, "Polish children playing beneath bright sunshine" only yards from the gates of Auschwitz; his recognizing his inability, at the trial of Himmler's adjutant, Karl Wolff, "to connect the appearance of the man with the war crimes he was accused of"; and his feeling "that uncanny sense of discontinuity, of a fact inaccessible to the imagination in any coherent or familiar form," when he stood before a pastoral painting entitled *Dachau*.[7]

Langer's interest is in "disjunction." The moments of dislocation he underwent make him wonder if the "literary intelligence" can "ever devise" forms "adequate to convey what the concentration camp experience implied for the contemporary now." As he sees it, the problem is how the disparate worlds of everyday life and of the Holocaust can be portrayed together in art. If "the existence of Dachau and Auschwitz as historical phenomena has altered not only our conception of reality, but its very nature," Langer believes that "the challenge to the literary imagination is to find a way of making this fundamental truth accessible to the mind and emotions of the reader." Looking at Paul Celan's poem "Fugue of Death," Jerzy Kozinski's *The Painted Bird*, and Wiesel's *Night*, he argues that the authors try to dislocate the reader, to ensure an initial reaction of discomfort rather than of aesthetic pleasure, before attempting a reorientation toward a perspective more appropriate to a post-Holocaust world.[8]

6. Lawrence L. Langer, *The Holocaust and the Literary Imagination* (New Haven, 1975), xii.

7. See Langer, *The Holocaust and the Literary Imagination*, xi.

8. Langer, *The Holocaust and the Literary Imagination*, xi, xii, 2–3.

In *Sophie's Choice*, Styron is, overtly and not, in dialogue with other accounts of Auschwitz and with Langer's view of the kind of art necessary for representing the world after the Holocaust.[9] In one sense, the novel adheres to Langer's view that the need is to place disparate worlds in a single, disjunctive frame. The direct references to schizophrenia, leading up to the news that Nathan is a "paranoid schizophrenic," are part of this.[10] Styron himself has called the novel a "split book."[11] Sophie has a "schizoid conscience" (348); Dürrfeld—echoing Hannah Arendt on self-pity—says that the Jewish problem gives them "all schizophrenia, especially me" (406); and Poland is "soul-split" (246). But in another sense, *Sophie's Choice* departs from the course Langer identifies. It begins not by dislocating the reader but by soothing the reader with the humorous preamble of a young man's angst, then unleashes the disturbing events at its core. Yet the opening chapters are set with traps, mines of minutiae, to catch the reader lulled by its casual air and encourage a reevaluation of Stingo's attitude once the details are set against the context of Auschwitz and the novel's pivotal events.[12]

The challenge of finding artistic means adequate to yoking the disjunction is recognized by several Holocaust commentators, and the goal is put most succinctly by Steiner in the present chapter's epigraph.[13] Styron quotes Steiner, who muses that when some were being

9. Appendix conversations, 216. Styron talks of the "unremitting" bleakness of previous accounts.

10. Styron, *Sophie's Choice*, 424, cited in the present chapter by page number, without title.

11. See William Heath, "I, Stingo: The Problem of Egotism in *Sophie's Choice*," *Southern Review*, XX (1984), 531.

12. Appendix conversations, 215.

13. Steiner, *Language and Silence*, 182. On the disjunction, see especially Tadeusz Borowski, *This Way for the Gas, Ladies and Gentlemen, and Other Stories*, comp. and trans. Barbara Vedder (London, 1967). In "The People Who Walked On," Borowski tells of how he played goalkeeper in a soccer game, with the train platform behind his goal. One minute a crowd was alighting, then nothing: "Between two throw-ins of a soccer game, three thousand people had been put to death" (p. 64). Among several critics of Styron's theme of disjunction is Ralph Tutt, who sees an "imbalance between" Styron's "tragic sense" and "comic inclination" ("Stingo's Complaint: Styron and the Politics of Self-Parody," *Modern Fiction Studies*, XXXIV [1988], 582).

killed at Treblinka, most, near or far, were getting on with everyday life. Steiner reflects, "The two orders of simultaneous experience are so different, so irreconcilable to any common norm of human values, their coexistence is so hideous a paradox—Treblinka *is* both because some men have built it and almost all other men let it be—that I puzzle over time. Are there, as science fiction and Gnostic speculation imply, different species of time in the same world, 'good time' and enveloping folds of inhuman time, in which men fall into the slow hands of the living damnation?" (216–17). Steiner differs from Langer on the proper reaction to the disjunction. He suggests either silence or else an attempt to write about it, because "the next best thing is to try to understand" (219). Rejecting silence, Styron begins by portraying a familiar world, and he seeks, in line and perhaps in response to Steiner, to connect Stingo's world view with the other reality, of Auschwitz—precisely to discover, in Steiner's words, the "relations between those done to death and those alive then." He strives "to locate, as exactly as record and imagination are able, the measure of unknowing, indifference, complicity, commission which relates the contemporary or survivor to the slain." But spurning the idea that the worlds are separate, Styron seeks to bare the conjunctive in the seemingly disjunctive—to indicate, in a recurrent image of the novel's, the sediment of evil inherent in everyday life.

This objective of displaying how the Holocaust connects with the rest of human behavior is evident throughout *Sophie's Choice.* Nathan observes that hydrogen cyanide exists in "Mother Nature in smothering abundance in the form of glycosides," which are found in pears, almonds, and peach pits (332). Here Styron has a metaphor for the evil he sees "at the *core*" of Stingo and Sophie (207). The novel perceives the best in life—"fellowship, familiarity, sweet times among friends" (68)—to be in intimacy with the worst, the "bitter bottom of things" (412). In the apparent conflict of existences—Steiner's "good time" and "inhuman time"—the commonality between them is at the cusp of the novel's attempt to grasp the "appalling enigma of human existence" (513).[14]

14. Styron's two-worlds approach is similar to Philip Roth's in *The Ghost Writer* (New York, 1979). For Styron's comment on this, see appendix conversations, 227. See

The novel's epigraphs fit Styron's theme. Rilke's reference to a child's death as something left in the "round mouth, like the choking core of a sweet apple," sets evil, like cyanide in fruit, at the core of life and relates as well, perhaps, to little Eva's death—the worst moment of evil, at the novel's core. Höss's daughter, Emmi, also springs to mind, since Sophie sees her as a "fetus, yet fully grown" (400), caught in the midst of absolute evil, in Rilke's phrase, "even before life's begun." In another epigraph, Malraux' reference to a search for "that essential region of the soul where absolute evil confronts brotherhood" captures Styron's idea of the proximity of the best and worst in mankind. Far from Auschwitz' being a separate world, *Sophie's Choice* suggests that the evil that allowed it is embedded in seemingly diverse but familiar realities, much as Styron's theme is embedded in the novel like a "choking core."[15]

In tying Stingo's story to Sophie's, the novel follows Steiner's suggestion of seeking connections between seemingly disparate worlds rather than that of Langer, according to which the expression of dislocation is the goal. Stingo's discomfort at the start is in the course of the narrative made to stand against experiences that shed ironic light on his "suffering" (513). His angst appears embarrassingly self-centered and trivial alongside the story Sophie tells him, but also connected to it. A somber disjunction thus succeeds the entertaining opening, as we realize that what we laugh at or identify with in Stingo is inseparable from the horrors that become the novel's focus.

But because the novel does not take the disjunction as final, a discourse toward harmony of a sort is still evident, if decentered. Although the novel at first seems to reverse the movement toward harmony in Styron's previous novels, which began by dramatizing discord and conflict, discord exists early on here too, at least for Stingo. It is he who is confused and unhappy in the opening pages, sweating with literary and sexual frustration as his ceiling vibrates from the unbridled

---

also especially Morris Dickstein, "The World in a Mirror: Problems of Distance in Recent American Fiction," *Sewanee Review,* LXXXIX (1981), 390–91.

15. On Styron and the epigraph from Malraux, see Robert K. Morris, "Interviews with William Styron," in *The Achievement of William Styron,* ed. Robert K. Morris and Irving Malin (Rev. ed.; Athens, Ga., 1981), 68–69.

coupling of Sophie and Nathan. The narrator, it turns out, also has an urge to connect—if not to reconcile—certain voices, but that arises from the later juxtaposition of Stingo's anxieties with the world of Auschwitz. Stingo's movement toward harmony is decentered by the double-voiced narration, in which the narrator constantly, often openly, contests the viewpoint of his younger self.

On one level, *Sophie's Choice* is about Stingo in 1947, his meeting with Sophie and Nathan and his attempts to write, get laid, and harmonize his world in light of his frustrations and conflicting interests. He is a central character struggling to make sense of the voices that compete around him, voices that include not only Sophie's and Nathan's but his father's (a voice, as Michael Kreyling suggests, from an older, stabler world, ever less available to Stingo), Leslie's and Mary Alice's (voices that, as Kreyling also observes, present a gross parody of the novel's language trope), Dr. Blackstock's (the voice of almost the "happiest man on earth" [97] until his wife dies in a car crash, illustrating the caprice of the world), and Morris Fink's (the voice of the worst specimen of ignorance ["What's Owswitch?"; 213] in all the unknowing, indifference, and complicity portrayed).[16] But taking Stingo as central leads some critics, like Joan Smith and Georgiana M. M. Colville, to refer, misleadingly, to "Stingo the narrator." The unnamed narrator explicitly states that he is not Stingo, in name or nature. Stingo, he says, "evaporat[ed] like a wan ghost" as the narrator aged, although Stingo he "still was" in the summer of 1947 (4). He thus lays stress on the gap that time has created between his present and former view of events, and varies his diction according to the viewpoint he adopts.[17] Still, however remotely connected with his former self, the narrator tells the story because his past self—the "insufferable" Stingo

16. See Michael Kreyling, "Speaking the Unspeakable in Styron's *Sophie's Choice*," *Southern Review*, XX (1984), 554, 550.

17. See especially Joan Smith, *Misogynies* (London, 1989), 87–88; Georgiana M. M. Colville, "Killing the Dead Mother: Women in *Sophie's Choice*," *Delta* (Montpellier), XXIII (1986), 112; and Francis S. Mathy, "Hell Reconsidered: William Styron's *Sophie's Choice*," *English Literature and Language* (Tokyo), XXI (1984), 121. Some critics, like Samuel Coale, note this distinction. See his *William Styron Revisited* (Boston, 1991), 126.

(206)—is, like the narrator's past self in Malraux' *Lazarus*, a moral "encumbrance."[18] The cleavage between Stingo and the narrator is vital, for the trials of "suffering Stingo" are told precisely because they are incommensurable with the real pain at the novel's core (513).

If it is misleading to describe Stingo as the narrator, it also obscures matters to say, without qualification, that the narrator is Styron. Certainly we are encouraged to draw analogies between Styron's life and what we come to learn of Stingo and the narrator, but *Sophie's Choice* is not just an autobiographical novel. Stingo's predicaments and dubious behavior are described in the service of the novel's aims and are not, as Smith believes, simply Styron's therapeutic attempt to "excuse" himself for what he did in the fairly distant past.[19] Among the other offices they serve in the novel, they depict by analogy the distance between Styron's earlier and later notions of art. The sleight of hand that makes the novel seem autobiography—a magic that appears to have worked too well—connects the disparate worlds of postwar America and Auschwitz, and gives a sense of immediacy to the novel as a meeting place for voices that did not meet but might have.

Like Styron's earlier novels, *Sophie's Choice* begins with scenes of discord and conflict. But by satirizing Stingo and his brand of suffering, it decenters the discourse toward harmony. In the opening sections, the narrator depicts Stingo—similarly to Culver, Peter, and Nat—in frustration and turmoil. Lonely, bored at work, then uneasy with freedom, he yearns for direction and encouragement. His untethered state is worsened by youthful mood swings; one moment he has the "faith of a child in the beauty" he feels "destined to bring forth," the next his future is "misty" and "obscure" (19). The emphasis in this comically turbulent opening is on language and voices. Stingo, retreating into his "cubicle," assuages his loneliness by reading widely and plunging into "make believe" (12), and he vents his frustrations on the unsolicited manuscripts that threaten to bury him. At first he is described as a "political neuter" (18), so oblivious is he of anything outside his immediate sphere of literature, southern history, and sex. His views on art keep political involvement at bay and validate a retreat from a men-

18. André Malraux, *Lazarus*, trans. Terence Kilmartin (1974; rpr. London, 1977), 5.
19. Smith, *Misogynies*, 90.

acing world. But what he will learn is that he has a responsibility to harness his yearnings to positive action and to act on his impulses, sexual and literary, not in isolation but in the context of society, of others, and of history.

Stingo's move to a "place as strange as Brooklyn" (25) adds to his turmoil. New voices invade his world, tumbling into his mind and lodgings. Through the summer he is beset not only by his father's advice, the words of the writers he would emulate, and the voices of his novel but by Nathan's insults, Sophie's confessions, and the lingual nonsense of Leslie Lapidus. He must sort out a din of competing interests and perspectives to find his own position in the world as a person and a writer. The experiences and opinions that Sophie and Nathan soon confront him with are at first like the "indistinct" sounds of their arguments through his ceiling: "voices rising in rage, uttering words" he is "only just able to comprehend" (38). But soon they invade his baby pink room, shattering his apathetic, largely southern, and literary outlook.

At the heart of his story is the impact of Sophie and Nathan on his world view. He feels that something is "inexplicably wrong" (45) in Yetta's house, but this has as much to do with his own standpoint as with Sophie and Nathan. His acquaintance with them will lead him to question his assumptions about life and the literary career he is set on. Closeted in his little room trying to create art, supposedly immured in his private space, he finds himself beset by a confusion of voices, noises, and moods that threaten to bring his ceiling down. His purist view of art is brought to curb by the events he becomes involved in.

The narrator's subject is not merely Stingo and Sophie but the connections between their lives, and between Brooklyn and Auschwitz. The distinction between the narrator and Stingo contributes a salutary schizophrenic dimension to a text that amasses a series of temporal, vocal, and spatial dislocations into a seemingly unbridgeable chasm between what Stingo and Sophie know. With irony, the narrator comments implicitly and explicitly on Stingo's reactions, raising questions about Stingo's voice through ironic juxtaposition and direct comment.

In Chapter 1, Stingo's and the narrator's voices—and their views about the world and language—mingle humorously. The narrator tells of Stingo's attitude to manuscript reading:

But at my age, with a snootful of English Lit. that made me as savagely demanding as Matthew Arnold in my insistence that the written word exemplify only the highest seriousness and truth, I treated these forlorn offspring of a thousand strangers' lonely and fragile desire with the magisterial, abstract loathing of an ape plucking vermin from his pelt. I was adamant, cutting, remorseless, insufferable. High in my glassed-in cubbyhole on the twentieth floor of the McGraw-Hill Building—an architecturally impressive but spiritually enervating green tower on West Forty-second street—I levelled the scorn that could only be mustered by one who had just finished reading *Seven Types of Ambiguity* upon these sad outpourings piled high on my desk, all of them so freighted with hope and clubfooted syntax. (5)

Stingo's voice here is put in its place by the ventriloquizing narrator. What Stingo considers his "savagely demanding" requirement that "the written word exemplify only the highest seriousness" is traced by the narrator to a "snootful of English Lit.," a flimsy basis for a sense of superiority. By falling in with Stingo's collegiate shorthand—"English Lit."—the narrator underlines the formulaic superficiality of Stingo's mind-set. He obliquely conveys his reaction to Stingo's viewpoint through details like the "spiritually enervating" tower, where Stingo has his "glassed-in cubbyhole." The tower bespeaks Stingo's ivory-tower mentality, which, if "architecturally impressive," offers little more than surface gloss. The diction is often Stingo's, but the details enable the narrator to undermine Stingo's position through ironic imagery.

Among the details is an indication of the kind of pure literary criticism Stingo has been exposed to, William Empson's *Seven Types of Ambiguity* being a classic of the New Criticism taught him in college. A conflict of viewpoints is evident here. For Stingo, Empson's text is a legitimate authority on which to base literary judgment. But for the narrator the text ironically reinforces the impression not only of Stingo's purist attitude toward art but of his limited receptivity to other things, for the disdain in which he holds unpublished work of others is inseparable from his later failure of sensitivity toward Sophie. As larded with humor as the conflict is, the passage prompts a wariness about Stingo's insight and dictum. When, later, the narrator refers to the "lyrical, muscular copy" that got Stingo his publishing job (12), he mimics the language Stingo might have used, turning it back on him. A few pages later, the narrator calls it a "snotty, freewheeling style" (16).

Gradually the divergence between viewpoints comes to touch more serious subjects. When Stingo lectures Nathan, the narrator again, with little but telling comment, lets him betray himself. The topic this time, however, is racism, and it relates to Stingo's area of specialty, southern history.

"You seem to have no sense of history at all," I went on rapidly, my voice scaling up an octave, "none at all! Could it be because you Jews, having so recently arrived here and living mostly in big Northern cities, are really *purblind,* and just have no interest in or awareness or any kind of comprehension whatever of the tragic concatenation of events that have produced the racial madness down there? You've read Faulkner, Nathan, and you still have this assy and intolerable attitude of superiority toward the place, and are unable to see how Bilbo is less a villain than a wretched offshoot of the whole benighted system?" I paused, drew a breath and said, "I pity your blindness." (206)

The narrator allows Stingo to hang himself in his own linguistic noose. In defending his precious South, he slips into stereotypes of Jews as bad as Nathan's of the South—imagining all Jews to be recent-immigrant city dwellers without any sense of the "tragic concatenation of events" in southern history. He has the insensitivity to expect them to recognize Governor Bilbo—and by extension, Eichmann, Höss, and their ilk—less as evil than as merely "wretched" by-products of the systems of which they are a part. Stingo's parochialism enables him to see southern history as both central and pardonable. It is not that his ideas are invalid—in another context, like the "college dissertation" rattling through his head (206), they might be defensible—but that his anger betrays the kind of shortcomings and hypocrisy of which he accuses Nathan.

Stingo, moreover, confuses high language with high sentiments; his pretentious diction is out of proportion with his childish indignation over Nathan's slighting of the South. Frederick R. Karl finds Stingo's use of the word *purblind* unlikely and so a narrative lapse, but his use of such a word is vivid testimony that he has the practical equipment to write—the verbal dexterity—but lacks the experience and judgment to put it to good use.[20] His rhetoric is by turn collegiate, abstract, and clichéd. His indignation reveals his immaturity just when he most feels he must impress. Instead of scorching Nathan with words like *concatenation* and *purblind* and shibboleths of sophistication like *racial madness* and *benighted system*, he wins only scorn—at the same time that he gauchely bumps into Faulknerian discourse. Having arrived in New York with an *American Collegiate Dictionary* among his few books, he is unwittingly constricted by it. His phrases are lifted from the senior-year papers he has only recently completed, and they compete—as in "assy and intolerable attitude"—with the slang of the college quadrangle. The narrator squeezes a last drop of irony out of Stingo's closing retort: "I pity your blindness." Accusing Nathan of "having no sense of history," Stingo, in his ivory tower, is the one who must learn to see himself, and his southern heritage, in its historic context.

Stingo displays some historical knowledge, but that is restricted to the South and is of a subjectively apologist complexion. "Outside of 'creative writing' . . . the history of the American South" was his "only serious academic concern" in college (190). Until he meets Sophie and Nathan, he does not venture beyond the narrow domain immediately concerning him. As the narrator says, "I had traveled great distances for one so young, but my spirit had remained landlocked" (24). Meeting Sophie, he discovers a far wider universe. With time and experience, this will let him see that, whether as victim or accomplice, he, like Sophie, is vulnerable to being caught up in political phenomena that, in the way of Auschwitz, seem "too abstract, too *foreign* . . . to register fully on the mind" (322). At this stage his historical sense is one of nationalism, which Steiner calls the "venom of our age."[21] Styron's humorous irony is, on another level, deadly serious, since Stingo manifests symptoms of the kind of bigotry and intolerance figuring in the historical context of the Holocaust. Because Styron seeks to under-

20. John Kenny Crane makes a similar point in *The Root of All Evil: The Thematic Unity of William Styron's Fiction* (Columbia, S.C., 1984). Styron, he says, portrays the "younger Stingo as having the drive, the desire, the cocksureness to write significant works of fiction, but neither the moral awareness nor the sensitivity to do so" (p. 4).

21. Steiner, *Language and Silence*, 153.

stand, in Steiner's words, the "relations between those done to death and those alive then," revealing the proximity between Stingo's callowness and a disastrous bigotry is a major purpose of the meandering, humorous opening.

What is also apparent in these early stages is Stingo's conception of the role of art. Though the subject has switched from literature to politics and history, Stingo's field of reference, and even his diction, remain largely literary. Typically, he refers to a southern novelist, Faulkner, whom he lauds, in modernist fashion, as almost a redeemer of the region's culture. He is incredulous that someone could read Faulkner and still have an "intolerable attitude of superiority toward the place," as if art could by itself redeem its shortcomings. But Stingo's modernist faith in art as a way to order reality is dialogized as the narrator continually points out the distance between himself and Stingo.[22] He has an irreverent cockroach wander across the page of Stingo's copy of Donne's poetry (11), and he offers explicit commentary on excerpts from Stingo's journal. In describing Stingo's evaluation of manuscripts, the narrator calls him a "supercilious young man" (6). All this is the broad counterpart of a much subtler dialogue. Stingo's determination to have language exemplify the "highest seriousness and truth" is set against the narrator's concern with a world in which the Nazis have cast doubt on the possibility of allying language with any seriousness and truth.[23] Stingo's later agonizing over whether to live in the South is about more than finding the most agreeable setting in which to live and write; it is in dialogue with the narrator's cares (see pp. 175–83 below).

It is clear that the narrator—and of course Styron—have very different concerns from their younger self. But, like Stingo, the narrator is seeking meanings in the young man's experiences, while, in a broader frame, also seeking connections between Brooklyn and Auschwitz. He is sorting out the aspects of Stingo's mentality that are "worth preserving" (513). He finds "vivid and valuable" the journal passages relating to "thwarted manhood," such as those dealing with Stingo's "black despair" over Leslie and Mary Alice. "So much of the rest," he says,

22. On Styron's changing vision, see appendix conversations, 226–27.

23. Steiner says his book is "about the pressures on language of totalitarian lies and cultural decay" (*Language and Silence*, 13).

consisted "of callow musings, pseudo-gnomic pretentiousness," and "silly excursions into philosophical seminars" that he consigned them years ago to a "backyard auto-da-fé" (512) in a symbolic act of purgation that is correlative with the novel itself. The "valuable" aspects of Stingo's voice, the narrator suggests, relate to "passions" rather than opinions. Stingo's feelings have value because they are genuine. His ideas and arguments, in contrast, are borrowed, and so, to use Sophie's phrase, "unearned" (130).

What, finally, the narrator finds "worth preserving" unsatirized are three sentences, "wrung like vital juices," that offer some connection between the younger and older man. "Artless as they now seem," they at least suggest the values he retains. However gauchely, they attest to the emotions Stingo has endured. *"Let your love flow over all things"* affirms the truism of "love," which Stingo must redefine. The three lines of poetry "'Neath cold sand I dreamed of death/but awoke at dawn to see/in glory, the bright, the morning star" (515), which he must reevaluate, affirm art. *"Someday I will understand Auschwitz,"* although naïvely stated, affirms the beginning of historical awareness and signals the direction the narrator's career will eventually take (513).

Nostalgic though the narrator is about his days of "first novelhood," he is also examining Stingo's behavior. He is not merely, as Crane puts it, "criticizing, and even humiliating," Stingo but striving to understand his young self—to trace the path by which the intolerant, often intolerable, Stingo matured.[24] The search for connections between the two conflicting voices in the apparently unitary narrative also marks a link between the narrator and Sophie, since, in a far more marked way, she too finds her past self an encumbrance.

Awareness of the double-voiced narration is vital to comprehending Stingo's relationship with Sophie and Nathan. Several critics have attacked the portrayal of Sophie after missing the distinction between voices. Colville calls the novel "one of the worst male chauvinist novels 'ever penned by man or beast'" because of the way "Stingo,

24. Crane, *The Root of All Evil*, 4.

the male narrator," treats Sophie.[25] William Heath complains about the "problem of egotism" precisely because he sees no distinction.[26] Judith Ruderman argues that Sophie's "sexual nature has many qualities of the postpubescent wish-fulfillment variety; Stingo's appropriately, Styron's less so," and Smith complains that Stingo's affection "manifests itself in a self-obsessed form which seems to have more to do with lust than affection." Smith conflates all three voices—Stingo's, Styron's, and the narrator's—when she says that it is hard "to read the book" without "cursing Styron/Stingo for his failure to give Sophie the help she needs; confronted with her despair and anguish, the narrator's main concern remains his now urgent sexual appetite."[27] The failure to distinguish between voices leads to misreadings. Ruderman, right about the presence of "postpubescent" fantasy in Sophie's sexuality, is left troubled at having to ascribe such thoughts to the narrator. Smith is right about Stingo's—but not the narrator's—"self-obsessed . . . lust." Colville ends up tarring Styron with—besides leaning to voyeurism, homosexuality, and nazism—being an overgrown child.[28]

Such criticism not only misses the gap between the narrator and Stingo but also fails to notice that the narrator, like Sophie, is involved in a confession. Heath deplores how Stingo's concerns "compete" with Sophie's story, when they should form an "understated ironic counterpoint."[29] But in tune with Langer and Steiner, surely such disjunction is the point; the reader is meant to feel discomfort at Stingo's language against the backdrop of Auschwitz. Although Stingo's views plainly

25. Colville, "Killing the Dead Mother," 113, 112. Colville argues that Stingo is "narrator, hero and implicit author, throughout the novel," and that "Styron appears to have deliberately eliminated all distance or difference between himself and the older narrating Stingo as well as between his former self and the younger Stingo" (p. 114).

26. Heath, "I, Stingo," 528.

27. Judith Ruderman, *William Styron* (New York, 1987), 124; Smith, *Misogynies*, 89–90.

28. See Colville, "Killing the Dead Mother." Colville portrays Stingo as a "confirmed voyeur" (p. 115) and Styron as a "Middle-aged Nazi" (p. 116). She argues that the narrator's—and so, for her, Styron's—"homosexuality" remains "latent" but is "hinted at" by "Stingo's references to Gide" and by his homosexual dream (p. 133).

29. Heath, "I, Stingo," 532.

color the description of Sophie, the narrator is constantly ventriloquizing Stingo's diction and arguing with it, to emphasize Stingo's often
ambivalent behavior. In retelling Sophie's confessions through Stingo,
he must confess the behavior and attitudes of his younger self, Sophie's
confessor, in a merging of roles that matches his concern with seemingly disparate worlds that are in fact linked.

In the triangular relationship between Stingo, Sophie, and Nathan,
Stingo's world view is pointedly juxtaposed against Sophie's and
against Auschwitz, and the relationship emerges through both Stingo's
voice and the narrator's. Stingo's focus is on the narrow question of
how, in different ways, he, Sophie, and Nathan can move toward personal and social harmony. In contrast, the narrator pays primary attention to the way Stingo's interest in Sophie leads her to recount her
experiences at Auschwitz, which puts Stingo's behavior and attitudes
during the Brooklyn summer in a different light. While Stingo struggles
to make sense of his feelings, the narrator is making connections between the supposedly disparate worlds of Brooklyn and Auschwitz.

On one level, Stingo, Sophie, and Nathan are all striving for personal harmony. Sophie and Nathan, who are in large measure at the
bottom of Stingo's distress, are themselves seeking coherence. Both
their lives are fragmented. Nathan, says Larry, has "never got his mind
in order" (424), and Sophie is an "incomplete" person (142), struggling
to come to terms with her past. The harmony the two of them at times
seem to possess, like Cass's alcohol-based harmony, is a "precarious
equilibrium" (91). Nathan is on drugs, and Sophie's reclothing of "herself in self-assurance and sanity" (93) drapes only a "thin outer layer"
(145) over inner disintegration. Her "chaotically" actuating love for
Nathan (147) and his "tormented underside" (187) compete with whatever is positive in their intimacy. Nathan says that Sophie has taught
him "about *everything*. Life!" (119); she says that she has experienced
"*rebirth*" through Nathan (91). He has brought her the "happiest days
she had ever known" (312), yet he is also partly her "destroyer" (316).
Unsurprisingly, then, Stingo's "elation," even at their best moments,
is "mixed with apprehension" (194). Their struggle is fundamental to
the novel's bittersweet schizophrenia, and the connection between the
best and worst of life.

Stingo's friendship with Sophie is dubious from the start. He befriends her for two reasons, both of which put in relief his limitations. In the first place, he, as a fledgling writer, is eager to hear about experiences he has not had himself; he has his own youthfully insensitive dose of the "ghoulish opportunism" writers are "prone to" (111). Moreover, he thinks Sophie has a "resemblance to Maria Hunt" (46), the girl whose suicide has given him a subject for his novel. In the second place, he wants to know her out of sexual motives. That makes him Nathan's rival as well as his friend. As, squirming "with mixed discomfort and delight" (311), he listens to stories of her "past love life," it becomes plain that the portrayal of Sophie is filtered through the mind of a young man of "staggeringly puerile inexperience" (203).

Here too Stingo's viewpoint is dialogized by the narrator, so that Stingo's and Sophie's differing uses of language are always conspicuous. At first, the play of voices is lighthearted. Stingo and Nathan literally have a word contest. Sophie is struck by the number of English words for the French word *vélocité* (67), and the two men compete with examples. Stingo, the budding writer, proves Nathan's equal, while Sophie looks on helpless. But as earlier, an amusing use of language takes on wider significance. Stingo may have a good command of English, whereas Sophie is new to it and far from adept, but because of the care she must take with her words and because of her experiences, she later shows a far greater awareness of the complexity and elusiveness of meaning. She has, after all, experienced a world where everyday language has been overturned, where a man like Höss can consign thousands a day to death but dismiss her attempt to get him "to contravene proper authority" as "disgusting" (285). In more ways than one she knows more languages than Stingo.

We have hints of Stingo's misproportioned diction when the narrator describes the young man's view of Sophie's sexuality: "Despite past famine," he observes, "her behind was as perfectly formed as some fantastic prize-winning pear" (51). The jarring caused by Stingo's reference to Sophie as a piece of fruit links with images elsewhere in the novel. If the epigraph from Rilke once more comes to mind, so does Nathan's observation that the seeds of evil exist at the core of everyday life. Stingo's view of Sophie as an edible object also places him uncomfortably close to the likes of Höss and Sophie's father, who both saw her as an object—an instrument for the achievement of their warped ends.

Similarly, Stingo's sexual use of her continues a pattern: she has been raped twice, once at Auschwitz, by Wilhelmine—a lingual rape that, as Kreyling suggests, is appropriate to the novel's emphasis on lingual domination—and then in Brooklyn, when she is finger-raped in the subway.[30] But she was also nearly used sexually by Höss, as she is finally used by Stingo. These last two events are hardly comparable in more specific terms, but in such parallels resides the connection between seemingly disparate worlds.

The narrator's implicit commentary on Stingo's perspective, through juxtaposition and images, shadows Stingo's entire relationship with Sophie. The jarring between the young man's diction of everyday life and the experiences she confronts him with propels the theme of disjunction. Stingo has the habit of describing minor events in highblown language; he sees his first sexual encounter with Sophie as "cataclysmic" (361). Unable to respond to Sophie's foreplay on their last night, he resolves "to commit suicide" (496), and after a night spent with her, he tells her that he slept "like a corpse" (459). Such discourse of collegiate angst becomes insensitive hyperbole in the context of Sophie's story.

Stingo's diction calls to mind the world of Auschwitz, emphasizing his naïve insensitivity, when he offers Sophie advice. On their trip south, he not only warns her that they must marry "to avoid ugly gossip" (491) but tells her that Nathan "is *insane*" and must "be *institutionalized*" (451). In both cases, his callow invocation of lawful institutions—his daring, even, to discuss morality and sanity—is out of bounds given the law Sophie has been subjected to, a kind that Höss dared not disobey, that governed the institution he ran. Stingo fails to make connections that are painfully obvious to Sophie and the narrator.

The narrator is ever reminding the reader that Stingo's activities are to be set against Auschwitz. Like the rotten core of the metaphorical apple, the language of atrocity is also at the center of Stingo's avowals of his determination to have his way with Leslie. In his journal, he describes how he finally manages to fondle a breast, which turns out

30. Kreyling, "Speaking the Unspeakable," 552–53. Styron invented Wilhelmine only when he learned that his original choice of rapist—Frau Höss—was still alive and a potential claimant of libel damages. See appendix conversations, 246–47.

to feel "like a soggy ball of dough beneath my hand, itself tightly im-
prisoned within the rim of a murderous brassiere made of wormwood
and wire" (178). The concentration-camp imagery connects his experiences with Sophie's even while the two worlds seem utterly distant.[31]

During Stingo and Sophie's trip south, Sophie tries to coax him out
of the narrow thoughtlessness his diction evinces. He is preoccupied
by thoughts of home and marriage, unaware of the reverberations that
the word *home* has for Sophie. She does not go along with his plans
passively. "Where are we truly going? What home?" she asks. By
"home," Stingo means not merely the peanut farm his father has offered him but an idealized vision of his youth that he would like to
return to—a comfortable, enclosed life away from modernity but
"with all the modern American conveniences." Quizzed by Sophie,
Stingo begins to see that his vision is illusory, although he still does
not understand that "home" might remind Sophie of her past—her father, her children—or that marriage might remind her of her just
aborted engagement to Nathan.

Sophie asks Stingo to spell out his notion of their future, again turning his own words back on him: "'Once we get settled'? What's going
to happen then? How do you mean 'get settled,' Stingo dear?" (460).
Previously, Sophie asked questions about the meanings of words because she was genuinely unsure. But now she does so because Stingo
is insensible to his ill choice of words. Caught in his fantasies, he
manages to become "thoughtlessly oblivious" to the effect her confession has had on her (491). The fissure between Sophie's discourse and
Stingo's understanding of it remains. When Sophie calls him "Stingo
dear," her words do not, as Stingo assumes, voice her love for him but
bespeak a motherly affection that, typically, he misinterprets.

But there are signs that Stingo is learning. Words, he begins to realize, must be reexamined, and sometimes redefined, in light of what
Sophie has told him. After one of Nathan's outbursts, the narrator says

---

31. Smith quotes this passage to argue that it divulges the "secret of the book's popu-
larity: the juxtaposition of sex and the Holocaust has been dressed up as art" (*Misogynies*, 88). Smith's interpretation perhaps results from trying to fit the novel into her thesis
that the British murderer Peter Sutcliffe went undiscovered for so long because he was a
normal man who merely carried out the misogynistic fantasies rife among men in Western society.

that he "would ever after define the word 'distraught' by the raw fear" in her face (202). Such is the disparity between Stingo's speech and Sophie's on that train ride south that, as he talks, he is aware that his words have the "exact timbre and quavering resonance of a proposal I had once seen and heard George Brent, of all the solemn assholes, make to Olivia de Havilland" (461). His recognition that his vocal forms are borrowed at least signals a growing awareness, although linguistic inadequacy continues to dog him as the shaky eloquence of youth tumbles into cliché: "You'll always be my—well, my . . . ," he begins, groping for a "properly tender" phrase. But the best he can come up with is "Number One," which even to him sounds "hopelessly banal"; in fact it is the same phrase he used, at age eighteen, in a letter to his father about his college football team. How his college vocabulary hobbles him is symptomatic of how far he still is from discovering a more mature outlook. When he does finally say, "I love you," the narrator, in a Flaubertian undercutting, has Sophie go "to the bathroom" (455).

There are, as can be expected in a novel of this length, some lapses in strategy. When the narrator tells us that he had "to torture" himself "by reading as much as I could find of the literature of *l'univers concentrationnaire*" (216), Heath rightly bridles.[32] The narrator rather than Stingo is speaking here, and his turn of phrase seems as exaggerated and arch and malformed as Stingo's. He also comes strikingly close to deploying the strategy he quotes Arendt as saying the Nazis adopted: the trick of turning sensibilities inward "so that instead of saying: what horrible things I did to people!, the murderers would be able to say: what horrible things I had to watch in the pursuance of my duties, how heavily the task weighed upon my shoulders!" (153). There is not, of course, an exact equivalence in what Styron does, but, like Stingo and Sophie as Styron portrays them, he too is directing tender feelings inward, rather than outward to the victims he is reading about. When the narrator—and implicitly the author—fall into approximately the modes of thought they are opposing, however, this fortifies rather than undermines the novel's theme of complicity.

Stingo's brash naïveté is an effective device in the novel precisely

---

32. Heath uses this example to criticize the novel. See "I, Stingo," 534.

because he has few qualms about prying into memories that Sophie more than once expresses a wish not to talk about and that Nathan is sensitive enough not to stir up. Stingo's thoughtlessness allows him to learn her secrets, and the tension the narrator creates between Stingo's voice and Sophie's story is conceptually fundamental. His voice comes to make its own confession: of the narrator's, Styron's, perhaps America's, perhaps most people's, ignorance, disengagement, and complicity through indifference or self-interest.

Although the viewpoints of Stingo and Sophie clash, however, the narrator also seeks connections, bringing out their similarities. They are physically united, of course, in the final sexual union but are more profoundly joined by the similarities of attitude toward people and events in what Stingo shows about himself in New York and in what Sophie reveals in her confessions.

A number of critics, including Smith, Alvin H. Rosenfeld, and Robert Alter, see their sexual union—and the general emphasis on Stingo's sexual strivings—as gratuitous or worse. But that aspect of the story has also been defended, not least by Rubenstein, who argues that "far from weakening the novel, Stingo's sexual struggles are integral to his unique voyage from innocence to experience."[33] Certainly, they are consistent with, and vital to, the display of transactions between dialogic worlds. His sexual union with Sophie is not only a final reminder of the immense gap between them but also encapsulates a further development in his "voyage of discovery" (25). His fantasy comes true, but ultimately it will have an unforeseen meaning for him, bringing his loss of political and historical as well as sexual innocence.

The scene is a natural culmination of the clashes on which the novel is built, since the sex act has utterly different meanings for the two characters. The narrator points out that Sophie's actions—as earlier, where Stingo is a "surrogate Josef" (361)—have little to do with Stingo and are scarcely more than "a plunge into carnal oblivion and a flight from memory" (496). Stingo himself appears less interested in Sophie than in practicing all that he has avidly read about. His dis-

33. Richard L. Rubenstein, "The South Encounters the Holocaust: William Styron's *Sophie's Choice*," *Michigan Quarterly Review*, XX (1981), 441. See Alvin H. Rosenfeld, *A Double Dying: Reflections on Holocaust Literature* (Bloomington, Ind., 1980), 163–66; and Robert Alter, "Styron's Stingo," *Saturday Review*, July 7, 1979, pp. 42–43.

course is at times more appropriate to a car enthusiast than to a passionate lover: "I was delighted that the 'female superior' posture was every bit as pleasurable as Dr. Ellis had claimed, not so much for its anatomical advantages . . . as for the view it afforded me of that wide-boned Slavic face brooding above me, her eyes closed and her expression so beautifully tender and drowned and abandoned in her passion that I had to avert my gaze" (497). In one sense, Sophie and Stingo could hardly be more separate as persons. Each is using the other, and experiencing the coupling in an unshared way. Stingo might as easily be musing over the merits of a stick shift with full-length front bench, while Sophie is privately "abandoned in her passion," letting carnal ecstasy shelter her from the consciousness on which her guilt feeds. For Sophie, sex, whether with Stingo or Nathan, allows her to escape her sense of self, by producing a transitory "inseparability of flesh" that prevents her from telling "whether she is lost in herself or in him" (331). But if Sophie begins as an object for Stingo ("as for the view . . . of"), he cannot avoid seeing her as a person too. He switches from surface description of her body and face to a contemplation of her expression—and so of Sophie as subject not just object—until he has to avert his gaze. No longer the technical enthusiast, he shows some slight shame over the advantage he—or she?—is taking. Stingo's dawning recognition that he is using Sophie is part of his journey toward understanding. Our human capacity to help or abuse others, depending on whether we identify with or dehumanize them, is, after all, what much of the novel is about. If Sophie's sexual nature is what motivates Stingo to listen to her—he is, after all, as usurious as he fancies Jews to be, since he hopes desperately for a return on his invested time, either sexualty or in a good story line—he gets much more than he was angling for, since she teaches him, directly and indirectly, about himself.

The sexual union between Sophie and Stingo amounts to a physical, not a mental, harmony. It is a union literally beyond language: a "kind of furious obsessed wordlessness finally—no Polish, no English, no language, only breath" (498)—and a momentary escape from the problems of verbal miscommunication. A truer understanding of the connections between Stingo's behavior and Sophie's story, prefigured by Stingo's evanescent recognition of Sophie as subject, matures only years later, when the narrator can admit that "at the time" he was "unable to see" that Sophie's actions were an attempt "to beat back death" (496). She may initiate him sexually, but his initiation into the complexities of life is vastly more important. Stingo and Sophie experience a "propinquity of flesh" (498), but the narrator's focus is on the unbridgeable gap left despite that. What for Stingo is a harmony only slightly tarnished by a vague uneasiness is for the narrator a crucial point in moving away from the dubious preoccupations and actions of his young manhood. The scene marks both Stingo's sexual initiation and the beginning of his growth out of political innocence. It affords him his first glimpse of the implications of his actions, and so opens the way to a truer knowledge of his position in the world.

The narrator is interested in more subtle, far reaching connections than the mere coupling of two individuals. He suggests a deeper connection between Stingo and Sophie in one of the failings they share: prejudice. Most of the characters—Wanda perhaps being the exception—are prejudiced to a degree. Some, like Höss and Sophie's father, are obviously so, but, too, Nathan's view of Poles can match the prejudice of any anti-Semite, and even Stingo's upright, moral "Southern liberal" father (289) yields to prejudice in reacting to New York's "barbarity" (188). Both Stingo and Sophie are more than ready, in moments of irritation or anger, to bring out a kind of hip-flask anti-Semitism. On their bus ride to the beach, Sophie complains about Nathan, and Stingo suspects Morris Fink of stealing. Earlier, what began as a possibly fair complaint by Sophie that Leslie and her friends were "picking their little scabs" (130) soon shifted to invective against the Jewishness of their behavior. Here, similarly, Sophie's personal grievances against Nathan—legitimate or not—soon center on his being Jewish. Upset for different reasons, Sophie and Stingo each launch into an anti-Semitic tirade.

But what might have constituted merely a recognition by the novel of the prejudice inherent in human life, turns into something more. Sophie and Stingo find themselves surrounded by "little deaf mutes" who form an "eerie, soundless retinue" as they cross the beach. With Stingo considering bringing charges against "that fucking little hebe," Morris Fink, the silent children suddenly disperse, "as if responding to some soundless signal" (353–54). The children call to mind the children of Auschwitz, including Sophie's own, and act as silent witnesses to the indulgence Sophie and Stingo allow themselves. The Holocaust, we are reminded, is with us still, and the conditions that led to it remain. The notion that Auschwitz is an aberration, of another world, is a dangerous fallacy.

Stingo and Sophie are also connected insofar as they share a fervent desire to remain uninvolved—a desire that the narrator consistently portrays as hopeless. Both try to avoid choices and the confrontation of issues, but both learn that apathy is complicity and that evasion may contribute to the disintegration of choice itself. Stingo considers himself "a writer, an artist," who by his definition has "more exalted goals" (179) than to "play the hapless supernumerary in some tortured melodrama" (62); Sophie masquerades as "the stainless, the inaccessible, the uninvolved" (376). Stingo sees himself as a "political neuter," and Wanda says Sophie has "no politics" (370). But as Stingo is "fated to get ensnared" (88) with Sophie and Nathan, so Sophie was "adventitiously ensnared" by a Nazi roundup of the resistance members she would not help (376). Throughout, the choice of political aloofness proves illusory or backfires: there is no sure escape. Suddenly, Sophie was plunged into the Auschwitz "selection" she had heard of, and suddenly Stingo's self-important selection and rejection of manuscripts—a source of humor early on—is seen to copy, if faintly, Von Niemand's doings. *Sophie's Choice* is partly about how Sophie and Stingo learn, like Rambert in Camus' *The Plague*, that such "business is everybody's business."[34]

Sophie's and Stingo's escapist tendencies link with the novel's title, and with the "choice" Sophie had to make between her children, Eva and Jan, on the platform at Auschwitz. That "choice" was no choice at all. She and her children were trapped in machinery where the individual has almost no leeway, so that Von Niemand's gesture was a gross parody of conceding an opportunity to choose. Probably both her children were to die, so all she could do was delay the death of one or the other and inevitably be saddled with guilt over what she had done. But the novel is also concerned with the real choices that result from rec-

34. Albert Camus, *The Plague*, trans. Stuart Gilbert (1948; rpr. New York, 1960), 188.

ognizing that the one choice we cannot make—but that Stingo and Sophie attempt—is to remain remote from political and historical forces. Both Sophie and Stingo are confronted by such choices. Sophie had to decide, among other things, whether to help the resistance, in and out of the camp, and whether to help her father by typing and distributing his racist tracts. Stingo, for his part, must decide whether to delay his novel by becoming involved with Sophie and Nathan—whether to stay, as Larry has asked him, to watch over Nathan or go up to New England and try to seduce Mary Alice Grimball. Given the kinds of decisions Sophie in Poland and Stingo in Brooklyn come to, the theme of choice raises questions of personal and social responsibility. Stingo begins to learn, in literary as well as personal terms, that nobody, let alone an artist, can be apart from society. Von Niemand's offer of a choice to Sophie reemphasizes how delusory is her belief in privileged detachment.

The friendship of Stingo and Sophie develops along lines similar to those of the novel as a whole. Starting with disjunction, it gradually yields connections. Stingo eventually recognizes an "intolerable distance" between them "preventing any real communion" (492). But Stingo's recognition of the gap is an assurance of its narrowing as he begins moving toward understanding. It also drives home that the narrator has all along been aware of the jarring he has portrayed. The reading of the narrative as double voiced, reflecting the novel's dialogic conflicts, is confirmed.

The novel's chronotopic pattern, especially that involving Stingo and Sophie, helps bring Auschwitz and the quotidian together. There are traces of the idyllic chronotope in Sophie's early portrayal of her father's house in Cracow and in Stingo's recall of the peanut farm, but these are subordinate.[35] The major time-space juxtaposition is of the Pink Palace in Brooklyn and Haus Höss at Auschwitz (260), both vari-

---

35. Bakhtin writes of the "destruction of the idyll" as being especially prevalent "in the *Bildungsroman*" (*The Dialogic Imagination: Four Essays*, trans. Michael Holquist and Caryl Emerson, ed. Michael Holquist [Austin, Tex., 1981], 229). Sophie's father's house, and Stingo's father's farm conform to this. At first Sophie talks of "wonderful times" at the house in Cracow (80), but she soon admits the truth about her father. Similarly, Stingo eventually comes to recognize the falseness of his idyllic vision where "no blowflies buzzed, no pumps broke down" (492).

ations on the castle chronotope deriving from the gothic genre. The two houses, like Gothic castles but with a difference, are linked by their peculiar capacity to disturb. Both houses—similarly to Sambuco—give a sense of their being set apart. The Pink Palace radiates vibrations that suggest something is "inexplicably wrong" (45). The Höss house, with its kitsch and its willfully oblivious family acting out a grim pastiche of normal family life, inspires horror precisely because of the banal normality of its fittings and of the behavior inside given the horrors surrounding it. Two planes of existence seem to intersect there: out of one window, a gallant stallion admired by Höss, and out of the other, the platform where Nazi selections take place. When the wind changes, the beauty of the woods is blanketed by "smoke from the ovens at Birkenau" (233).[36]

The contrast between the houses, especially with regard to the place Sophie has had in each, bears on the story. In the Pink Palace, at least when Nathan is sane, Sophie is queen. Living on the second floor, she is adored by Stingo below and celebrated by Nathan, and she dines on steak and burgundy. At Auschwitz, considered privileged just to be in Haus Höss, she was a "piece of Polish *Dreck*" (412), "among the lowliest of the low" (404), and she lived "deep in the ground" nibbling cold slops (253). Up in the attic was Rudolph Höss himself, on whose commonplace and indifferent mind she vainly rested her hopes. If individualism is celebrated in Brooklyn, in Auschwitz the individual was a cipher, clawing for survival. Because we see only the least brutal side of Auschwitz, as we saw the least brutal side of slavery in *The Confessions*—Sophie was a house slave—the real horror remains outside the novel's bounds. For the months in the main camp that Stingo is not told about, we must turn to Wiesel, Levi, or the countless documentary studies like Martin Gilbert's *The Holocaust* or Elie A. Cohen's *Human Behaviour in the Concentration Camp*.

Auschwitz and the quotidian also come together to batter each other in the chronotope of the train. The misunderstandings between

36. "The girl wears a little white dress. Her arms are brown and suntanned. The dog is a black Dobermann Pinscher. The girl is the daughter of the Unterschafürer, the boss of Harmenz, and the little house with its little window-boxes and its ruffled curtains is his house" (Borowski, "A Day at Harmenz," in *This Way for the Gas, Ladies and Gentlemen*, 41).

Stingo and Sophie climax on the ride south. For both it is a journey home, even though the word *home* is a battleground of meaning. For both it is a journey into the past. But what for Stingo is nostalgic, is for Sophie horrific: "The train sped across New Jersey's satanic industrial barrens, the clickey-clack momentum hurling us past squalid slums, sheet-metal sheds, goofy drive-ins with whirling signs, warehouses, bowling alleys built like crematoriums, crematoriums built like roller rinks, swamps of green chemical slime, parking lots, barbarous oil refineries with their spindly upright nozzles ejaculating flame and mustard-yellow fumes" (451). Their escape by train becomes simultaneously her journey to Auschwitz. Discourse from that earlier world—*crematorium, fumes*—invades the description of the everyday world. Sophie's stumble to the end of the car is the physical correlate of her mental movement backward. She ends up slumped "on the floor" in a railroad car with a "padlocked glass door crisscrossed by wire mesh," as if in a train to Auschwitz (456). But in another interpenetration of Auschwitz and the ordinary, her actual journey to the camp was by elegant carriage. Again the idea that Auschwitz and everyday life can be segregated—that we can discount the Holocaust as an aberration—is subverted.

Nathan, the schizophrenic in whom the "attractive and compelling" seem in "equipoise with the subtly and indefinably sinister" (116), personifies the novel's theme. If two conflicting forms of human experience are juxtaposed in *Sophie's Choice*, Nathan's schizophrenia encapsulates the clash, since in him, to quote the novel's epigraph from Malraux, "evil confronts brotherhood." Through him, seemingly disparate worlds beyond him are set in dialogue. Nathan is both Sophie's "savior" and her "destroyer" (136). A "golem" as far as Morris Fink is concerned, he is for Stingo alternately a "monstrous Caliban" (309), a "mentor, pal, savior, sorcerer" (187), and a "colossal prick" (203). His nursing of Sophie back to health is the antithesis of the Nazi nihilism she has been subjected to. Yet in his violent moods his voice booms through Stingo's ceiling with the "measured cadence of booted footfalls" (77), in an image that joins him to the world Sophie has escaped.

Stingo's initial attraction to Nathan is as selfish as his early friendship with Sophie. He is only too ready to lap up the praise Nathan offers, and to accept Nathan's handout. For him, Nathan is a resource along the road to literary success. Their friendship is shaped by a "puerile inexperience" that keeps him from wondering about Nathan's mental state, and a "guilelessness" that stops him from distinguishing between insights and ravings (203). Won over by Nathan's praise, he is ready to believe Nathan's ludicrous stories, and to see his tale of having been the "only Jewish Albigensian monk . . . St. Nathan le Bon" as merely an "extravagant piece of waggery" (185).

Stingo's friendship with Nathan is bound up with Sophie to such an extent that there are no conversations between them without Sophie present. But when Nathan and Stingo talk together, Nathan's schizophrenic personality invariably catches him off guard, thereby revealing aspects of his character. Nathan's gift for mimicry often amuses Stingo, but when Nathan gets venomous, he threatens "certain crucial underpinnings" of Stingo's outlook (208). Nathan's attacks on the South goad Stingo into showing how muddled his outlook is (see pp. 167–68 above). And when Stingo refuses to toast the death of Governor Bilbo, of Mississippi, Nathan baits him into defending Bilbo, and then mimics him. As governor, argues Stingo, Bilbo's "important reforms" included establishing a "highway commission," a "board of pardons," and the "first tuberculosis sanatorium."

"He added manual training and farm mechanics to the curriculum of the schools. And finally he introduced a program to combat ticks . . ." My voice trailed off.

"He introduced a program to combat ticks," Nathan said.

Startled, I realized that Nathan's gifted voice was in perfect mockery of my own—pedantic, pompous, insufferable. "There was a widespread outbreak of something called Texas fever among the Mississippi cows," I persisted uncontrollably. "Bilbo was instrumental—"

"You fool," Nathan interrupted, "you silly klutz. Texas fever! You *clown!* You want me to point out that the glory of the Third Reich was a highway system unsurpassed in the world and that Mussolini made the trains run on time?" (206–207)

Like Sophie, only more brutally, Nathan tests Stingo's complacent and narrowly southern viewpoint by turning his words back on him and setting them in a broader context. His questioning is integral to Stingo's growth in awareness. Sophie and Nathan not only invade the physical privacy of Stingo's room but also apply pressure to the narrow viewpoint he has on art and life in general. Nathan especially, with the encyclopedic knowledge of a brilliant obsessive, gets Stingo to realize how narrow his own interests have been but also challenges him on his own terms, making him reflect on everything from Nazism to what Nathan calls the "worn-out tradition" of southern writing (115).

For the novel, Nathan's Nazi obsessions enable further connections between the world of Auschwitz and American society. The upheaval Nathan visits on Stingo extends well beyond his initial foot-in-the-door insistence that Stingo leave his novel and enjoy their company. Nathan's madness also explodes Stingo's Sophie-like hope that he can remain uninvolved, solitary in his creativity. The revelation of Nathan's illness shows him that his rejection of the "raw dirty world" (193) for the sanctuary of art cannot be sustained. Much as Sophie had heard of Nazi selections but "thrust them out of her mind" since they seemed so "unlikely to happen to her" (182), Stingo has "heard of madness" but always "considered it an unspeakable condition . . . safely beyond [his] concern." Like Sophie, though, he finds that what seemed safely distanced from his life has become a part of it. The abstraction of madness is suddenly "squatting in [his] lap" (427), in the way the abstractions of Auschwitz and selections suddenly beset Sophie. His hope of remaining aloof, protected by the "armor" he has "wrapped around" himself (438), is dashed.

Prized from his self-imposed incarceration in art, Stingo becomes involved with Sophie and Nathan. But he retains a degree of detachment, and it is this, the narrator shows us, that gives him a large responsibility for the final tragedy. Nathan, during his telephone tirade before Stingo and Sophie flee south, accuses Stingo of "betraying" him by sleeping with Sophie (444). His accusation is mistaken at the time, but he is right in believing that he cannot depend on Stingo. Larry had asked Stingo specifically to "keep an eye on Nathan," since he was probably his "best friend" (423). Had Stingo stayed, says the narrator, he might have prevented Nathan's "last slide to ruin" (428). But both then, when he instead went to visit Jack Brown, hoping for sexual fulfillment with Mary Alice, and at the end, when he heads south alone before returning to Brooklyn, he shirks the obligations he has been trusted with.

Sophie's unwillingness to help her "dearest friend," Wanda, with the resistance outside or inside the camp (468) is reprised—at a lower level of risk—by Stingo's unreadiness to help Nathan at a crucial moment. Stingo's instinct is the same as the one Sophie displayed in Cracow and at Auschwitz. The narrator makes that easy to see. When Larry says to Stingo, "I wouldn't ask you to be a spy if Nathan weren't in such a perilous condition" (427), it is necessary only to replace the word *Nathan* with *Poland* or *we* to obtain a remark that Wanda could have made to Sophie. Nathan's unpredictable nature tests Stingo's fiber to the limit and proves it wanting, so the narrator's story is partly a confession of complicity in the tragedy. Just as Sophie was not merely a victim but also an accomplice in events in Poland, so Stingo is both the distraught survivor and a complicit party to the tragedy in Brooklyn.

The discourse toward harmony is still apparent in the main characters of *Sophie's Choice*—in Sophie's and Nathan's failed struggle toward wholeness and in Stingo's attempt "to collect and put back together the shards" of their friendship (210)—but it has been dislodged from its central position as the shaper of the narrative. In prominence now is the price all three pay for harmony through evasion, force, and repression. Sophie's experiences and Nathan's knowledge force Stingo to confront issues he would rather avoid. The urge to harmonize is still alive at the end and is implicit in the narrator, but the narrator also retains his distance from Stingo and ends the novel with more questions asked than answered, and with the accent not on closure but on the future.

Throughout the novel, attempts at harmony are shown to be either largely unworkable or highly ambivalent. Sophie and Stingo both find not only that they cannot avoid the "raw dirty world" but that in trying to avoid it they may contribute to its dirt. Stingo, in his effort to shape events into a coherent picture, shows tendencies as violent as Nathan's. When Sophie's behavior becomes "unruly and difficult" on the final journey south, he finds consolation in saying to himself, "Wait till we're married" (454), as earlier he wanted "to beat the living shit out of" Leslie for not conforming to his plans (175). Moments like these remind us that to strive to shape the world toward harmony may be a basic human and artistic urge but one that can also lead to violent suppression or to evasion—Lukács' "withdrawal before the contradictory problems thrown up by life"—and so to complicity. It is an urge that, in a sense, the Nazis took to an extreme.

But in *Sophie's Choice,* as in Styron's other novels, despair and affirmation sit together. There is an element of hope even in the deaths of Sophie and Nathan. Given the odds ranged against them, they die to some degree on their own terms. Their bodies are found to the boisterous sound of "Purcell's *Trumpet Voluntary* . . . filled with a resignation almost like joy" (508). Sophie's smile, as seen by Morris only moments before the suicide, suggests a "curious fleeting glimpse of mild amusement," almost a "gentle laugh" (500)—harking back to her "soft peals of laughter as she sank earthward with Nathan" (514) at the fairground in happier days. There is an air of existential defiance. Since, as Nathan says, "Death is a necessity," they go "downward to darkness on extended wings."[37] Consequently, Stingo witnesses not so much their disintegration from health as their courageous rebirth and swan song, as each gives the other a short but memorable stay before the inevitable.

Or is this impression of defiance just a result of the narrator's—and Styron's—need to end on a positive note? The phrasing he ascribes to Morris—the "glimpse of mild amusement"—is really his own, for Morris' eloquence never exceeds his pithy summary of Sophie and Nathan's life together: all they do is "hump and fight" (42). The remark attributed to Morris betrays the narrator's need to discern the possibility of meaning where none may exist. That too, is undercut, however: Sophie and Nathan die in each other's arms in the costumes they wore to celebrate "being human" (63), but Larry warns Stingo not to look at their faces. Yet the mystery of death at least allows the narrator some purchase for avoiding total negation.

Despair is also contained insofar as Stingo ends the novel griefstricken but in a position to begin anew. If "Sophie's attempts to gain a hold on the confusion of her past" (381) were doomed and Nathan "never got his mind in order," a "fragile yet perdurable hope" (514) of

37. The phrase is Wallace Stevens', in "Sunday Morning," in *The Collected Poems of Wallace Stevens* (London, 1955), 70.

regeneration remains. There are times when nothing but silence is appropriate. After Sophie's revelations, Stingo—fortunately—can "say nothing" (492), and then he resorts to discussing peanuts, in a southern version of Kurt Vonnegut's *"poo-tee-weet!"* in *Slaughterhouse-Five.* He awakens the morning after the funerals from dreams of "speechlessness." But what wakes him are the boisterous shouts of children. Their mimicry of their elders—"Fuuu-ck you!" shouts one, but they have also buried Stingo in the sand protectively—attests the generative cycle that, for Styron, makes tragedy "so provisional."[38] Stingo's eventual arrival among the older generation is promised by his now "frail and rickety" legs (515). His small recognitions are grounds for optimism that he is on the way to a maturer understanding of his relationship to society and history.

The cleavage between Stingo and the narrator, however, persists to the end. Stingo's archly poetic discourse is set off from the main narrative by italics, punctuating how the clash of voices remains:

It was then that in my mind I inscribed the words: *'Neath cold sand I dreamed of death / but awoke at dawn to see / in glory, the bright, the morning star.*

This was not Judgment Day—only morning. Morning: excellent and fair.

Stingo's focus, as so often, is on himself: it is he who dreams of death, and he who awakens. He is concerned, too, with meter and rhythm—with the artistic form over the subject: hence *'Neath,* and *the bright, the morning.* In contrast, the narrator stresses not the personal but the more generally significant. Open-endedness is what is on the mind of someone who reminds us that Judgment Day is not here. The repetition of *morning,* unlike Stingo's repetition of *the,* has nothing to do with meter and everything to do with renewal and affirmation. The narrator ends not with his own words but with Emily Dickinson's phrase *excellent and fair.*[39] While Stingo struggles for independence from the discourse of other writers, the narrator is content with a turn away from himself and toward another. He is aware that the dialogue

38. Appendix conversations, 215.

39. Emily Dickinson, "Ample make this bed," in *The Complete Poems of Emily Dickinson,* ed. Thomas H. Johnson (London, 1970), 402. Styron quotes the entire poem (512).

must remain open, not merely over Auschwitz but over his, and our, connection with events such as it. For our understanding of the sum and potential of human behavior, it is still only morning.

The allusion to future generations allows the novel to end at least at the junction between hope and despair, between the promise of life and the inevitability of death, the best and worst of human nature and experience. Styron's melding of Stingo's story with Sophie's permits this, but also embeds the horror of Auschwitz in an American context. It lays bare the relevance of that atrocity to the lives of people like Stingo. It also underlines that "absolute evil" is "never extinguished from the world," because its seeds exist not in "monsters" but in the unwitting attitudes of normal people like Stingo, like the victim and accessory Sophie, and like the bureaucrats Dürrfeld and Höss. Stingo, with his self-centered determination, incarnates much of the schizophrenic potential of humanity. When he asks Sophie to "love me . . . love *Life!*" (452), he exhibits the two sides of that potential at once, since he is both selfishly homing in on Sophie for himself and illustrating the necessary optimism of youth.

A sense of rebirth might seem facile on the part of an author who has experienced nothing approaching Auschwitz. But the accounts of survivors demonstrate that even at Auschwitz there were two sides to existence. In *If This Is a Man*, Levi wrote that "sooner or later in life everyone discovers that perfect happiness is unrealizable, but there are few who pause to consider the antithesis: that perfect unhappiness is equally unobtainable."[40] Many survivors of Auschwitz retained their hope in life. If taken literally, Adorno's comment that there is "no poetry after Auschwitz" would be a denial of the human spirit.[41] In any case, it is countered by the facts: Levi begins his account of Auschwitz with a poem, and a spool of writing has been produced by survivors—very often, it appears, as a way of sustaining life. In the camps themselves, inmates gained comfort from storytelling and singing. That is the historical basis for the novel's hopeful, regenerative ending: the idea is that art sustains life, as music does for Sophie—and as it does for Juliek in Wiesel's *Night*, who after the march from Buna to

40. Primo Levi, *If This Is a Man/The Truce*, trans. Stuart Woolf (1960; rpr. London, 1987), 23.

41. Steiner, *Language and Silence*, 53.

Gleiwitz played his violin for others on the night of his death.[42] That such hope is fragile, however, and that art has its limits are made equally clear.

When the narrator seeks, if not harmony, at least understandable connections between himself and the "suffering Stingo whom I once inhabited, or who once inhabited me" (513), his concerns are far wider than the largely personal preoccupations of Sophie, Nathan, and Stingo. Stingo—prior to his glimmers of understanding—is only fleetingly concerned with the historical context of Sophie's trauma. His desire for her overrides a concern for her feelings. He laps up the "desperately needed" and "vivid encouragement" that Nathan proffers (187) but has little insight into Nathan's madness even after Larry's revelations. The narrator's broader focus takes in the connection between Auschwitz and everyday experience and behavior. At times in the narrative, he—or Styron, as we can call him at such times— dispenses with the characters and amplifies the dialogue.

"For those of us who were not there," the narrator writes, the "nexus" between the differing orders of time that Steiner talks of is "someone who *was* there" (218). Whatever the problems of subjectivity, language, and textual layering, experience is finally nothing if not personal. However impossible it is for us, as James E. Young puts it, "to know these events outside the way they are passed down to us," real people suffered real experiences in millions of personal ways.[43] To mediate some idea of that sort of experience is one of the ends of the novel. But elsewhere Styron—who there becomes one with the narrator—pushes out into wider sociohistorical regions. Sophie's and Stingo's stories recede from the narrative, giving way to a different dialogue conducted in essay form. When Styron brings in books such as Rubenstein's *The Cunning of History* and Steiner's *Language and Silence*, there is a wider purview than the characters', with Auschwitz seen as a historical event re-created through its survivors and commentators.

The short but wide-ranging *Cunning of History* is a disturbing ex-

42. See Levi, *If This Is a Man*, 118–21; and Elie Wiesel, *Night*, trans. Stella Rodway (1960; rpr. Harmondsworth, Eng., 1988), 107.

43. James E. Young, *Writing and Rewriting the Holocaust: Narrative and the Consequences of Interpretation* (Bloomington, Ind., 1988), vii.

amination of the Holocaust not as an aberration nor as something of preeminently Semitic concern but "as the expression of some of the most profound tendencies of Western civilization in the twentieth century." Writing shortly after the fall of the Nixon administration, Rubenstein argues that the Holocaust is directly linked both to Western religious traditions and to the increasing rationalization, secularization, and bureaucracy of Western society. For Rubenstein, it was an event that, far from being the "work of a small group of irresponsible criminals," not only directly involved ordinary businessmen and bureaucrats, who for the most part returned to executive jobs after the war, but also "required the cooperation of every sector of German society."[44]

Rubenstein suggests that the mentality behind Auschwitz is still evident in Western society. He writes that "the American system can be seen as a link in the process of the progressive rationalization of a system of total domination that reached its full development in the Nazi camps," since any system based on "rational efficiency and calculated results" and intent on "minimum costs and maximum profits" will be subject to pressures to evolve in this way. In working slaves to death at minimum cost and maximum productivity, the executives of I. G. Farben "merely carried the logic of corporate rationality to its ultimate conclusion."[45]

Sophie's two meetings with Walter Dürrfeld, the second of which the narrator calls a "fragment, among the most odd and unsettling" (381), of her story, plainly flow from Rubenstein's book. The historical Dürrfeld was a director of I. G. Farben who survived the war and an eight-year prison term to become an industrial executive in postwar Germany.[46] The two encounters of Sophie and Dürrfeld relate to the bureaucratic apparatus of Auschwitz that managed the production of synthetic rubber. The details that Styron develops, including the af-

---

44. Richard L. Rubenstein, *The Cunning of History: Mass Death and the American Future* (1975; rpr. New York, 1978), 21, 4. This edition has an introduction by Styron.

45. *Ibid.,* 58.

46. *Ibid.,* 60–63. On the connection between German industry and Auschwitz, see also Eli Cohen, *Human Behaviour in the Concentration Camp* (London, 1954), 10–11, 33; and Borowski, "Auschwitz, Our Home (A Letter)," in *This Way for the Gas, Ladies and Gentlemen,* 113.

finities between German and American industry, are largely from Rubenstein, and constitute still another link between apparently disparate worlds.

It was at the second meeting, at Auschwitz, that Sophie heard Dürrfeld speak of the "schizophrenia" caused him by trying to reconcile the "Special Action" of genocide with the "need for labor" (406). But the schizophrenia that Styron probes is not this, which lends itself to the kind of self-pity about which Arendt writes, but that arising from the divergence between Dürrfeld's prewar concerns and his concerns at Auschwitz. Sophie remembered that when they first met, the attractive Dürrfeld not only did "not in the least resemble the paradigmatic Nazi" (386) but also "uttered not a word about Jews." At Auschwitz, in contrast, where he did not recognize Sophie, "almost all that she heard from his lips concerned Jews and their consignment to oblivion" (388). Everything Dürrfeld said was couched in terms of bureaucratic efficiency, to the point that he referred to human beings as "thermal units of energy." He told Höss, "I am answerable to a corporate authority which is now simply insisting on one thing, that I be supplied with more Jews in order to maintain a predetermined rate of production" (405). Styron dramatizes Rubenstein's argument that a few years before the war "I. G. Farben was not an anti-Semitic corporation" and that the Nazis harnessed the outlook and efficiency of ordinary bureaucrats to murderous ends. Both books thus articulate the conviction that what appears disjunctive is really, ominously, in Rubenstein's words, "part of the same world."[47]

Styron is convinced that to see Auschwitz as an aberration—as Bruno Bettelheim does, for example, in *The Informed Heart*—is far more dangerous than to examine the continuities between it and the rest of Western life.[48]

Sophie's actions in the war, and Stingo's friendship with her and Nathan, not least his failure to comply with Larry's request, also illustrate Rubenstein's argument. Complicity through indifference riddles the consciences of both Sophie and the confessing narrator. For both

47. Rubenstein, *The Cunning of History*, 60.
48. "Although much of this book deals with the oppressive state of man, I believe that the Hitler variety was a passing phenomenon" (Bruno Bettelheim, *The Informed Heart: Autonomy in a Mass Age* [London, 1961], 105).

Styron and Rubenstein, the complicity of the victim can be through ignorance. Rubenstein argues that "even the most innocent victim is part of the process of his own undoing by virtue of the fact that he did not or could not take protective measures. The very helplessness or ignorance of the victim is an indispensable part of what takes place."[49] Styron exhibits not only how "absolute evil" is "at the core" of us all but also how our destinies can depend on whether we choose, like the "political neuter" Stingo or the "naïf in politics" Sophie (386), to empower evil through evasion and apathy or, like Wanda, to fight it. It is also true that the consequences of action and inaction have no guaranteed outcome—there is uncertainty as much in speaking as in keeping silent, as Sophie finds to great cost with Von Niemand—but silence, by a social rather than individual measure, must be the more dangerous, since it does nothing to dispel "helplessness or ignorance." There can be no more compelling answer than this to Steiner's musing that the best response to an atrocity like the Holocaust may be silence. The idea that "nothing speaks louder than the unwritten poem" is palpably untrue; unwritten poems do not speak at all.

The Cunning of History also has ties with the novel's dialogizing of the discourse toward harmony and its assessment of the ambivalent worth of ordering activities in the face of historical and political realities. Rubenstein argues, partly by invoking Max Weber, that a movement toward order is in alliance with the logic and progress of capitalism. He endorses Weber's view in "Bureaucracy" that bureaucracy's *"specific nature which is welcomed by capitalism develops the more perfectly the more bureaucracy is 'dehumanized.'"*[50] In *Sophie's Choice*, Höss, with his arms around Sophie, is like a "mechanical fly" (281). When she senses a breakthrough it is like an "aperture clinking open" (275). Höss is part of a system that tries to impose order on Europe: the "first technocratic state, with its *Regulierungen und Gesetzverordnungen*, its electrified filing-card systems and classification procedures, its faceless chains of command and mechanical methods of data processing" (250).

In the novel's musical trope, Nazi order is compared to musical

49. Rubenstein, *The Cunning of History*, 69.
50. *Ibid.*, 22.

discord—Auschwitz has "symphonic death sounds: of metal clangor, of the boxcars' remote colliding booms and the faint keening of a locomotive whistle" (280–81)—whereas music itself is Sophie's "life blood" (464). It sustains her from the start against the "discordant strains of her father's obsession" (243). She sees her father as "everything that music cannot be" (387). Contrasting with the sharp dissonance of Nazi technocracy is her memory of "Beethoven's violin concerto played one night at the stadium Yehudi Menuhin with such wild, voracious passion and tenderness that as she sat there alone high on the rim of the amphitheatre, shivering a little beneath the blazing stars, she felt a serenity, a sense of inner solace that amazed her, along with the awareness that there were things to live for, and that she might actually be able to reclaim the scattered pieces of her life and compose of them a new self, given half a chance" (89). This is the urge toward harmony at perhaps its best: the impulse not to impose order on others but only to compose a "new self" better equipped to deal with a world always under threat from drives toward totalitarian order (79).[51]

The use Styron makes of The Cunning of History confirms that the future is a central concern of this historical novel in the same way that, according to Carlos Fuentes, it is a central concern of The Confessions. Styron calls Rubenstein's book an "urgent consideration of our own uncertain tomorrows" (235). The object in seeking connections between Auschwitz and Brooklyn must be to reduce the potential of such an atrocity's recurring. As Steiner writes, quoting Kierkegaard, "it is not worthwhile remembering that past which cannot become a present."[52] Styron, like Rubenstein, shows how the individual is at the mercy of events seemingly beyond immediate concern. The implicit conclusion is that we cannot afford to be the political naïfs and neuters that Sophie and Stingo start out as, and that art cannot afford to languish in the deluded vision of an apolitical purity. In 1974, a year before Rubenstein's book appeared, Styron wrote that he could not "accept anti-Semitism as the sole touchstone" by which to examine Ausch-

51. On music in the novel, see Nancy Chinn, "William Styron's Sophie's Choice: A Study" (Ph.D. dissertation, Florida State University, 1982), 73–103.

52. Steiner, Language and Silence, 87.

witz.[53] In Rubenstein's book, Styron could find spelled out some of the universal implications of the conditions that conduced to the Holocaust.

That Steiner's polemical *Language and Silence* ironically engages in and fans the discussion it purports to reject is recognized by Styron when he says that there is a "touch of piety" in Steiner's call for silence since Steiner himself "has not remained silent" (218). Styron's novel seems to enter into dialogue with three major components of Steiner's argument: his comments on the study of literature, his assertion that much of modern art is a "retreat from the word," and his call for silence.[54]

Steiner asks if, given that a man like Höss can read Goethe and Rilke and then "go to his day's work at Auschwitz," the conception of art as a liberalizer and enlightener is tenable. He goes on to inquire whether a "wide gap" exists "between the tenor of moral intelligence developed in the study of literature and that required in social and political choice": "There is some evidence that a trained, persistent commitment to the life of the printed word, a capacity to identify deeply and critically with imaginary personages or sentiments, diminishes the immediacy, the hard edge of actual circumstance. We come to respond more acutely to the literary sorrow than to the misery next door."[55] To the first point, it is possible to respond that atrocities by some who read literature do not prove that no one is affected positively by reading it. Meaning exists between the work and the reader; literature is a tool we find uses for. By Steiner's logic, the possibility of killing with knives should call such instruments' social utility into question. But knives can also be used for surgery, and you can strangle someone with a bandage. The second question, however— about whether a commitment to literature diminishes a person's response to the misery next door—requires more than a perfunctory answer.

The second question also has greater pertinence to *Sophie's Choice*,

53. William Styron, *This Quiet Dust and Other Writings* (Rev. ed.; New York, 1993), 338.

54. Steiner, *Language and Silence*, 30.

55. *Ibid.*, 15, 23.

since Stingo's early attitudes seem to substantiate Steiner's suggestion. Stingo certainly begins as one who cares more about literature than people. He deals mercilessly with the hopeful authors who bring their manuscripts to McGraw-Hill, and when he meets Sophie and Nathan, he wants to "nudge them" out of his life because he has other, literary, "fish to fry" (62). But *Sophie's Choice* also affords a partial answer to Steiner. For Stingo begins to learn that art, and the artist, rather than superseding or transcending life, are integral to it. Steiner's argument rests on a monolithic idea of literary study, whereas Styron's novel makes a distinction: Stingo learns the limitations not of the study or practice of literature but of his attitude toward it.

Steiner likens the "retreat from the word" that he sees in literature to developments in postimpressionist and abstract painting and what he sees as the loss of "organization" in modern music.[56] He detects a "retreat from the authority and range of verbal language" in contemporary writing. "The writer today," he says, "tends to use far fewer and simpler words, both because mass culture has watered down the concept of literacy and because the sum of realities of which words can give a necessary and sufficient account has sharply diminished." Only a few writers, suggests Steiner, including Faulkner, Joyce, and Stevens—all influences on Styron—have mounted "brilliant rearguard actions" against the "pressures on language of totalitarian lies and cultural decay."[57]

Language is at the fore in *The Confessions,* and in *Sophie's Choice* there are indications that Styron has in his use of language reacted to Steiner's lament. Not only has Styron mounted a rearguard action of his own but he has done that through a clash of languages, thereby enhancing the textual schizophrenia. Styron's style has often commanded mention by his admirers, critics, and rivals alike. Dorothy Parker, early in his career, said that he "writes like a God," and Norman Mailer remarked that he wrote like "an angel about landscape, and an adolescent about people."[58] More recently, Ruderman has com-

56. *Ibid.,* 42. See also pp. 30–54 ("The Retreat from the Word").

57. *Ibid.,* 13.

58. See Andrew Fielding, "An 'Unfamous' Great Writer Brings Out a New Novel, *Sophie's Choice,*" *Horizon,* XXIII (June, 1979), 62; and Norman Mailer, *Cannibals and Christians* (1966; rpr. London, 1967), 103.

plained that his novels have an "overabundance of words, words, words." Anthony Burgess has a concern about *Sophie's Choice* similar to the one Ruderman has expressed, but he acknowledges that there could be the same concern about "James, Dickens and Melville." In his view, *Sophie's Choice* "is powerfully moving, despite the Southern tendency to grandiloquence, the decking of [Styron's] prose with magnolia blossoms where starkness was more in order."[59] The gravamen of the charge against Styron is usually that, if his eloquent prose is admirable in itself, it either seems to camouflage a lack of substance or is inappropriate to the subject.

There may be truth in the imputation of excess. Unlike much current American writing, Styron's prose has a voluptuous fluidity deriving partly from the grandiloquent southerners Wolfe and Faulkner. But just as there is a subtle use of language in *The Confessions*, there is far less extraneous or inappropriate language in *Sophie's Choice* than many imagine. It is easy to see what Burgess means by magnolian language, both in the narrator's discourse—*thaumaturges* (234), *prosthodontia* (313), *unguentary* (457)—and rather differently, in the gross hyperbole of Stingo's desperate episodes with Leslie. But it also needs repeating that a novel can have many styles in contest with one another. In *Sophie's Choice*, a variety of styles are enlisted in furtherance of the theme of apparently disparate worlds. What Burgess epitomizes as magnolian phrasing is really a dynamic of differing styles for differing outlooks. In this, Styron highlights the ambivalences but also celebrates the powers of language.

Acquaintance with the novel banishes the idea that the style is uniformly grand—and inappropriate. The long passages of Sophie's narration do not overflow with stylish prose. Consider: "These long years, in 1945, when the war was over and I was in this center for displaced persons in Sweden, I would think back to that time when my father and Kazik were murdered and think of the tears I cried, and wonder

59. Ruderman, *William Styron*, 128; Anthony Burgess, "Brooklyn Liebestod," *Observer*, September 9, 1979, p. 15; and Anthony Burgess, *Ninety-Nine Novels: The Best in English Since 1939* (London, 1984), 121. Frederick R. Karl says Styron's "thick rhetoric often works against, not with, the starkness of the internal story related by Sophie" (*American Fictions, 1940–1980: A Comprehensive History and Critical Evaluation* [New York, 1983], 539).

why after all that had happened to me I couldn't cry no longer" (86). Nor does the direct discourse on Auschwitz come across as florid, except in irony, as in Höss's description of his house at Auschwitz as making the place seem like an "enchanted bower" (208). The novel is a heteroglossia of competing styles, ranging from Stingo's, in speaking of the need "to stifle [his] monumental anticipation" and "slow [his] galloping pulse" (210), to the reportage of camp conditions: "The stripping and searching of prisoners that invariably took place as soon as they arrived at Auschwitz seldom allowed inmates to retain any of their former possessions. Due to the chaotic and often slipshod nature of the process, there were occasions when a newcomer was lucky enough to hold on to some small personal treasure or article of clothing" (237). Lapses occur in this narrative technique. But given the novel's length and complexity, and the slipperiness of language, it would be remarkable if this did not happen. What is important is that Styron is not subordinating the heteroglossia to one overriding language—as Faulkner perhaps tried to do—but is juxtaposing discourses and levels of experience to bring out connections between them.

Burgess is right to say that in writing about the Holocaust, starkness is in order, but the subject of *Sophie's Choice* is not directly the Holocaust but Stingo's marginal connection with that atrocity. Styron's careful use of language to portray the clash of world views can be seen as an attempt to reaffirm the power of language that Steiner believes attenuated, as well as to incorporate its ambiguities.

Steiner asks whether "our civilization, by virtue of the inhumanity it has carried out and condoned," has "forfeited its claims to that indispensable luxury which we call literature." He argues that silence "*is* an alternative." He suggests that "the best *now*, after so much has been set forth, is, perhaps, to be silent; not to add the trivia of literary, sociological debate, to the unspeakable. So argues Elie Wiesel." Wiesel does indeed argue this. He proclaims, "I write to denounce writing."[60] But the paradox of that proclamation and the oxymoron of Steiner's phrase *indispensable luxury* illustrate that their positions are more nearly gestures of despair than viable proposals.

60. Steiner, *Language and Silence*, 72–73, 74, 188; Elie Wiesel, "Does the Holocaust Lie Beyond the Reach of Art?" New York *Times*, April 17, 1983, p. 12.

Steiner, for all his polemics, is not silent, nor is it an advocacy of silence for him to admit that, if nothing else, the "compelling reason" for reading more about the Holocaust is "to make oneself concretely aware that the 'solution' was not 'final.'" Where Styron and Steiner seem to agree is not just in recognizing the personal and national complicity that leads to atrocities but in believing that art is important because it is regenerative. A person can engage in the arts and then "go to his day's work at Auschwitz," but art still has *some* power. As Steiner says, "Men who burn books know what they are doing. The artist is the uncontrollable force." Literature's reputation as a "humanizing force" may be damaged, but great writing springs from the "harsh contrivance of spirit against death."[61]

If Stingo's self-understanding is embryonic at the end of the novel, Styron's focus has been on the transformation Stingo begins to, and must, undergo as man and novelist. The story of Stingo and Sophie means to illuminate what Steiner describes as "the artist's primary material—the sum and potential of human behaviour"—in light of the Holocaust. The focus on the self is not "egotism," as Heath calls it and as Leslie Fiedler implies, but it shows something about egotism, just as the novel is not by but about Stingo.[62]

Sophie's Choice is a journey of recognition—or to the beginnings of recognition—a Bildungsroman perhaps but, really, as David D. Galloway, Rhoda Sirlin, and others say, a *Künstlerroman*.[63] It condenses the path of Styron's career that this study has traced: the movement of his novels away from the stable world of Stingo's father and from Stingo's faith in pure art toward complexity and linguistic ambiguity that continually frustrate any attempt to find a solid base. Above all it charts the distance between Styron's early view "of literature as just pure lit-

61. Steiner, *Language and Silence*, 182, 28–29, 15, 21. See also pp. 183–93.

62. Leslie A. Fiedler talks of the "writer's selfish pleasure that one, at least, has lived to tell the tale" ("Styron's Choice: A Novel About Auschwitz," *Psychology Today*, XIII [July, 1979], 107).

63. David D. Galloway, *The Absurd Hero in American Fiction* (London, 1981), 123; Rhoda Sirlin, *William Styron's "Sophie's Choice": Crime and Self-Punishment* (Ann Arbor, Mich., 1990), 57. Several critics call the novel a Bildungsroman. See especially John L. Cobbs, "Bearing the Unbearable: William Styron and the Problem of Pain," *Mississippi Quarterly*, IV (1980–81), 23; and Richard Gray, *Writing the South: Ideas of an American Region* (New York, 1986), 234.

erature" and his eventual engagement with political and historical topics such as the subject matter of the novel itself. Only by coming to terms with the individual's responsibility through complicity, ignorance, or unrealized potential can we hope to avoid a recurrence of an atrocity on the scale of the Holocaust. The effort, however inadequate, to see the individual in integration with society is necessary and appeals, as Malraux says, to "that element in man which today is fumbling for an identity, and is certainly not the individual."[64] People need to see themselves as part of a wider historical context, and humanity as part of a world structure. Stingo needs to gain an awareness far beyond the "lilac *fin de siècle* hours" with which he begins his career.

If, after all, there seem to be, as Langer suggests, two worlds, or as Steiner says, two levels of existence, all the more reason to try to connect them, however jarringly, into one conceptual frame. The aim must be to locate the points of contact between the best and the worst, between normality and events like the Holocaust that seem to stick "like some fatal embolism in the bloodstream of mankind" (514).

The novel looks not merely to Stingo's future but to "our own uncertain tomorrows," which are ever more insecure—and for reasons now beyond what man can do to man, in view of what humanity is doing to the planet. We cannot say we are not responsible, that we can do nothing, that we have no choice. For one choice we do not have is whether to be involved. If, like Sophie and Stingo, we deny our involvement, the choices that we do have may themselves dissolve.

Rubenstein points out that *Sophie's Choice* "is less a novel about the Holocaust than a novel about how the Holocaust" affects a young writer. Given Styron's southern Wasp background, his response, says Rubenstein, is bound to be different from that of Jewish writers, but "this does not mean that Styron's story is necessarily more or less significant." For Rubenstein, "every honest interpretation represents the weaving of the interpreter's own history and experience with what he or she knows of the event."[65] That, we have seen, is what takes place between the book's two levels—the competing voices of the narrator, Stingo, Sophie, and others on one level, and those of commentators on

64. Malraux, *Lazarus*, 4.
65. Rubenstein, "The South Encounters the Holocaust," 425, 441–42.

another. If we can approach any kind of understanding of the Holo-caust, it must come from such a textually layered multiplicity of view-points, of which *Sophie's Choice* is now one small cluster among others.[66]

The novel therefore must end with Stingo, and with the morning star—a tired symbol, repeated from *The Confessions*, that perhaps be-trays the exhausting effort needed to retain such hope. History, Stingo at last realizes, is not, as Stephen Dedalus would have it, the "night-mare" from which he should try "to awake," nor language something merely to be played with, to immerse himself in like some pleasure-oozing postmodernist bubble bath.[67] History is instead the nightmare that he must awaken *to*, and language—inadequate, flawed, mislead-ing but also powerful—a writer's only means for doing that.

66. Compare Lawrence L. Langer: "We err if we hope to find the essence of the Ho-locaust in a single voice. The most we can wish from a writer is a particular point of view" ("The Divided Voice: Elie Wiesel and the Challenge of the Holocaust," in *Con-fronting the Holocaust: The Impact of Elie Wiesel*, ed. Alvin Rosenfeld and Irving Green-berg [Bloomington, Ind., 1978], 32).

67. "History, Stephen said, is a nightmare from which I am trying to awake" (James Joyce, *Ulysses* [1922; rpr. Harmondsworth, Eng., 1984], 40).

Conclusion

Styron and Risk: *This Quiet Dust, Darkness Visible, A Tidewater Morning,* and an Overview in Context

NOT *silence, but curiously enough, only thing worth* Risking *a word.*
                                    —*Note scrawled on* Sophie's Choice MS

He has taken the risk of creating a novel as a meeting place.
                                    —*Carlos Fuentes, on* The Confessions

He has taken tremendous risks.

                                    —*Frederick R. Karl, on* Sophie's Choice

Norman Mailer once likened writers to pole-vaulters. "The man who wins is the man who jumps the highest without knocking off the bar. And a man who clears the stick with precise form but eighteen inches below the record commands less of our attention."[1] Few contemporary writers have aimed as high as William Styron, and it is clear that much of the harsh criticism directed at his novels stems from his taking on subjects that expose him to the chance of serious failure. As Frederick R. Karl says of *Sophie's Choice,* "The effort is of such overwhelming ambition that any reservations [must take into account Styron's] attempt to go beyond any previous undertaking."[2] *The Confessions* and *Sophie's Choice* show that, in contrast to Leslie Fiedler's opinion that we should be "less serious, more frivolous," Styron thinks novel writing matters most when it tackles subjects that render frivolity obscene.[3] It is when it risks setting voices of historical and political controversy against one another, and so enters the vital arenas of sociohistorical debate, that the novelist reaches full potential.

1. Norman Mailer, *Cannibals and Christians* (1966; rpr. London, 1967), 101.
2. Frederick R. Karl, *American Fictions, 1940–1980: A Comprehensive History and Critical Evaluation* (New York, 1983), 535.
3. Leslie A. Fiedler, "Cross the Border—Close the Gap: Postmodernism," in *America Since 1900,* ed. Marcus Cunliffe (London, 1975), 348.

Sophie's Choice is on that criterion a culminant novel. In contrasting Stingo's narrowly literary outlook with the narrator's broader view of a novelist's role, it reflects the author's own journey of self-discovery. Stingo and the author learn not only that, in Lukács' words, a "yearning for inner harmony" can be a "retreat" from the contradictions of life and society but also that it can contribute to the problems the yearner would withdraw from.

Once there is the recognition that each of us, artist or not, is implicated in the "sum and potential of human behaviour," the notion of art as chiefly a way to harmonize existence becomes redolent of escapism or suppressive hegemony.[4] More and more apparent become the affinities it has with notions of order and stability that are at best self-satisfying but delusory and at worst reminiscent of the solipsistic self-pity that contributes to the growth of "purifying" movements like Nazism.

Sophie's Choice is the culmination of Styron's shift away from modernist forms of aesthetic experimentation and personal isolation and toward the necessity of engagement with society and history. The novelist who retreats into self-examination or an overly cerebral examination of technique or who, as Ihab Hassan has said of John Barth's characters, wants to inhabit "some pure self-delighting realm of the verbal mind" has become for Styron an indirect accomplice to personal and social forces we must guard against.[5]

Styron's later work thus goes a long way toward meeting Lukács' ideal of the novel as engaging with history by representing the "interaction of character and environment." For Lukács, that "is the exact opposite" of projecting the image of man as "solitary, asocial, unable to enter into relationships with other human beings," in the way "leading modernist writers" do. Like Lukács' modernist hero, both Stingo and Styron start out "strictly confined within the limits of [their] own experience," but their journey takes them toward awareness of how they relate to and affect the lives of others.[6] Far from negating history, as Lukács maintains modernist writers do, Styron has, at least in his

4. George Steiner, *Language and Silence: Essays, 1958–1966* (London, 1967), 23.
5. Ihab Hassan, *Contemporary American Literature, 1945–1972: An Introduction* (New York, 1973), 57.
6. Georg Lukács, *The Meaning of Contemporary Realism*, trans. John Mander and Necke Mander (London, 1978), 24, 20, 21.

later work, "sought to grapple with" the "big issues."[7] George Orwell
said in "Why I Write" that his own career moved away from an ornate
and apolitical view of art.[8] Styron's is like Orwell's in that regard.

From the pivotal *Set This House on Fire* onward, Styron has in life
as well as letters taken an increasingly committed stance. The essays
collected in *This Quiet Dust and Other Writings* witness to that—not
least some of those selected for the expanded edition of 1993. "Death
Row," from 1987, and "The Wreckage of an American War," from 1991,
are especially notable for their political content. From the sixties onward, Styron became a "more active, visible and politically involved
writer," fighting capital punishment, taking up the cause and writing
about the plight of Benjamin Reid and Shabaka Sundiata Waglini, and
speaking out on civil rights and the persecution of writers in other
countries.[9] More recently, he has spoken of taking part "in a lot of
extraliterary things" that he finds "irresistible." In 1988, he visited
Chile to support the opposition in Pinochet's plebiscite.[10] In recent
years he has been as likely to spend his time writing about a historical,
political, or social issue as to be at work on new fiction. Almost never
is he to be found pondering such questions as the exhaustion or replenishment of literature.

This Quiet Dust leads Melvin J. Friedman to conclude that Styron
"seems to approach his craft from a different direction" from that of
his American contemporaries. Friedman compares the essays in the
collection to those of French writers—André Malraux, Jean Paul Sartre, Michel Butor, and especially Albert Camus in *Resistance, Rebellion, and Death*—and contrasts them with the essays of American contemporaries like Barth and John Updike.[11] When Styron was asked by

7. Richard Gray, *The Literature of Memory: Modern Writers of the American South* (London, 1977), 285.

8. See George Orwell, *The Collected Essays of George Orwell* (London, 1948), 419–26.

9. See James L. W. West III, "William Styron in Mid-Career," in *Critical Essays on William Styron*, ed. Arthur D. Casciato and James L. W. West III (Boston, 1982), 6. On Benjamin Reid, see William Styron, *This Quiet Dust and Other Writings* (Rev. ed.; New York, 1993), 122–52.

10. Appendix conversations, 225.

11. See Melvin J. Friedman, "William Styron's Criticism: More French Than American," *Delta* (Montpellier), XXIII (1986), 61–76.

the *Times Literary Supplement* to comment on his favorite book of 1988, he chose Roy Gutman's *Banana Republic*, an account of American involvement in Nicaragua. That choice not only attests to his sense of engagement but also reflects the attention to American foreign policy that marks the published extracts from his long-awaited novel, *The Way of the Warrior*.[12]

Apart from *This Quiet Dust*, Styron's published work since *Sophie's Choice* includes not only the extracts from *The Way of the Warrior* but also *A Tidewater Morning: Three Tales from Early Youth* and *Darkness Visible: A Memoir of Madness*. The three tales of *A Tidewater Morning* were published together late in 1993, but they appeared separately in *Esquire* magazine long before that. The earliest, "Shadrach," was written during the composition of *Sophie's Choice* and came out in the magazine in 1978. "Love Day" and "A Tidewater Morning" first appeared in 1985 and 1987 respectively, as extracts from Styron's work in progress.

In keeping with the pattern of the later novels, all three stories set individuals' situations in a context of larger historical events. "Shadrach" recounts the story of an ancient former slave who turned up during the narrator's childhood, having trekked from Alabama to his original home in Virginia to die. "A Tidewater Morning" is a strongly autobiographical story of a young boy, Paul Whitehurst, facing his cancer-ridden mother's painful last days in September, 1938, as the world slides inexorably toward all-out war. "Love Day" leads up to the horror that Stingo, as a young marine eager for battle, feels when he witnesses a kamikaze attack on a neighboring ship. The collection is consistent with the historical preoccupations that have come to shape Styron's career.

Personal though Styron's account of his clinical depression, in *Darkness Visible*, is, it equally shows his concern to reengage literature with pertinent human issues, and to use his literary skills to explore social as well as political and historical questions. *Darkness Visible* offers a vivid depiction of what Styron sees as the almost indescribable agonies of a much-misunderstood illness. But, in a very different way from *Sophie's Choice*, it also offers a retrospective on his

---

12. "Books of the Year," *Times Literary Supplement*, December 2–8, 1988, p. 1342.

career and reveals an achieved clarity on Styron's part about the meaning of his work.

The influence of Styron's latent depression through the years is evident in the structure of the novels. "Doubtless depression had hovered near me for years, waiting to swoop down," he writes. Indeed, the "stifling anxiety" and "dread" that this "mood disorder" brought with it, full of "anarchic disconnections" and a "sense of something having gone cockeyed in the domestic universe," is more than reminiscent of the various forms of discord—ranging from unease to confusion to despair—felt by Peyton, Culver, Peter, Nat, and Stingo as they set out in their search for mental and social harmony.[13]

But *Darkness Visible* also addresses the transformation of Styron's artistic vision as his career has developed. Discussing other writers who have suffered from clinical depression, he returns to the impact of Camus on his work. In line with Friedman's comments on *This Quiet Dust*, Styron makes particular reference to "Reflections on the Guillotine," an essay in *Resistance, Rebellion, and Death*: "I know my thinking was forever altered by that work, not only turning me around completely, convincing me of the essential barbarism of capital punishment, but establishing substantial claims on my conscience in regard to matters of responsibility at large. Camus was a great cleanser of my intellect, ridding me of countless sluggish ideas, and through some of the most unsettling pessimism I had ever encountered causing me to be aroused anew by life's enigmatic purpose" (21–22). "Reflections on the Guillotine" was first published in 1957; *Resistance, Rebellion, and Death* came out in translation in 1961, and Styron tells of plans he had to meet Camus, through Romain Gary, before Camus' fatal crash in January, 1960. It seems no coincidence that the time at which this essay caused Styron to be "aroused anew" was also the time of the writing and publication of *Set This House on Fire* and then *The Confessions. Set This House on Fire*, we have seen, was the pivotal novel, concerned with an awakening to a new vision of responsibility. Just as reading Camus set Styron's artistic and political soul on fire, that novel is also Styron's great "cleanser," his first work in which the

13. William Styron, *Darkness Visible: A Memoir of Madness* (New York, 1990), 43, 12, 12, 42, 14, 42, cited in the Conclusion by page numbers, without title.

movement toward harmony is opposed by social, historical, and political realities.

Moreover, as Styron repeats in *Darkness Visible*, the "cosmic loneliness of Meursault" in *The Stranger* "so haunted" him that he chose in *The Confessions* to employ "Camus' device of having the story flow from the point of view of a narrator isolated in his jail cell during the hours before his execution" (21). That decision led naturally to *Sophie's Choice*, involving Styron's retrospective examination of his literary journey from harmony to history. If *Set This House on Fire* is the one novel Styron does not mention here, that is perhaps because in it he was working out his direction rather than reacting to an insight fully conceived.[14]

Where does this leave Styron's work in relation to his contemporaries'? Is he, as Barth puts it in "The Literature of Replenishment," a writer who "repudiates the whole modernist enterprise as an aberration and sets to work as if it hadn't happened," beating a technical retreat into "nineteenth-century middle-class realism"? Barth certainly tries to consign Styron to "premodernist" company, along with Updike, John Cheever, "most of Bellow, and the Mailer of *The Naked and the Dead*." But it should be plain by now that Styron not only incorporates modernist techniques but responds to a more urgent need to make the novel a meeting place for controversial voices. Modernists do "set very high standards of artistry" in giving voice to "their preoccupation with the special remove of the artist from his or her society," but they take the novel form to its limits in only one direction.[15]

In reengaging fiction with history, Styron works against one of the long-standing traditions of American writing. It is possible to say of Styron what Craig Werner has said of Ralph Ellison, in *Invisible Man*: that he is a novelist who "repudiates the implications of the classic American retreat from society."[16] Tony Tanner characterizes the retreat of the modern American novel as one pursuing an escape from

14. "It was a kind of novel less in search of completion than a creation in itself without a fully established metaphor" (Appendix conversations, 221).

15. John Barth, "The Literature of Replenishment," *Atlantic Monthly*, January, 1980, pp. 70, 69.

16. Craig H. Werner, *Paradoxical Resolutions: American Fiction Since James Joyce* (Chicago, 1982), 196.

society and history into an "unpatterned, unconditioned life" where "choices and repudiations" and movements "are all your own." "A typical American hero," says Tanner in his study of modern American literature, *City of Words*, wants to find a "house by the side of the road of history and society" so as to secure the freedom to "create himself in some private space not in the grip of historical forces."[17] Writing before *Sophie's Choice*, Tanner had nothing whatever to say about Styron's work. In any case, the journey between *Lie Down in Darkness* and *Sophie's Choice* is directly away from the private space Tanner identifies.

It is true that *Lie Down in Darkness* is, in Tanner's language, partly about Peyton's desire "to be free of" the "imprisoning constructs of society," that *The Long March* is about the "problematical relationship of the American hero to the systems in which he finds himself," and that *Set This House on Fire* is partly a manifestation, in the tradition of Natty Bumppo, Huck Finn, and Augie March, of the archetypal attempt to "secure the self against the coercions and intrusive persuasions of society."[18] But the overall force of Styron's work is to assert not just the impossibility but the moral irresponsibility of anything like that. If the harmony sought by Styron's characters appears comparable with Yossarian's Sweden, Augie March's Greenland, or Holden Caulfield's "nice and peaceful" place, the thrust of Styron's career is to disqualify such an assimilation.[19] In contrast to Salinger, whose *Catcher in the Rye* appeared the same year as *Lie Down in Darkness*, Styron was working away from the illusory sense of having the right, or even the ability, to stand apart or, like such modernist figures as Eugene Gant and Jake Barnes, be "lost."

Styron's work lies closest to that of American novelists who see a role for fiction in the sociohistorical arena. James Baldwin and Toni Morrison have already been mentioned, but there are also E. L. Doctorow and Kurt Vonnegut—both usually designated postmodernists—as well as Walker Percy, John Irving, Joyce Carol Oates, and Philip Roth. Doctorow's approach to history differs radically from Styron's but evinces a similar concern to wrench fiction back to mattering. *Rag-*

17. Tony Tanner, *City of Words* (London, 1971), 15, 182, 58.
18. *Ibid.*, 55, 31, 147.
19. J. D. Salinger, *The Catcher in the Rye* (1951; rpr. New York, 1976), 204.

time and *The Book of Daniel* set different voices in dialogue to re-create eras and connect them with contemporary concerns. Not unlike Sophie, the Isaacsons' "self-deception," in Paul Levine's words, makes them "accomplices in their own destruction."[20] Like Styron, Docto-row conveys how "innocence is complicity," as is the "failure to make connections."[21] Styron's determination to show that the Holocaust was no aberration is not dissimilar from Doctorow's insistence on making clear that, as Michelle M. Tokarcyzk puts it, "the anti-communist hysteria of the 1950s was not, as many Americans would like to believe, a brief aberration washed away by the political progres-sion of the 1960s."[22]

Although Vonnegut may, in Tanner's words, have "sympathy with" the "quietistic impulses" of Billy Pilgrim in *Slaughterhouse-Five* and Howard Campbell in *Mother Night,* his "whole work suggests that if man doesn't do something about the conditions and quality of human life on earth, no one and nothing else will."[23] In Percy's *The Thanatos Syndrome,* Father Smith's confession of possible complicity in the Nazi atrocities, and the thread of connections between current science and the events of World War II, bespeak an authorial concern to reen-gage fiction with sociohistorical issues. In *A Prayer for Owen Meany,* Irving's strategy is similar to Styron's in *Sophie's Choice.* To ease the reader into his main subject, the Vietnam era, Irving opens in a light vein, but the novel grows steadily more disturbing until, with the reader caught, the author directly introduces voices relating to Ameri-can foreign policy from Kennedy onward. Oates, whose work has ex-plored a huge variety of social and political issues, begins *American Appetites* by depicting a world similar—in values if not geography—to the complacent suburban milieu of *Lie Down in Darkness.* But the comfortably benign opening, like that of *Sophie's Choice,* is delusory. The Eden of the successful, self-satisfied Ian McCullough collapses as he crashes through the facade of ordinary life into a hell on earth.

Roth's and Styron's work has parallels beyond those between *The*

20. Paul Levine, *E. L. Doctorow* (London, 1985), 43.

21. E. L. Doctorow, *The Book of Daniel* (1971; rpr. London, 1982), 234, 236.

22. Michelle M. Tokarcyzk, "From the Lions' Den: Survivors in E. L. Doctorow's *The Book of Daniel, Critique,* XXVIII (1987), 4.

23. Tanner, *City of Words,* 200.

Ghost Writer and *Sophie's Choice*. Most recently, Roth's *Operation Shylock*—in which Styron's name appears more than once—deliberately blurs the line between biography and fiction to involve the reader in a journey from personal reminiscence into a broader political and historical debate. Roth exploits the device of uncertain identity to pull the reader into a polyphonic debate concerning Israel and the Middle East.

Consequently, Styron's deviation from modernism is not retrograde, or to a premodernist sensibility, but builds on the modernist legacy, in a manner made familiar by several of his contemporaries. Far from being a throwback to Faulkner, Styron in his later work engages issues that reflect concern about the future as much as about the past, and he counsels involvement with, rather than alienation from, politics and history. Active responsibility is his ferment, rather than romantic notions of a fugitive arcadia, stoicism, or decay.

Moreover, even though his work seems at odds with certain kinds of postmodernism, the convergences between him and Vonnegut, and especially between him and Doctorow, establish that some of his main themes are precisely those of so-called postmodernists of a more *engagé* stripe. In Europe, as well as the United States, writers like Milan Kundera, in *The Unbearable Lightness of Being*, and Julian Barnes, in *A History of the World in 10 1/2 Chapters*, deal with history, with the textual element of history, and with the indistinct line between the public and the private self in ways that are comparable to Styron's. Those writers are at one in seeing the inanity in calls for frivolity when, in Percy's words, there are "one hundred million dead" in our scientific century.[24] All of them, though through differing means, are committed to addressing problems of history and textuality, and to extending the novel in subject matter as much as form. To do that—to grapple with issues that matter—they must take risks, opening their work to the possible hostility of others who either do not share their social ardor or disagree with the sort of expression they give it.

Alain Robbe-Grillet has said that the contemporary novel is an "exploration" seeking the reader's "active, conscious, *creative* assistance."

24. Walker Percy, *The Thanatos Syndrome* (1987; rpr. London, 1989), 373. See also Richard L. Rubenstein, *The Cunning of History: Mass Death and the American Future* (1975; rpr. New York, 1978), 7.

The author invites the reader to join in a "creation, to invent in his turn the work—and the world—and thus to learn to invent his own life."[25] Styron, in his later novels, takes the risk of exploring what some would rather see left untouched: the life of a historical black rebel—which blacks in the late sixties said Styron had no right to explore—and the "unspeakable" realm of the Holocaust. He thereby summons us to look again at connections between apparently distant events and our own lives—to peer more closely at the ways that such events are inescapable for us. The feat of fantasy by which we are brought to this in *Sophie's Choice* and *The Confessions* requires the reader's "conscious, *creative* assistance." It is only when critics see the novels as retailing statements rather than tendering exploratory reflections that they can believe Styron, or any writer examining historical or political events, is seeking the definitive word.

The Way of the Warrior has evolved through myriad forms since the end of the sixties. Styron broke off from work on it in 1974 to write *Sophie's Choice* and was then dogged by the illness he describes in *Darkness Visible*. Excerpts from various versions, such as "The Suicide Run," "Marriot, the Marine," and "Saipan, July 1945," have appeared in magazines.[26] But the decision to make "Love Day" an autonomous story in *A Tidewater Morning* lets us gather that the novel he began writing has metamorphosed. That is not unconnected with the upheavals that, since the late 1980s, have neutralized the Cold War polarities of forty years' standing. Until 1986, the novel—as "Love Day," among other stories, testifies—was at its heart about World War II. But Styron has now refocused it to deal, in some way or other, with American foreign policy since the war.

He has talked about his progress on the novel as he saw it when he spoke.[27] Since then it has apparently continued a radical evolution. Whatever its final form, *The Way of the Warrior* seems sure to con-

25. Alain Robbe-Grillet, *For a New Novel: Essays in Fiction*, trans. Richard Howard (Freeport, N.Y., 1970), 134, 156.

26. William Styron, "Marriott, the Marine," *Esquire*, LXXVI (September, 1971), 101–210, not continuous; William Styron, "The Suicide Run," *American Poetry Review*, III (May–June, 1974), 20–22; William Styron, "Saipan, July 1945," *Paris Review*, CIII (Summer, 1987), 16–29.

27. Appendix conversations, 231–43.

tinue the shift this study has tracked and to deal with the themes of complicity and responsibility basic to his work from *Set This House on Fire* onward. Styron wrote on the manuscript for *Sophie's Choice,* "Note to myself: 'Bring in Soviet, Gulag, Viet Nam etc.' REJECTED."[28] The inference is that *The War of the Warrior* and *Sophie's Choice* are works stemming from the same sense of historical awareness.

As in *Sophie's Choice,* there is a reflexive strain in the new novel that measures the distance Styron has come. History is a decorative backdrop in *Lie Down in Darkness* but invades the characters' lives in *Sophie's Choice.* Similarly, the atom bomb and foreign policy in general, which are subsidiary in *Lie Down in Darkness* and *Set This House on Fire,* have become central in *The Way of the Warrior.* The yielding of harmony to history persists and promises to become even less ambiguous.

28. "Sophie's Choice" (Manuscript in Styron Papers, William R. Perkins Library, Duke University).

Appendix
Extracts from Conversations with William Styron

These extracts, taken verbatim from several hours of taped conversation with William Styron, were recorded either in interview sessions or on walks and car journeys. The first two sections are from conversations during visits to Styron's home in Roxbury, Connecticut, on April 6 and April 22–26, 1988. Styron's wife, Rose, was present on some occasions, and at one point I have included a couple of questions that she asked about Sophie's Choice. *The third section consists of brief extracts from our conversations during his visit to Britain between November 26 and November 28, 1991. This appendix is intended to provide primary material of general interest, as well as a context for some of the quotations within my study. I have therefore sought to remove discontinuities, repetitions, and grammatical inaccuracies only where they hamper understanding.*

Roxbury: First Visit, April 6, 1988

GCB: It strikes me there is a move in your career from the highly literary preoccupations of Stingo—from a Flaubertian notion of "art for art's sake"—toward some notion of an artistic commitment to social and historical issues.

WS: I think immediately after a major war like World War II people like to retreat. The commitment is enormous. When you have a major enterprise like that—a savage involvement in events—the tendency, especially if you're young, as I was, is to withdraw, and to become hermetically sealed.

GCB: As Paul Whitehurst does in "A Tidewater Morning"?

WS: Yeah. The ivory tower beckons.

GCB: At the Start of *Sophie's Choice,* Stingo is always in one form of cubbyhole or another: the green tower of the McGraw-Hill building, his pink room.

WS: Yes, exactly, and such a retreat is quite natural. Right after World War II there was a large desire to give high regard to the kind of worship of pure intellect and pure criticism of T. S. Eliot—who was of course a great poet—but this kind of worship of intellectual endeavor is very natural after a huge world upheaval. That's where I was, and that's why I was in retreat, and why academe beckoned.

GCB: Would it also have something to do with Flaubert, and then the high modernists: with Faulkner's—presumably humorous—idea of "Ode on a Grecian Urn"'s being worth any number of little old ladies?

WS: I think so.

GCB: So you were imbued with a modernist ethos?

WS: Yes, I think I was. It was very natural to want to do that, and not entirely pernicious.

GCB: Your writing is very different from what critics call postmodernist writers: John Barth and so on. How do you feel about their writing and its value, given that it's so different from yours?

WS: I'm not attracted to that kind of writing. It's just not something I have much regard for. I can find some enjoyment in it. It's not counterproductive. It has its own raison d'être and plainly satisfies both writer and some readers. But to me it's like the famous Supreme Court justice who tried to define pornography. He said, "I don't know what it is, but I can tell what it is when I see it." Well this is the way I feel about good writing. I can hardly define it. It can cross boundaries, but I know it when I see it. I know the kind that moves me, that I consider important writing, and more often than not it does not include postmodernist forms of writing. John Barth, to my mind, is a totally self-preoccupied writer, to the extent that he virtually lacks any interest for me.

GCB: What about the idea that since our world changes, so forms have to change? Have you felt the need through your career to change the way you write?

WS: I don't think so. I think I write with a fairly simple premise. That I want to communicate, that I want to tell a story. It need not be a simple-*minded* story, but there has to be some kind of narrative.

GCB: So would you disagree with the modernist idea that the complexity of reality should be reflected in the art? That it's got to be opaque, or difficult to grasp, because that's the way reality is?

WS: I believe in limited opacity, which is to say that once you have "conned" the reader into reading you and getting engrossed in your work, then you can do all sorts of things. This is the time-honored tradition. Tolstoy did it.

GCB: So you'll bring in Steiner, say?

WS: You can indulge yourself only when you indulge the reader. There has to be a sense of communion. I don't intentionally want to start out obfuscating the reader, and making demands on the reader that are completely unnecessary. But if later on I want to unburden myself of something important, which is not strictly "traditional" narrative, I go ahead and do it.

GCB: Like Roethke you learn by going where you have to go?

WS: Yeah, in a sense. I think you follow your own nose.

GCB: And learn part way through, that, for instance, Sophie is lying. But you must have some kind of general plan?

WS: Obviously you have a general plan. You have point *A* where you start and *Z* where you end, but the letters are not necessarily in order between *A* and *Z*.

GCB: You end your latter two novels with the morning star. How do you see those two endings? I'm always reminded of Wallace Stevens' phrase "downward to darkness on extended wings." The endings of both novels are both tragic and uplifting.

WS: I suppose I have always felt that tragedy is so provisional. Tragedy is real, but it is not final, simply because, despite the most horrendous tragedies you can imagine, people go on. It seems to me there's no ultimate bleak vision you can entertain of life. Even the most bleak modern vision of Eliot, or Beckett, has a grain of hope in it.

GCB: *Sophie's Choice* is both bleak and at other times exhilarating, and it seems to me that these two "worlds" you focus on make the novel more effective than it might otherwise have been. Did you have this chiaroscuro effect in mind?

WS: Yeah, of course. I knew from the start that if I was writing about something as grim as Auschwitz, there would be no possible way to make it work as meaningful narrative unless I embedded it in another context. What had bothered me about previous narratives I had read about Auschwitz was that, being narratives of personal experiences, and usually very honest and extremely effective ones, they were almost *too* effective. They were unremitting descriptions of what it was like to live in those barracks, to be constantly beaten, to have people dying around you, and to have the constant presence of the people going off to the gas chamber. I wanted to avoid that, because I felt that if I could strike another kind of metaphor, not only of the choice and the children, but one that would remove me from the horror, I could be effective in a different way.

GCB: I'm trying to see how you were thinking during the writing. There's a moment when Stingo and Sophie are making love, and with Sophie deep in her own world, oblivious to Stingo, Stingo looks away, slightly embarrassed. Am I way off the mark if I suggest that this is some kind of metaphor for the unease one might feel at engaging with the Holocaust as a subject for art? At the fact that, since art is partly about enjoyment, you are capitalizing on the suffering of others?

WS: I think that's implicit about anything anyone writes. You're a surrogate victim when you're a writer. An artist has to appear remote and safe, because that's his function. He has to write about other people's horrors, and there must be always an element of slight embarrassment, I suppose, in being a voyeur, a viewer who has not himself experienced the thing. There's no way out of that dilemma. But I never really had any basic problems with embarrassment over my subject matter. As you'll be aware from what I said of Steiner, this has always seemed to me an absolutely hollow deception, on the part of Steiner, Elie Wiesel, and others, that we can't write about Auschwitz.

GCB: There's a sense in *Sophie's Choice* of art as a sustainer of life, an idea supported in the work of Wiesel, or of Primo Levi, belying Adorno's comment that to write poetry after Auschwitz is "barbaric."

WS: I think people have quoted that Adorno line very glibly, without realizing it's a rather dumb statement. It's quoted like Holy Writ, but I think it's stupid. It's a thoroughly hollow idea.

GCB: Are you willing to talk about what you're doing at the moment?
WS: No, I don't really like to deal with that if I can help it. I've got my finger in so many pies right now.

GCB: Will it be a while before we see another novel from you?

WS: I'm not really sure. It's a question I usually sidestep, because it's not something I like to think about. It either happens or it doesn't.

GCB: Fair enough. Another question: E. L. Doctorow. What do you think of his writing? His use of history?

WS: Well, I'll tell you. I will answer that question, but I don't like to talk about my contemporaries if I can help it. That's an exception about Ed Doctorow. I think he's dealt with history very well. *Ragtime* was an interesting experiment and one that worked.

GCB: Do you feel a commitment to getting the role of the writer back among historical, political issues?

WS: I suppose I do. I'm going back to what I said originally. I know what grabs me, what moves me, what I find central and important, and it is the course of human events. I am moved by moments when human lives intersect with large historical events and become metaphors. I think these things have meaning. Even when we live in a backwater, we're moved by the tides of history. I don't think a writer can program himself to say this is the way he should write. But I'm attracted to these moments.

GCB: A question about your writing technique: I've been curious in the time that I've studied your work about the way you talk of perfecting a page before moving on, and building up the novel in this way. Don't you feel a need to move faster, to catch a scene, say, to ensure your prose flows, knowing you can go back and rework the looser parts?

WS: I think my concern for the language is so obsessive that I can't just let myself flow. I have to pick and choose among words so meticulously, and writing doesn't come easily. When I let it flow, I find myself writing like an idiot.

GCB: Has your career gone the way you envisaged it?

WS: I never knew what the hell I was up to. When you look at your career, it's rather puzzling. What can you say? You've done your best. You wish you'd done better. But you've done what you've done, and it's a great deal better than some other people, and not as good as others. So what? You've made your mark.

GCB: Can you say something about your techniques regarding language in *The Confessions of Nat Turner?*

WS: I think I was trying to establish in a kind of subtle way the very obvious fact that a black slave was not going to think and feel in the way I was writing. It was a kind of transcription, in which, however, language was of very large importance. I was creating an illusion. That book conceivably could have been written in a primitive way. I deliberately chose a kind of orotund, classical style. A writer has to at some point assume that readers are either going to accept it or not. If they accept it, fine, if they don't then they should go to a movie or read something else. You have a contract with a reader. Readers who, totally aside from the attack on it, objected to *The Confessions of Nat Turner* on literary grounds just didn't accept the contract. That's their right and, from my point of view, their loss.

GCB: As I see it, your movement toward harmony, even though you show it to be problematic, remains evident enough in the novel to conflict with the assertion of self-identity taking place in the late sixties. So your novel was going to clash with the interests of black radicals whatever.

WS: That's quite true. There was very little . . . Well, that's an entirely different subject, the whole political attack. The language thing, though, was a closed subject. You either accepted it, or you didn't.

GCB: Do you have anything to add about James Baldwin's role in your formation of the novel?

WS: Only that he encouraged me. He was a great friend of Toni Morrison's, whom we talked of earlier.

GCB: You do have a mild homosexual incident in the novel, which one or two of the ten black writers attacked. What was its significance?

WS: I don't think there was any significance other than that it indicated the transitional phase that many—if not most—young boys go through. That was one of their more ludicrous attacks. You know, abstract phrases like "Styron made our hero a homosexual." Well, come on!

GCB: Obviously you'd read Erikson on the frustrated man with a vision.

WS: Yes, it's that famous thing that Norman O. Brown investigated. A point when you don't know where your sexuality is. He was going through a thoroughly normal transitional phase.

GCB: Did you read Frederick Douglass?

WS: Sure.

GCB: How about Franz Fanon?

WS: Yeah, I had read all those people. Du Bois and so on. Even fanatics like Marcus Garvey. There's hardly anyone I hadn't read.

GCB: Eldridge Cleaver came later, didn't he?

WS: That's right. *Soul on Ice* was published in 1968, when I was beginning to get this drubbing. They had claimed that I had suggested that a black man could actually prefer a white woman over a black woman. This was the extent of my mendacity. That I had taken their hero and caused him to have sexual desires for a white girl. Then along came Eldridge Cleaver. You pick up that book, and the first chapter is an ecstatic vision of white women.

GCB: That disdain for one's own people in a situation of oppression comes out in the work of Maya Angelou, it comes out in Toni Morrison's *The Bluest Eye.* The culturally received idea of beauty as blond hair, blue eyes.

WS: Yeah, and I think that that was among the things I hated most, the hypocrisy—that they were accusing me of expressing emotions which were impossible when, indeed, everything they wrote validated what I said.

GCB: In "This Quiet Dust," you ask whether Nat Turner found his humanity or lost it. Is this a central question?

WS: I think it's unresolved. I never gave it much thought after my speculation in that essay. I don't know whether you gain or lose your humanity by killing someone else.

GCB: But Nat's actions were justified?

WS: Sure. The killing of a human being is appalling, but it's not necessarily the most horrible thing on earth. It's too common an event. The wanton, sadistic killing of someone is something. But in war, in combat . . .

GCB: So Nat was in combat?

WS: Yeah. I mean, he had chosen this route. He had deliberately said, "I'm going to have to kill to make whatever statement I'm going to make."

GCB: Is he a hero?

WS: Well, I don't think the question is necessarily answerable.

GCB: When, and why, did you write the Author's Note?

WS: I wanted to orient the reader, and tell the reader that this was based on actual history, that's all. I don't know when I wrote it. I think I wrote it after the book. A postscript.

GCB: Do you see our ancestors as people like us, dressed up differently, or do you think people are very much part of their historical context?

WS: I think both. I think certain basic emotions are common to us, and to our ancestors, however far back. This is demonstrated by the great witnesses: the poets. Homer tells us that the Greeks had the same emotions as we do. But certainly there's warping and bending of attitudes, and it's largely created by our institutions. An example might be the evangelical, charismatic Christian, who at this moment in history has profoundly different behavior patterns compared to you and me, because of what he's been educated and conditioned to feel and to react to. An entirely different series of responses to life, let's say to sex, or to anything.

GCB: *The Confessions* has a very strong religious aspect. Do you have any views regarding religion, agnostic or whatever? You seem to leave the way open, where many writers wouldn't.

WS: Well, I know one thing, that I've been profoundly anti–institutional religion. I think it's an appalling fraud that human beings have perpetrated on themselves, and I'm basically mistrustful of Christianity.

GCB: But toward the end of *The Confessions,* he says, "I would have spared one person, the person who showed me the figure of Jesus," and you have the alpha-omega sign at the start, and the references to Revelation toward the end, and so on. Would you distance yourself from Nat's feelings toward the end of the novel?

WS: Uhuh.

GCB: There is certainly a jarring there, because he says he would have killed them all, except for the one who introduces him to Jesus, who would have said, "Don't kill anybody."

WS: Right. I understood that paradox. The idea of Jesus is a great idea, and I've never (I'm beginning to sound like a corporate executive) I have nothing but great respect for the idea—for Jesus. I mean, the concept, the man himself, seems extraordinarily fabulous. It's goodness. A man is trying to deal with life with as much goodness as he can summon. It's an extraordinary view, and the Gospels are very telling documents in that we do see a good man. But it's a cliché now. The thing has gotten so perverted that it's become sickening.

GCB: Though it's what society has done with the message, rather than the message itself.

WS: Of course, yeah, and this is why Christianity to me is a basically hollow concept. Jesus remains, but the institutions, to my mind, are hollow, especially their personnel.

GCB: Did you have any trouble with the title of *The Confessions?*

WS: I was never going to call it anything else.

GCB: Do you feel there was anything positive behind the black critics' arguments? Do you feel they had a case at all?

WS: I suppose if one read meticulously through their charges, one could find one or two things in which they had a point. But I never had any problem with what I did. Naturally, I wasn't very happy. It was extremely disconcerting, but I never had any philosophical doubts whatsoever, in addition to which, I had such staunch support from people who knew better.

GCB: John Hope Franklin wrote a favorable piece, didn't he?

WS: He wrote a glowing, favorable review. I don't know him at all well, but I've seen him once or twice in the subsequent years, and he's always said something like "Are they still on you? I can't figure that out."

GCB: Set This House on Fire is particularly interesting to me as what I see as a turning point in your career, a novel where you're seeking to shed certain ideas and find a new direction.

WS: I think you're accurate that there's a transitional quality to it. I was trying to feel my way in certain directions, and I don't think I fully understood what those directions were.

GCB: You were still awakening, like Roethke?

WS: Yeah, and it was a kind of novel less in search of completion than a creation in itself without a fully established metaphor, and that gives it perhaps a less substantial quality. It may have been due to the fact that I'd written a first novel, in which I *had* said rather basic, and to me important, things, about my life and art, and that I just didn't have the resources to fully conceive of another one at that time.

GCB: There's evidence of your going to Schopenhauer, Sartre, and so on, but there's a very strong satiric element to the novel too. Windgasser says it's "twagic! Like the Gweeks!" and so on. So how seriously should the reader take the references to Sartre and others? Is there an element of parody in your use of all this?

WS: I think so. I think you've nailed it.

GCB: You end with a choice between being and nothingness, which is in a sense an echo of the end of the penultimate chapter in *The Wild Palms.*

WS: Yeah, of course.

GCB: So you were still exorcising Faulkner?

WS: I think to some degree, yeah.

GCB: So you would go along with the idea of some sort of "anxiety of influence"?

WS: Probably, with that book. I'd have to think that one over.

GCB: Which writers seem to you important in having helped determine the direction of your career?

WS: That triumvirate: Malraux, Orwell, and Koestler. I think these are writers who've tried to grab the issues that are important to me. All writing is important when it's good, but there's an added dimension when it tries to grapple with these virtually incomprehensible things that go on in history.

GCB: Harnessing the talent you have toward something worth dealing with?

WS: Yes, you can follow your intuition; we're all groping. But that's why it seems more and more irrelevant to me the questions of what modernism is, or postmodernism. This is ultimately of no importance to me. I happen to think, for instance, that Orwell is one of the very important writers of the twentieth century, but who could have been less tied to a school, who could have been more spontaneous, who could have been more himself?

GCB: And because of that he's occasionally clumsy in the writing, but that's not the important thing.

WS: Of course, that's not the point; the point is you read him for what he is, communicating the way he's saying it, the way he wants to say it. That, to me, is the only important thing about a writer. I've long since abandoned worrying about how I'm going to write. In what mode of introspection.

GCB: So Orwell.

WS: Very much. A book that impressed me enormously was Koestler's *Darkness at Noon.*

GCB: What about it?

WS: Just that rigorous view of evil, which Orwell had too.

GCB: How about Camus's *The Rebel?*

WS: Yeah.

GCB: It seems to me there are echoes of *The Rebel* in *The Confessions,* in particular the idea that man is constantly struggling to be recognized by other men. That seems to be happening where Judge Cobb and Nat recognize each other as human beings, and where Gray and Nat shake hands and Gray in some way finds his humanity.

WS: In shaking hands with Nat, I see, yes.

GCB: You've mentioned elsewhere that *The Stranger* gave you the idea for the novel's structure, but has Camus been an important influence overall?

WS: Yes, I think there's a kind of ultimate vision that Camus had that helped form my own, a bleak, bleak view. Essentially Camus was a writer who had abandoned almost but not all hope. He saw his society, and Western society, as being a big con job, which it is. We're victims of ourselves, of the advertisers, and the con men, and the media monkeys, and it's very hard to be an individual in this world, and he saw human destiny as being redeemed individually in terms of self-reliance, the only thing we've got. There's a desperate desire for self-identity.

GCB: But you have talked elsewhere of Flaubert as your "master."

WS: Well, I do think there is something about that deliberate pain and determination to wrench out of every scene its absolute substance that Flaubert has that appeals to me.

GCB: Can you tell me anything about your present writing interests?

WS: I intend to write about the time I went to Trieste on a cattle boat in 1946. In fact it's under way.

GCB: You wrote a story when you were young called "A Moment in Trieste."

WS: Yeah, I'm going to elaborate on that. I'm going to describe the cattle boat part of the whole thing. In fact, I may interrupt what I'm doing now to write that as a short novel.

GCB: Can I ask about that? Is it still *The Way of the Warrior?*

WS: The main piece, yes.

GCB: What's the significance of that title?

WS: It's a free translation of the Japanese word *mushido,* which is the code of honor, the *Way,* meaning the lifelong journey of the warrior.

GCB: You began "Love Day" with a Melville quotation: "All wars are boyish and are fought by boys."

WS: Well, it's quite true. They're the ones who not only get sent but who often even enjoy it, and suffer in it and die in it. You look at the faces of these warriors, on television, and they look like my—about-to-be—grandchildren.

GCB: You once spoke of recent English writing as "frivolous and evasive." Can you expand on that?

WS: I guess the larger picture is that there are moments in history which allow for the creation of certain works. The two coincide, and this is why they happen. I think that British writing . . . Phil [Roth] is sort of grandiose about it; he says that the last great writer was Orwell. He may or may not be right about that. I would not go that far. But I do find, as I mentioned in a letter to you, that these lady writers like Anita Brookner seem to me to be the kind of reading that I would expect nice British ladies to have with them when they're taking a long plane ride to South America or something. It's that sort of thing. But it's mainly a commentary on this wave of history rather than anything else. History, I keep insisting, has a great deal to do with what writing becomes. There are moments when history is a wave, and otherwise history is sort of a backwater too.

GCB: So you see English writing as having been channeled into the still waters, bumping against sandbars, as it were?

WS: After this majestic course. I think that this is probably a reason that, unless I'm mistaken, there has been a degree of hostility in England to certain voices in American writing. An example might be Doctorow, who once told me that he never received any kind of reception.

GCB: He has some . . .

WS: Well, maybe after a time things are changing. But if the public reception is any gauge, I remember he was just roasted for *Ragtime.* I was with him when he received the reviews, and it was as if he had written some travesty.

GCB: Do you read a lot of fiction?

WS: It depends. I go through phases. I like to see what's going on.

GCB: Have your interests shifted since *Sophie's Choice* toward other areas?

WS: Well, there's always this famous argument about whether a writer should be *engagé,* they used to say, and I've gotten myself involved in a lot of extraliterary things which I probably shouldn't have, but which I find irresistible. I'll give you an example, since the word *Chile* came up. For some reason the opposition to Pinochet has summoned enough clout, after being dormant for a long time, to have forced a plebiscite, which is going to take place some time next year, and they want support. You have to understand about Latin America. They have this absolute worship of writers. The United States, and maybe England, are about the only places where writers are not cultural heroes. We just are not. It has to do with history again. On much of the continent and certainly in Latin America, a writer is a figure: they have clout, in the same way that in France, just in our time, people like Camus and Sartre and Malraux could all wheel and deal on a public level.

GCB: Malraux in the government and so on?

WS: Yes, cultural minister under de Gaulle.

GCB: Would you like to have more political influence?

WS: I wouldn't particularly. Even if I could, I wouldn't. I would absolutely shudder at becoming some kind of figure. But I'm not talking about that so much, as about the effect that one can have. Now, they want me to come down to Chile in a few weeks, on the first of June, just to be there to lend support to the opposition, the reason being that my work is very well known there, better known than that of almost any other American writer. I don't know why, but it shows you how these things work, these strange currents. And I think there's a very good chance I might do that, because if this *is* a possibility, why not avail oneself of that? It's something that most American writers and perhaps British writers have never taken into consideration, because it's never fallen their lot. But I believe a writer can be anything he wants. If he wants to be in an ivory tower and write *Ulysses*, fine. Or if he wants, like Faulkner, to stay on the lot down there in Oxford and write, that's fine too. And there's much to be said for that. But there should not be a quarrel about it. If the writer on the other hand wants to be engaged, it seems to me he has a perfect right, and even obligation, to do it that way too.

GCB: Do you like to think of yourself as an engaged writer?

WS: To some extent I do. I've noticed that what I have done in the last couple of years, and not only me but people like Ed Doctorow, who feels this way, and Kurt Vonnegut, that we get things done. It may be that we're getting a bit more clout.

GCB: This is what I was getting at when we started talking: this move through your career from largely aesthetic interests to a commitment to historical and social arenas of discussion.

WS: I never began as a writer in order to become an operative. Never. But I'm beginning to realize, almost in retrospect, that my work has addressed large social issues, and for some reason, in various contexts in other countries, this has reached out and grabbed people. That is, somehow what I've said in my work, in Chile let's say, has arrested people's imagination. Not to say it hasn't to some extent here, but you get lost in the shuffle, and this engaged posture that I'm talking about I think can be very valuable if it is literally going to help in some way. I mean, I've been told, over and over again, from the impeccable authority of the people who want me to come down there, that my coming there would make a huge difference. Pinochet, of all people, would learn I was there, aiding the opposition. This might alter events to some extent.

GCB: Has your career been a learning process? Do you have different notions now to those with which you began it?

WS: Yes, I've learned a lot, I suppose. I've learned proportion and balance.

GCB: Are you less solipsistic?

WS: Yeah, much.

GCB: You've mentioned Philip Roth a few times. I recently read *The Ghost Writer*, and it struck me that there were a number of similarities between that and *Sophie's Choice*, in terms of their concerns. Both were also published the same year, weren't they?

WS: That's right, yeah. That's a coincidence, I think. I knew Philip was working on something vaguely similar. We rarely talked much about each other's work. But I sensed that, and I think he sensed it.

GCB: There are one or two uncanny echoes.

WS: Yeah.

GCB: Like when he's listening to what's going on in the room above.

WS: Quite true, yeah.

GCB: A wonderful stylistic device.

WS: Audio-voyeurism [*laughs*].

GCB: And the fantasy about the Auschwitz survivor, all that struck me.

GCB: You once had lunch with Faulkner. What did you talk about?

WS: We talked about Truman Capote, whom he didn't like very much. He called him the big flea [*laughs*]. We talked about horses; he was going to the Kentucky Derby, so we talked a great deal about horses. He couldn't have been nicer. He was just as nice as could be. He had read *Lie Down in Darkness*, I know that, and had liked it very much. I know because he confided in his then editor, who was at lunch with us, Bob Linscott, that it was the best first novel he'd ever read. In fact, Linscott told me later that in one of his later books, Faulkner was influenced by *Lie Down in Darkness*.

GCB: Which one was that?

WS: I can't remember. A later one, obviously. *The Mansion*, or one of those.

GCB: So, you clearly were influenced by him, but you can almost claim that it was a reciprocal thing. Bloom and people talk about anxiety of influence, but no one's really talked about the idea that older people can be influenced by younger writers—fathers by sons.

WS: Sure. There's no formula.

GCB: You've talked about our blind belief in science. Do you value instinct over this? In your novels—for instance, in *Sophie's Choice*—

you have orderers, striving for order, but often in very negative ways, and put in terms of cacophony and metallic structures, as against the imagination and instinct. Is that something you're conscious of?

WS: Yeah, I think that plainly the society that gets computerized is in desperate danger. We're all becoming—you were talking about Oliver Sacks and Lewis Thomas and so on—well, there's a new theory that some scientific philosopher has conceived that the universe is a computer, that it has a meaning only insofar as you assume that it's a computer, and that everything in existence is part of a program. Who knows? But if so, it means all the more reason why we should try and seek our own individual identities. To me the worst fate is to lose that ability to assert oneself, to do that Camusian thing, which in effect is merely saying, "Kilroy was here," but to do it with a sense of nobility and dignity.

GCB: "Downward to darkness on extended wings."

WS: Yeah. It's something that . . . to be swallowed up into the gorge of this existence, and not to have . . . well, plainly, taking the broadest philosophical view of human destiny, you realize you're a speck of dust. We know that. Unless our institutions are totally haywire, we know that the earth is going to be turned into a cinder.

GCB: We know there are probably countless other planets just like ours.

WS: Just like us, and we know from experience as human animals that to seek only for pleasure is also a dead end, because that's completely self-defeating.

GCB: You would be against the hedonism of Hemingway's characters?

WS: It doesn't work, it's provable, except for a few gifted idiots, who have no moral center anyway. But we're not talking about people like that. We're talking about you and me and most people. Yet the struggle for pure self-transcendental experience is also a dead end, the search for spiritual ecstasy seems to me a dead end. So we have to learn to live somewhere in a precarious balance between ourselves as victims of our own desires, weaknesses, and lusts, and this glorious, transcendental dream of becoming one with the universe.

GCB: You wouldn't rule out that possibility?

WS: I wouldn't know.

GCB: Would you go along with Henry James and say that "our doubt is our passion, our passion is our task, and the rest is the madness of art"?

WS: Sure, you keep struggling, and just take some kind of hope that if one is an artist, your art will have some tiny but meaningful effect on this whole blindly mysterious process that we are all caught up in.

GCB: Do you see yourself as an optimist?

WS: I suppose, because ultimately I wouldn't continue to be the writer I am if I didn't have some sense of optimism.

GCB: And art is perhaps an act of affirmation?

WS: It is, otherwise you lay down your tools and do nothing, and one can't do that.

Roxbury: Second Visit, April 22–26, 1988

GCB: We talked before of critical reaction to *The Confessions*, and the differing views of Alice Walker and Toni Morrison on the novel. You didn't get so much flak for *Sophie's Choice*, but you did get some from, say, Alvin Rosenfeld and Georgiana Colville. How do you react to the idea that what you attempt to write about, or the way you do it, is somehow illegitimate or presumptuous?

WS: When writers or critics make these terrible limiting statements, they don't understand how severely they're limiting their own potential. It's tantamount to saying, "You should not try." Not that you cannot do it, but that you *shouldn't*.

GCB: When in some ways that's the essence of art.

WS: Look at Shakespeare. These incredible leaps of the imagination. Cleopatra. I love that hysterical attack on me in *Delta*.

GCB: Colville's piece?

WS: It's so high-pitched and shrill that you can't . . . I mean there's a tip-off in the first paragraph. She says she's seen a photograph of me looking fat. Now by any standards this is unacceptable. There are hateful people I would attack, but I would never attack them for their physique. Rosenfeld talked about me writing pornography on the Holocaust. But the point is that what I took enormous pains *not* to do was to describe any erotic connection of any importance between Sophie and the commandant. I could have chosen to have him have relations with her if I had wanted to, but I chose not to.

RS: And why, at the moment of choice, did you choose not to?

WS: Because I thought it *would* be a total jarring. I could have had the fearful Nazi blond, you know, describing his coupling, but I chose not to.

GCB: But it was important, you felt, to have Sophie and Stingo?

WS: It was important to have. I could have easily done the Nazi element to demonstrate their power. It was a temptation. I had it very briefly: was I going to describe the Nazi screwing Sophie in the same detail that I later did with Stingo? It just seemed inappropriate. But what I'm saying is that I still celebrated the fact that I had the choice, in our era, since World War II, which Tolstoy did not have.

GCB: And of course the scenes between Sophie and Stingo are important.

WS: Of course.

GCB: Though there are critics who have taken issue with this, usually by confusing the narrator with young Stingo.

WS: It was important if for nothing other than to finally say explicitly all the things that had been building up implicitly in his erotic fantasies throughout the book. And that's where this guy Rosenfeld missed the point by accusing me of bringing a pornographic aspect to the Holocaust. The point is I leaned over backwards to avoid this. He has the partially acceptable view that there have been frequent film versions of the Holocaust which have overly emphasized the sexual. I find it questionable but at least it's arguable. For instance, in movies like *The Night Porter* and *Southern Beauty*, which do bring sex into the concentration camps. This guy Rosenfeld said that I took part in the same nasty pornographic vision.

RS: But you so clearly didn't. What evidence did he have for tarring you with that brush?

WS: People want to do that.

GCB: If I was to ask you to put in a couple of sentences to get the purpose of writing, to sum up how you feel about writing, what would you say?

WS: Let me think about that, will you?

GCB: Well, you have Farrell saying to Stingo, "Write your guts out." Then there's James Michener, who, whatever one thinks of his writing, has written an incredible amount, and all since the age of forty. He was in a plane crash, and he wrote that he realized that he didn't matter. There's a sense that when people realize that their lives aren't important, that it doesn't matter what they do, that that can be an instigation to write.

WS: I think that of course that's an element; the "Kilroy was here" syndrome. I don't think that there's any doubt that you want to leave your mark. You'd be a liar if you said otherwise. You're dealing in something that you hope will survive and live on, and that's certainly one of the reasons, that when you're gone you're going to have a monument that people will connect you with, not just a piece of marble.

GCB: And why do you want that monument?

WS: You've seen something, presumably. You're registered your view of life, and you've made a statement about it. You've said, "I was here, and I saw it in such and such a way. I hope you too, by reading my work, can be moved, or exhilarated or whatever the same way I was." That's part of the motivation.

GCB: Is the ego involved?

WS: The ego is very much involved.

GCB: So how can Joyce Carol Oates talk of having no ego?

WS: She's not telling the truth.

GCB: Do you feel that a writer is someone who intentionally gives, or is it very much selfish—something one needs to do but that other people gain from because they need the same thing?

WS: I would say that what you're saying is accurate. It's symbiotic. But the effect on another person is very rewarding.

The following discussion took place in two parts. In the first part, Styron outlines a version of his novel in progress, The Way of the Warrior. *In the second part, he has read aloud the first chapter of the manuscript and then agrees to reread the first paragraph on tape, but the conversation ranges over that whole chapter. Although some of the references might seem to appear from nowhere and although Sty-*

ron has since told me that the novel has moved on from the version he discusses here, I have left the whole conversation in with minimal editing, for the interest it will hold after the novel is published.

WS: My problem is that I always find it extremely difficult to find a framework for hanging the vision on, so to speak.

GCB: What do you mean by that?

WS: To find the architecture of the work which allows you to thread your various visions and perceptions about life into a fabric that makes a coherent whole.

GCB: Are you reticent about talking about writing before it's done?

WS: I don't think so.

GCB: Do you now have that sense of the architecture you've been looking for?

WS: I have a story. Let me outline it to you. This guy is totally footloose. He's just come back from the war, and is delighted to be back because he feared the fact of going into the invasion of Japan. So he's lying around in Virginia, trying to make peace with himself, living with his father and stepmother, who bugs him, and he is sexually frustrated, since after the war he was going to have this erotic feast, and nothing happened. Girls are just like they were before, you know, they're all . . . so he gets in touch with—and here are the two figures—this other young guy, Stiles, who's from a different background, quite rich, went to Yale, of whom the narrator rather disapproves, but is fascinated by him, in the same way that Stingo was with Nathan, although it's an entirely different book. The other guy has a large streak of fascism in him, à la so many Americans of that class. So there's a flashback to the two of them on Saipan, and the narrator sees this guy hound . . . first there's a scene in which there's a suspected homosexual in the Marine Corps unit, in which they're both young lieutenants. The narrator is ready to be tolerant; not so this other guy, who unsuccessfully mounts a campaign to find out about this suspected homosexual. Similarly, there's this older enlisted man who's been suspected of spying. He's been taking pictures in this unauthorized area. And this causes the other guy to get very upset and root out this guy's Communist past, although basically it's nearer to a Red-bait. The guy's not Communist, he's just left-wing. That amounts to very little too, but nonetheless it reveals the kind of person this man is. So a year or so later, in Virginia, in this desperate situation, the narrator calls this other guy, or vice versa, they get in touch with one another, and decide to go on a cattle boat, leaving that port of Newport News. You see that there are some autobiographical elements in it, although it's not in any sense autobiographical, any more than was *Sophie's Choice.* So they take off together on this cattle boat, heading for Trieste, and this inspires this other fellow because he knows that Trieste is under the domination at that moment of Tito, the Communist ruler of Yugoslavia, and this brings out his anti-Communist phobia. But the crux of this thing is that on the way over on this cattle boat— and this I had visualized as a very rich part of the whole story—the narrator is the victim of an unsuccessful homosexual grope by one of the guys in the crew, among the cattle handlers, which most of these guys are. (I'm compressing this.) The other guy learns this, and this is on the voyage over . . . the narrator lets this guy know, which provokes the Yale fellow into a real, semimurderous assault on the guy. He beats him *mercilessly.* The narrator swallows his terrible distaste over this act of almost murder; the kid is badly beaten up, and in Trieste they embark on this sexual orgy. They pick up these girls who are being bought for virtually nothing—for cigarettes—and, you know, act the role of conqueror, and go on this extraordinary orgiastic debauch. This leaves the narrator feeling very vulnerable. He's got rid of his pent-up erotic feeling, but nonetheless he's exploited heavily these defenseless girls. On the way back on the ship, now unloaded from the cattle, making its way back through the Mediterranean, the Yale fellow, once again . . . he's not so sadistic that he once again beats this guy up, but he mercilessly misuses him again, and the kid jumps overboard. He commits suicide. And then there are some subsidiary characters. There's a minister, much older than these guys, who comes along because he's bred some of these cattle. He's a figure who runs through this story as a kind of wiser, older man, and after this horrible night when the kid jumps overboard, the narrator has an intensely erotic vision, or experience, or dream, or culmination of the three, in which he realizes, first, that he could have easily succumbed to this homosexual approach by this kid, he's overwhelmed by a postmortem, retrospective desire for this kid, and he realizes for the first time in his life, at the age of twenty-one, that this impulse is buried deep inside him, and it causes him the revelation of his life. He realizes that he's been in effect a coconspirator with the Yaley fellow in the kind of marauding, bigoted, fascistic journey. That's more or less the end of the story. He goes to this older guy, and says, "You know, I'm homosexual, am I not?" The guy says, "No, you're not." How does that strike you as the framework for a story?

GCB: I think it sounds great, but I think it sounds like it will be a lot longer than a novella.

WS: Yeah, I do too. But I think on the other hand it could be a brief novel.

GCB: My guess is . . . I'm beginning to see a little bit about how you work; I mean, *Sophie's Choice* was going to be short, wasn't it?

WS: Yeah [*laughs*].

GCB: If you start thinking it's going to be short, then you're going to be thinking tight, and you're not going to allow things in that aren't necessary. That way it doesn't matter if it does explode, because then you've got into it, so it's probably easier to think you don't have a very big canvas on which to work, and add extensions as you need.

WS: Yeah, I think you're right, and absolutely right. The danger is to think small, and to restrict. I think this has led to a great amount of constipated fiction in our time. Works that somehow fail because the writer . . .

GCB: They intellectually constrict, when they won't allow themselves free range.

WS: That's right, and it shows to the reader. The reader says, "Well, where's the guts here?" And the wonderful exceptions to this—and I think *The Great Gatsby* is a great example—

GCB: But of course he wrote big and reduced, so he still has the elements.

WS: Yeah, there's a kind of absolute control that he had which is quite uncanny.

GCB: I see how the story fits your concerns as a novelist. It strikes me that it's almost as if you've worked on *The Way of the Warrior* just to keep your mind rolling; it's exercise.

WS: Well, this would include, interestingly enough, if it worked out, parts of *The Way of the Warrior.* It would have a new setting, but there would be little snippets of Saipan, nothing much, but the themes intertwined here are . . . the most important one, really, is a portrait of what to me is our major flaw as a nation: this incipient fascism. As well as this, there's a theme which is subsidiary, but I think quite important too, which is this awareness that . . . it's something Gore Vidal, for instance, has been shamelessly wrong about: the assumption that all males are really bisexuals and can go both ways. The point is he's totally wrong about that, but he is right to the extent that all males at a certain point in their development have the capacity to be that, and this is part of the whole biological picture.

WS: Would you like to hear some of it?

GCB: I'd love to, yes.

WS: Would you? Just a few pages to see how it starts? It may be inflicting too much on you.

GCB: It isn't, as long as you don't expect any reaction.

WS: Of course not. I feel that since you're at least partially on a quest to see what I'm up to, this might be helpful. I haven't read a word of it to anyone. I'm trying to establish the voice, the tone, and it may be that I'll have to discard some of this.

GCB: What exactly is the main thing you're preoccupied with?

WS: I have been obsessed by a notion which I share with a lot of other people—it's certainly nothing new—that the tragedy of our nation in my lifetime has resulted from the paranoid reaction to the Communist menace.

GCB: The domino theory and so on.

WS: The whole thing. I mean, one has to be realistic, there is plainly a Communist menace. One doesn't have to be a Red-lover to say this. They're up to no good too. But we have been trained to hate them.

GCB: Without seeing them in us, and us in them?

WS: Yeah.

GCB: Which you show, I imagine, through a personal level in the book?

WS: That's right, and also that our foreign policy—our whole career as a nation—has been seriously compromised and undermined by this view, which led to the war in Vietnam, it led to our alienation of the people in Cuba. Certainly, had we been less rigorous, Castro would have been on our side.

GCB: And the whole attitude, the whole situation in South America.

WS: Of course. In other words this desperate Red-baiting that has been central to our failures as a nation. It's nothing new, but what I'm trying to do is to dramatize it, without being didactic, pointing out this attractive rich young guy who's quite beguiling and seductive yet who, when shown a couple of things, is like a bull being shown a red cape.

GCB: He's got a couple of blind spots.

WS: Well, the homosexuals . . . the homosexual thing is not necessarily a part of that . . .

GCB: Well, it relates in a sense.

WS: It does relate.

GCB: These people are threats to his whole world view.

WS: Yeah, that's right. I don't know, it's been bugging me for a long time. *The Way of the Warrior,* as you quite properly analyze it, has been percolating along in a curious unfulfilled way for a long time, but what I plan to do, if this thing goes well, is to incorporate what I've already written into this story, which I've figured out I can do very easily. But the main thing is to focus on the kind of love-hate relationship between the narrator and this guy, and the wonderful trip on the cattle boat. As you can tell, some of this is autobiographical; I was on a cattle boat in forty-six; it was an amazing, wonderful trip, and I *did* have this—God!—orgiastic sex feast in Trieste. I mean that's when I first discovered that women really *did it!* You know, that they weren't little girls that sat around with their legs closed, sweating and vomiting fear. They really *like* it. I was twenty, twenty-one, but it was in Europe that I discovered that. So that's another subpoint I'm going to try to make.

GCB: Do you make notes, or is this all in your head?

WS: I've made some notes, but I've written quite a bit of it.

GCB: Joyce Carol Oates says one thing she does, and advises others to do, is to pretend you're not doing it, yet do it. You pretend you're not at the crucial point of writing the great novel or whatever, and you build to the point where you're ready.

WS: Yeah, oh absolutely.

GCB: So what will you do? You'll have so much in your head, and then you'll sit down one day and you'll write the first three pages?

WS: Well, I've already done that, as a matter of fact. I've written the first forty or fifty.

GCB: Do you have an estimate of the length of a book before you start?

WS: I really don't. For instance, I had no idea *Sophie's Choice* would be quite such a long, long book. Again, I thought it was going to be a novella, then I got into it and realized it wasn't going to be that but I had no idea it was going to be so long. It's a very long book by any standards.

GCB: I guess doors open up, and the possibilities and options unfold.

WS: Absolutely. But I want to make ultimately a statement about various things—and I don't mean to say I'm suddenly in the twilight years and I'm summing up—but I want to make statements about my feelings about things that bubble up in the subconscious: life and death and God knows what else.

GCB: There seems to be a connection in your work between the subconscious and the historical: the largest and the smallest, and the effect of one on the other.

WS: Well, certainly the history has been a central preoccupation. I don't think very well unless I relate it to historical events.

WS: [*reading*] In the year following the end of World War II, having returned from the Pacific to my home in Tidewater Virginia, I was in moral and physical disarray. My existence had become so aimless as to give new meaning to that gray old phrase "at loose ends." For the first time in my life I was faced with what appeared to be almost nothing to occupy my hours intelligently, or enliven my days. It was early summer. Before this the Marine Corps had taken care of my summer, long before that there had been summer school, and before that places like summer camp. Now, in the early months of my official manhood, I was drifting through the steamy Virginia mornings and afternoons as sluggishly as a boat without a rudder, and I felt like a bum. Actually there was deeper trouble than this mere idleness. Two realities had spread their somber shadows over my life. One of these was the atomic bomb. The other was my stepmother.

GCB: What you're doing here seems to me to fit in with the pattern of how, as I see it, your work usually develops. Again you have a narrator who for one reason or another is at loose ends, or has specific discord in his life, and again you equate the personal with the historical: the stepmother and the atomic bomb.

WS: Yeah. I'm aware of how what I'm writing now fits what you've written about my work, and of that combination.

GCB: You go from a time present to a memory. Is that right? He's come back from his experience in the Pacific.

WS: Yeah. I'm letting these things flow. It would probably be better if you could sit to read it, instead of hear it, but I'm hoping that this going back and forth, you know the memory of going to bed with a WAC, these things . . . in effect, I'm doing something which I've done before, but I don't know if I'm doing it as well as I can, free-associating them in a curious way, so that once I get on a thing, I don't want it to be too tight, I want it to flow. I want to make observations about my stepmother, and if I do, I let it go.

GCB: One of the things I like about your writing anyway is that, as we talked about before, some writers at the present time don't give themselves that kind of free rein. And I can see already the way in which the equations are made. For instance the miserable sex with a WAC, which is not much better than a "WAC-off."

WS: [*laughs*] Yeah.

GCB: Again you've got the problem of order and freedom, and the uniform sex seems to relate to the whole army experience. Now, this is the piece that will be involved with Trieste?

WS: Yeah, I thought it would be interesting maybe to read this and then tell you, or sound you out as to what I'm going to. I've already told you on one of our walks of what I thought I might do. But you see this is a prelude. I should say that the Longerbone sequence is a spacer. I begin once again at home. I'm lying in bed, and I have this long talk with my father. In other words, the first part of the book is a slow revelation of a day, and the antagonism between this guy, the narrator, Paul Whitehurst, and his stepmother, and the mounting tension, the miserable animosity, which in itself is not terribly important, but which leads to other situations. It reveals mainly the narrator's character. It's a story of alienation. The kid is alienated. He's twenty-one years old, and trying to find himself.

GCB: A number of your narrators begin in that kind of a position.

WS: That's right. In fact he's alienated because it's the end of the war, because he's footloose, he's sexually totally bottled up, and I'm going to take him through this day. This'll be the first chapter, during which he does get in touch with this guy Stiles, who has not come up yet but who will gradually assume more and more major importance in the story. Stiles being that Yale guy I told you about.

GCB: The fascist.

WS: Yeah, who is up North in the rich part of Connecticut, and gets the narrator to join him on this trip on a cattle boat to Trieste. And there'll be several flashbacks to Saipan, where the narrator remembers the time when Stiles, the Yaley, is trying to root out the homosexuals from the outfit, unsuccessfully, and also the place where he unsuccessfully tries to Red-bait this older enlisted man who is of an ethnic background.

GCB: One gets the feeling reading your books that while they're free-flowing, you also pack them. Each part has illustrations, characterizations, minor caricatures, mild echoes of the central themes to do with a kind of loss of a sense of order or harmony in the world, which would relate not only to his experience in the war but to his stepmother and so on.

WS: Yes.

GCB: So, what about Longerbone? Will he be significant later?

WS: He will be a minor figure later on. He will be the enlisted man, kind of on the sidelines.

GCB: But in some ways an exacerbation of what exists within Stiles?

WS: Yeah. Longerbone will have no basic importance, of course. He's not a central figure. He's metaphorical. He's there. He's important to that extent. The only thing I was slightly troubled with in reading this to you was whether the Longerbone sequence seems to come naturally. Does it jar you intensely to have it at that point?

GCB: Where does it come out of?

WS: Well, all I mean is to have it introduced in that rather possibly dragged-in way.

GCB: Is that where you say, "An illustration"?

WS: Well, where I say, let me see. I'll just read two or three sentences to give you the gist: [*reads*] One July day I resolved to clear out of the house for good. It was a day of great upheaval involving my conflict with Isabel, Stiles and so on. (I'm just improvising.) It began as I woke in bed with a reverie of Saipan. Not a dream, a memory. I often thought of my months in the Pacific, the recollections cropping up at random as memories do, with no particular rationale or order. On the morning of which I speak I found myself thinking of Sergeant J. C. Longerbone. Sometimes I would conjure up military images as a means to quell my waking randiness, to put my tumescence to rest. It usually worked. Nothing is less sexually arousing than someone like J. C. Longerbone. Longerbone had been my platoon sergeant . . . And so on. Does that seem okay to you?

GCB: It seems okay because this is the point where he decides to get out and get away, and you do a kind of full circle because you come back to when the birds are blown away, and he says, "Jesus Christ," or, "What the hell is going on?" or whatever he says.

WS: Yes.

GCB: And that's the point, as I take it, of the reverie. It's important to his state of mind, the memory of Longerbone, when he gets up and decides he's got to get the hell out of . . .

WS: The house.

GCB: The house. So far that's . . . yes.

WS: So it doesn't seem too horribly yanked in by the ears, does it, that episode?

GCB: No, I think that you often seem to work like that in your fiction. It's refreshing that you don't smooth in necessarily, because you have a natural speaking voice, a narrator who says, "And now I'm going to talk about this," or, "Now I'm going to bring in Rubenstein," or whoever.

WS: So take it or leave it. In other words, to the reader: "Please accept this."

GCB: Accept the contract. Yes.

WS: Yeah. Well, good. You did not then feel . . . that was the only thing I was going to quiz you on . . . on whether you felt a horrible jar.

GCB: No.

WS: You don't?

GCB: I would say if I did. No, I found that, as I say, I visualize it in a circular fashion, and I thought it was a powerful ending to the Longerbone episode, where your narrators will often start with this chaotic sense of rootlessness and strive to find some order, so it's symptomatic, it's one example of why he is in this turbulent state right now.

WS: You weren't then troubled by an overdiscursiveness? This is discursive in a sense that when a little sidetrack beguiles me, I go along it. When I want to talk about Isabel, I go along the track, and when I want to talk about Longerbone, I go along that.

GCB: But you do that as a novelist, I think. You do that in *Sophie's Choice*. I don't see anything that you're doing now that is in any way worse than what you do in *Sophie's Choice*.

WS: So, in other words, you follow the narrative without distractions?

GCB: Yes, I know exactly why you bring in . . . it makes perfect sense to me that you bring in the Longerbone episode.

WS: You see, what I'm trying to do here is to . . . there are several themes I'm working on. You can already tell. Most of them are already there. The Stiles theme has yet to develop. I intentionally left out the one or two references to Stiles when I was reading it to you, for fear of distracting you. But if you were reading it in print you would see that that too fits. But if this novel, if it is indeed so, as I think it will be, instead of a short novel or novella, has these related themes, which will come in later in the day, I intend to have Isabel leaning hard on the atomic bomb, and the poor narrator has to be exposed to the fact that her nephew was horribly wounded in some I-don't-know-what. She also throws up to him the atomic bomb, and there's a preacher who comes to the house and argues that the dropping of the atomic bomb was an atrocious piece of inhumanity on the part of the American people.

GCB: So the narrator has something to resolve.

WS: Yeah, well, of course, because his life, his ass . . .

GCB: Is saved by this.

WS: And he has guilt over it, naturally. Anyone who was in that position would. But also he has a sense of . . . so this is a theme that is a kind of . . . it's not a major theme, but it's there. It's already been introduced in this chapter.

GCB: Will Isabel remain an important figure?

WS: Not really.

GCB: She's a base?

WS: She's a foil. But she's interesting in herself. She's important for the narrator to bounce his frustrations on.

GCB: My impression is that you've set out a picture. There are these two different worlds, and it's vital that one knows this about the narrator, that he has these two different worlds in his head, and that one can't know about Paul Whitehurst without knowing about what's going on both in the historical area, in Saipan, and with his family, because there's a kind of microcosm-macrocosm tension, and that you see the same tensions in family life as you see in historical events. That's how I see it. It's all part of his discord.

WS: Yes, and it's a matter of trying to make them mesh, to bring them into harmony—*aesthetic* harmony—without getting too distracted in one direction or another. The major theme, though, has been barely introduced, which is this protofascist. I have already written a great deal which I've put aside, which I'm going to resurrect and bring back and embed it later on in the narrative. I realized in my original version of this story that I was too far off the target. Now I see a kind of consolidation, a way to bring these themes in as episodes.

GCB: So what you'll end up doing will be a combination of the Trieste story, and parts of *The Way of the Warrior* you've already written?

WS: Yeah. That was in a different mode, a lot of the original *The Way of the Warrior* was laid on Saipan. I'm going to take some of the scenes that I've written, which I think are very good, like this Longerbone piece, and pull them out of the narrative I've already written and embed them in the new framework. But they have to do with Stiles—with his Red-baiting and homophobia. Maybe you recall that piece in *Esquire* called "Love Day." I'm going to use some of that material.

GCB: "Nice gal, too. I should have cut her throat."

WS: Yes [*laughs*].

GCB: So in a sense, what you're doing is a little like what the narrator's doing, which is pulling together the different elements to try and move toward some form of harmony, but with the ironic distance and awareness of the elements that cannot and should not be reconciled.

WS: Yeah, that's right, and as I view it, I think, without deluding myself, these flashback sequences are strong enough to be able to pull them out of what I've already written and embed them in the new narrative.

GCB: It's important if you're going to break and tell the reader, "Well, I'm going to do this now, I'm going to give you an example," or whatever, that it has a very big impact. The blowing the birds away, for instance, is a very strong image.

WS: I think it's a good way to establish what I'm going to do again, more than once, which is to go back to Saipan.

GCB: Paul Whitehurst has had his own flock of birds—block of words—blown away, in a sense; his little picture of life has been blown up.

WS: Yeah. So in terms of narrative and foreshadowing I think my strategy is right at this point, at bringing in the Longerbone, the bird stuff, because this will prepare the reader for the fact that there will be other stuff on Saipan. This is their first knowledge of this guy's experience.

GCB: So there will be elements that go toward Saipan, and at the same time he's moving toward Trieste, so you have a kind of pulling apart there, with the narrator seeking to find overall connections.

WS: That's right. If it works, and I hope it will, I intend the stuff having to do with Saipan will be done during the day here in this town of Newport News, all heading toward this guy's . . . the first chapter being this guy's disaffection with his homelife. He also tries to get laid, and he can't; that's another thing. Plus the conflict with Isabel, all of this melding and building up with the flashbacks about Stiles. Finally the day ends with the two of them agreeing that they're going off on a cattle boat. So I'll have practically all the major stuff already built when I get on this cattle boat.

GCB: Will there be a major female character in the book?

WS: I don't believe so.

GCB: It's basically the relationship and tension between Stiles and Paul?

WS: Yes.

GCB: When you wrote *Sophie's Choice*, which has a discursive opening in some ways, did you have these kinds of decisions to make? Did you have to think, "Do I want this here now?" in this same way?

WS: I did, yeah. I had no, you know . . . it was a *tabula rasa* except for certain things. I didn't know what the hell was going to come. I just started inventing things.

GCB: You have basic lines, but you don't know how it's going to fill out.

WS: Yeah, I knew where it was headed. But all the other stuff came as I wrote it.

GCB: So you were reading people like Steiner as you wrote.

WS: Yeah.

GCB: Well, of course, you read Steiner when it came out, but you . . .

WS: I recapitulate. So it's a matter of choice, of choosing the right episodes. These episodes, as I say, several of them I've already written. I can very easily use some of the "Love Day" stuff.

GCB: So you're working through, and how many pages have you written straight through, as it were?

WS: Several hundred, I'd say.

GCB: Several hundred?

WS: Yeah, but I'm not sure whether I'm going to retain all that. This is a new departure for me.

GCB: But you've stopped what you were doing and begun this, and yet it's all related.

WS: It's all related. It's stuff I can draw on. It's a matter of recasting it. This is what I'm going to try and do, keeping Stiles in the foreground, because he's so important.

GCB: It seems like it's all related to what you've had in your mind all along, but that you're finding the pattern.

WS: Exactly.

GCB: You know exactly what to say, but have to work out how to go about it.

WS: The architecture.

GCB: For me it's very comforting because it seems so like the kind of process that I've been going through. You know, you write lots that doesn't seem to go anywhere, but it's all just a question, as you say, of the architecture.

WS: Of getting it together. It's like a jigsaw puzzle. You know, and finding that it actually *does* fit.

GCB: Is this your common experience in writing novels?

WS: Yes. I've had it over and over again.

GCB: But you're feeling fairly good.

WS: I'm feeling pretty good about it. The important thing is that I think I have an understanding of what I'm heading toward. The unifying factor is the voice. To be able to keep the voice. I think I have a consistent voice in this passage. I think it will make the rest of the book fall into place.

GCB: There's a wonderful, slightly dry tone, as you have had in other things, where you undercut the voice of the younger self.

WS: Well, when you're dealing with a very young person it's necessary to either do the Huck Finn route, which Mark Twain did, and become a fourteen-year-old boy, or you become a middle-aged man recounting, and being able to shift from his own point of view to his youthful point of view.

GCB: Walker Percy talks about the difficulty of writing about this century because it's the worst and the best. We're sheltered now, we have far more leisure, and yet things seem so terrible. But as I see it, most people, in the West at least, are pretty lucky to be living in this century. We tend to forget what it must have been like to have lived in the fifteenth century.

WS: Oh yes, oh God. Or the fourteenth century, where again two out of three people died pretty quickly.

GCB: Do you feel that you're writing in a time of crisis? Or is that idea just part of the neurotic modern character?

WS: [*laughs*] I think we've been through so many crises that we're numbed to them. I was so naïve that I thought that the end of World War II, when I was twenty years old . . . that the atomic bomb . . . was the end of all wars. There was such a sigh of relief after that war, because it had been a *horrible* war, totally aside from the Holocaust part, which wasn't even known about then, just the exhaustion of fighting, guys dying, before and after the five years, six years really, and then to have this hiatus, and that was not only not the end, but we've had crisis after crisis.

GCB: Do you see it as a never-ending thing, just going on this way until something catastrophic happens?

WS: I think we're always teetering. You see, I think . . . I have a suspicion that the threat of nuclear destruction becomes less to some degree. I think we're finally getting ourselves together into an understanding, with recent developments in the Soviet Union and here. Reagan certainly didn't help anything with this terrible buildup of weaponry, but I think we've suddenly come to our senses and are headed in a direction which will be less menacing in terms of nuclear destruction. I think there'll be more universal supervision. I don't mean to say it will ever entirely disappear. Aside from that, I can't really feel much optimism about the abolition of war.

Britain: Styron's Visit, November 26–28, 1991

WS: Certainly when I started *Sophie's Choice,* I felt that, you know, that sense of possible guilt, or possible *unease,* in dealing with a subject like the Holocaust. But it was very important to me that you never ever in the whole book actually enter Auschwitz. I knew that I had to all the time keep my distance from the direct experience, which, of course, is not something that you or I have actually experienced.

GCB: And you kept this in mind all the time?

WS: Yes, if you want to put that in the record, I think it's important. At no point does the reader enter the boundaries of the camp.

GCB: It's the older Stingo remembering the younger Stingo, remembering Sophie, remembering her own experiences and what she's heard.

WS: Exactly. Layer on layer, which is just how we—those who weren't there—have to experience the Holocaust.

WS: Something else I maybe never told you about *Sophie's Choice* is that originally—you remember that Sophie is raped by a woman at the camp—well, originally I had Frau Höss as the rapist. But when it went to Bob Loomis and Random House, they said, "We're afraid you can't use that, because she's still alive living in a suburb in Germany and she may sue for libel." So I had to change it, and that's why I created the character of Wilhelmine.

GCB: Did it matter—to change it?

WS: It did at the time, sure, but not really, not when I think about it now.

GCB: Was there any reason why you wanted to have Frau Höss, or was it simply that you wanted to streamline—that you didn't want to bring in an unnecessary new character?

WS: Yes, that's right. Something like that.

GCB: I like the comments you made earlier today about the whole idea of risk. I talk about this idea in my conclusion. I picked up something you wrote on your manuscript of *Sophie's Choice,* at the start of Chapter 4. You scrawled across the page, "Only thing worth *Risking* a word." Writing about the Holocaust, presumably.

WS: I wrote something like that?

GCB: Yes, on the title page of Chapter 4 you've got various notes about what's in your mind. It also has your recognition that Sophie's lying, and that her father's really an anti-Semite. Though you put that with a question mark at the time.

WS: Yes.

GCB: But on the risk issue, you must have had this idea in your mind—that if it's worth doing anything, you might as well give it everything.

WS: I'd forgotten that comment. Well, you live one life, you do your best to make a difference. You might as well take a chance. Otherwise what's the point?

GCB: Given, for instance, that the *Voyager 2* spacecraft, having left our solar system won't reach its next destination—Sirius, the dog star—until, whenever, about A.D. 295,000.

WS: Yes, there's nothing out there. You know, some people are appalled at the idea that we're some little freak of a planet, marooned in the middle of nowhere. But I kind of like it. It appeals to my sense of life. We're on our own, and it just seems to me that, since you're alive, you've just got to do what you can do to help in the understanding of the world. You might fall flat on your face, but you've got to take the risk.

Selected Bibliography

With both primary and secondary sources, I list those most pertinent to the aspects of Styron's novels explored here. I have included from Styron's early stories only those of special interest to this study. The same principle has guided my selection of his essays and articles, the best of which appear in the original and expanded editions of *This Quiet Dust and Other Writings*, both cited here. For more complete bibliographies, see *The Achievement of William Styron*, edited by Robert K. Morris and Irving Malin, and *William Styron*, by Judith Ruderman, both cited here.

Works by William Styron

Novels

Lie Down in Darkness. New York, 1951.
The Long March. New York, 1952.
Set This House on Fire. New York, 1960.
The Confessions of Nat Turner. New York, 1967.
Sophie's Choice. New York, 1979.

Stories

"A Moment in Trieste." In *American Vanguard,* edited by Don M. Wolfe, 214–47. Ithaca, N.Y., 1948.
"Marriott, the Marine." *Esquire,* LXXVI (September, 1971), 101–210, not continuous.
"The Suicide Run." *American Poetry Review,* III (May–June, 1974), 20–22.
"Saipan, July 1945." *Paris Review,* CIII (Summer, 1987), 16–29.
"Blankenship." *Papers on Language and Literature,* XXIII (1987), 430–48.
A Tidewater Morning: Three Tales from Youth. New York, 1993.

Nonfiction Volumes

This Quiet Dust and Other Writings. New York, 1982. Rev. ed., New York, 1993.

Darkness Visible: A Memoir of Madness. New York, 1990.

Drama

In the Clap Shack. New York, 1973.

Dead! Esquire, LXXX (December, 1973), 161–290, not continuous. This screenplay was written with John Phillips.

Uncollected Essays and Articles

"My Generation." *Esquire,* LXX (October, 1968), 123–24.

"Social Animal of Manic Gusto." *Observer,* December 6, 1987, p. 10.

"Nat Turner Revisited." *American Heritage,* XLIII (October, 1992), 64–73. This essay also now appears as an afterword to *The Confessions of Nat Turner* (1967; rpr. New York, 1993), 434–55.

Secondary Sources

Books

Aldridge, John W. *The Devil in the Fire: Retrospective Essays on American Literature and Culture, 1951–1971.* New York, 1972.

Bakhtin, Mikhail M. *The Dialogic Imagination: Four Essays.* Translated by Michael Holquist and Caryl Emerson; edited by Michael Holquist. Austin, Tex., 1981.

Baldwin, James. *Nobody Knows My Name: More Notes of a Native Son.* 1961; rpr. London, 1964.

———. *Notes of a Native Son.* 1955; rpr. London, 1964.

Borowski, Tadeusz. *This Way for the Gas, Ladies and Gentlemen, and Other Stories.* Compiled and translated by Barbara Vedder. London, 1967.

Camus, Albert. *The Myth of of Sisyphus.* Translated by Justin O'Brien. London, 1955.

———. *Resistance, Rebellion, and Death.* Translated by Justin O'Brien. London, 1961.

Casciato, Arthur D., and James L. W. West III, eds. *Critical Essays on William Styron.* Boston, 1982.

Chaufour-Verheyen, Christine. *William Styron: Le 7e Jour.* Paris, 1991.

Chefdor, Monique, Richard Quinones, and Albert Watchel, eds. *Modernism: Challenges and Perspectives.* Urbana, Ill., 1986.

Clarke, John H., ed. *William Styron's Nat Turner: Ten Black Writers Respond.* Boston, 1968.

Cleaver, Eldridge. *Soul on Ice.* New York, 1968.

Coale, Samuel. *William Styron Revisited.* Boston, 1991.

Crane, John Kenny. *The Root of All Evil: The Thematic Unity of William Styron's Fiction.* Columbia, S.C., 1984.

Douglass, Frederick. *Narrative of the Life of Frederick Douglass, an American Slave.* Edited by Houston A. Baker, Jr. 1845; Harmondsworth, Eng., 1986.

Duff, John B., and Peter M. Mitchell, eds. *The Nat Turner Rebellion: The Historical Event and the Modern Controversy.* New York, 1971.

Erikson, Erik H. *Young Man Luther: A Study in Psychoanalysis and History.* London, 1958.

Finkelstein, Sidney. *Existentialism and Alienation in American Literature.* New York, 1965.

Fisher, Philip. *Hard Facts: Setting and Form in the American Novel.* New York, 1985.

Foner, Eric, ed. *Nat Turner.* Englewood Cliffs, N.J., 1971.

Fossum, Robert H. *William Styron: A Critical Essay.* Grand Rapids, 1968.

Friedman, Melvin J. *William Styron: An Interim Appraisal.* Bowling Green, Ohio, 1974.

Friedman, Melvin J., and Irving Malin, eds. *William Styron's "The Confessions of Nat Turner": A Critical Handbook.* Belmont, Calif., 1970.

Friedman, Melvin J., and August Nigro, eds. *Configuration Critique de William Styron.* Paris, 1967.

Galloway, David D. *The Absurd Hero in American Fiction.* London, 1981.

Gray, Richard. *The Literature of Memory: Modern Writers of the American South.* London, 1977.

———. *Writing the South: Ideas of an American Region.* New York, 1986.

Harding, Vincent. *There Is a River: The Black Struggle for Freedom in America.* New York, 1981.

Henderson, Harry B., III. *Versions of the Past: The Historical Imagination in American Fiction.* New York, 1974.

Karl, Frederick R. *American Fictions, 1940–1980: A Comprehensive History and Critical Evaluation.* New York, 1983.

Kenner, Hugh. *A Homemade World: The American Modernist Writers.* New York, 1975.

King, Richard H. *A Southern Renascence: The Cultural Awakening of the American South, 1930–1955.* New York, 1980.

Langer, Lawrence L. *The Holocaust and the Literary Imagination.* New Haven, 1975.

Leon, Philip W. *William Styron: An Annotated Bibliography of Criticism.* Westwood, Conn., 1978.

Lukács, Georg. *The Historical Novel.* Translated by Hannah Mitchell and Stanley Mitchell. 1962; rpr. Harmondsworth, Eng., 1986.

———. *The Meaning of Contemporary Realism.* Translated by John Mander and Necke Mander. London, 1963.

———. *Writer and Critic, and Other Essays.* Translated by Arthur Kahn. London, 1978.

Mackin, Cooper R. *William Styron.* Austin, Tex., 1969.

Morris, Robert K., and Irving Malin, eds. *The Achievement of William Styron.* Rev. ed. Athens, Ga., 1981.

Morrison, Toni. *Playing in the Dark: Whiteness and the Literary Imagination.* Cambridge, Mass., 1992.

Orr, John. *The Making of the Twentieth-Century Novel: Lawrence, Joyce, Faulkner, and Beyond.* London, 1987.

Pearce, Richard. *William Styron.* Minneapolis, 1971.

Ratner, Marc L. *William Styron.* Boston, 1972.

Rosenfeld, Alvin H. *A Double Dying: Reflections on Holocaust Literature.* Bloomington, Ind., 1980.

Rubenstein, Richard L. *The Cunning of History: Mass Death and the American Future.* 1975; rpr. New York, 1978, with introduction by William Styron.

Ruderman, Judith. *William Styron.* New York, 1987.

Sirlin, Rhoda. *William Styron's "Sophie's Choice": Crime and Self-Punishment.* Ann Arbor, Mich., 1990.

Smith, Joan. *Misogynies.* London, 1989.

Steiner, George. *Language and Silence: Essays, 1958–1966.* London, 1967.

Stevens, Wallace. *The Collected Poems of Wallace Stevens.* London, 1955.

Stone, Albert E. *The Return of Nat Turner: History, Literature, and Cultural Politics in Sixties America.* Athens, Ga., 1992.

Tanner, Tony. *City of Words.* London, 1971.

Tragle, Henry I. *The Southampton Slave Revolt of 1831: A Compilation of Source Material.* Amherst, Mass., 1971.

West, James L. W., III, ed. *Conversations with William Styron.* Jackson, Miss., 1985.

Woodward, C. Vann. *The Burden of Southern History.* New York, 1960.

Young, James E. *Writing and Rewriting the Holocaust: Narrative and the Consequences of Interpretation.* Bloomington, Ind., 1988.

Articles and Reviews

Akin, William E. "Toward an Impressionistic History: Pitfalls and Possibilities in William Styron's Meditation on History." *American Quarterly,* XXI (1969), 805–12.

Arms, Valarie M. "A French View of William Styron: Topicality Versus Universality." *Southern Review,* XXIX (1990), 47–69.

————. "William Styron and the Spell of the South." *Mississippi Quarterly,* XXXIV (1980–81), 25–36.

Barth, John. "The Literature of Replenishment." *Atlantic Monthly,* CCXX (1980), 65–71.

Bradbury, Malcolm. "The Nonhomemade World: European and American Modernism." *American Quarterly,* XXXIX (1987), 27–36.

Brandriff, Welles T. "The Role of Order and Disorder in *The Long March.*" *English Journal,* LVI (1967), 54–59.

Burgess, Anthony. "Brooklyn Liebestod." *Observer,* September 9, 1979, p. 15.

Caputo, Philip. "Styron's Choices." *Esquire,* CVI (December, 1986), 136–59.

Coale, Samuel. "Styron's Choice: Hawthorne's Guilt in Poe's Palaces." *Papers on Language and Literature,* XXIII (1987), 514–22.

————. "Styron's Disguises: A Provisional Rebel in Christian Masquerade." *Critique,* XXVI (1985), 57–66.

Cobbs, John L. "Bearing the Unbearable: William Styron and the Problem of Pain." *Mississippi Quarterly,* IV (1980–81), 15–24.

Coles, Robert. "Arguments: The Turner Thesis." *Partisan Review,* XXXV (1968), 412–14.

Colville, Georgiana M. M. "Killing the Dead Mother: Women in *Sophie's Choice.*" *Delta* (Montpellier), XXIII (1986), 111–36.

Cooke, Michael. "Nat Turner: Another Response." *Yale Review,* LVIII (1969), 295–301.

Dickstein, Morris. "The World in a Mirror: Problems of Distance in Recent American Fictions." *Sewanee Review,* LXXXIX (1981), 386–400.

Eggenschwiler, David. "Tragedy and Melodrama in *The Confessions of Nat Turner.*" *Twentieth-Century Literature,* XX (1974), 19–33.

Fiedler, Leslie A. "Styron's Choice: A Novel About Auschwitz." *Psychology Today,* XIII (July, 1979), 102–107.

Foster, Richard. "An Orgy of Commerce: William Styron's *Set This House on Fire.*" *Critique,* III (1960), 59–70.

Friedman, Melvin J. "The French Face of William Styron." *International Fiction Review*, X (1983), 33–37.

———. "William Styron's Criticism: More French Than American." *Delta* (Montpellier), XXIII (1966), 61–76.

———. "William Styron in Eden." *Papers on Language and Literature*, XXIII (1987), 544–48.

Fuentes, Carlos. "Unslavish Fidelity." *Times Literary Supplement*, May 16, 1968, p. 505.

———. "Words Apart." *Guardian*, February 24, 1989, pp. 29–30.

Hays, Peter L. "The Nature of Rebellion in *The Long March*." *Critique*, VIII (1965–66), 70–74.

Heath, William. "I, Stingo: The Problem of Egotism in *Sophie's Choice*." *Southern Review*, XX (1984), 528–45.

Kreyling, Michael. "Speaking the Unspeakable in Styron's *Sophie's Choice*." *Southern Review*, XX (1984), 546–61.

Lang, John. "The Alpha and the Omega: Styron's *The Confessions of Nat Turner*." *American Literature*, LIII (1981), 499–503.

———. "God's Averted Face: Styron's *Sophie's Choice*." *American Literature*, LV (1983), 215–32.

Leon, Philip W. "The Lost Boy and a Lost Girl." *Southern Literary Journal*, IX (Fall, 1976), 61–69.

McNamara, Eugene. "William Styron's *Long March*: Absurdity and Authority." *Western Humanities Review*, XV (1961), 267–72.

Mathy, Francis S. "Hell Reconsidered: William Styron's *Sophie's Choice*." *English Literature and Language* (Tokyo), XXI (1984), 119–44.

Mellard, James M. "This *Un*quiet Dust: The Problem of History in Styron's *The Confessions of Nat Turner*." *Mississippi Quarterly*, XXXVI (1983), 525–43.

Moore, Hugh L. "Robert Penn Warren, William Styron, and the Use of Greek Myth." *Critique*, VIII (1965–66), 75–87.

Mudrick, Marvin. "Mailer and Styron: Guests of the Establishment." *Hudson Review*, XVII (1964), 346–66.

Nagel, Gwen L. "Illusion and Identity in *Sophie's Choice*." *Delta* (Montpellier), XXIII (1986), 91–109.

O'Connell, Shaun V. "Expense of Spirit: The Vision of William Styron." *Critique*, VIII (1965–66), 20–33.

Reitz, Bernhard. "Fearful Ambiguities of Time and History: *The Confessions of Nat Turner* and the Delineation of the Past in Postmodern Historical Narrative." *Papers on Language and Literature*, XXIII (1987), 465–79.

Robb, Kenneth A. "William Styron's Don Juan." *Critique*, VIII (1965–66), 34–46.

Rubenstein, Richard L. "The South Encounters the Holocaust: William Styron's *Sophie's Choice*." *Michigan Quarterly Review*, XX (1981), 425–42.

Saposnik, Irving S. "Bellow, Malamud, Roth . . . and Styron? Or One Jewish Writer's Response." *Judaism*, XXXI (1982), 322–32.

Scheick, William J. "Discarded Watermelon Rinds: The Rainbow Aesthetic of William Styron's *Lie Down in Darkness*." *Modern Fiction Studies*, XXIV (1978), 247–54.

Searle, John R. "The Logical Status of Fictional Discourse." *New Literary History*, VI (1975), 319–32.

Shapiro, Herbert. "*The Confessions of Nat Turner:* William Styron and His Critics." *Negro American Literature Forum*, IX (1975), 99–104.

Smith, Frederick N. "Bach Versus Brooklyn's Clamorous Yawp: Sound in *Sophie's Choice*." *Papers on Language and Literature*, XXIII (1987), 523–30.

Stone, Albert E. "The Return of Nat Turner in Sixties America." *Prospects*, XII, (1987), 223–53.

Tragle, Henry I. "Styron and His Sources." *Massachusetts Review*, XI (1970), 134–53.

Trouard, Dawn. "Styron's Historical Pre-Text: Nat Turner, Sophie, and the Beginnings of a Postmodern Career." *Papers on Language and Literature*, XXIII (1987), 489–97.

Tutt, Ralph. "Stingo's Complaint: Styron and the Politics of Self-Parody." *Modern Fiction Studies*, XXXIV (1988), 575–86.

Urang, Gunnar. "The Broader Vision: William Styron's *Set This House on Fire*." *Critique*, VIII (1965–66), 47–69.

West, James L. W., III. "William Styron: A Biographical Account." *Mississippi Quarterly*, XXXIV (1980–81), 2–7.

———. "William Styron's *Inheritance of Night:* Predecessor of *Lie Down in Darkness*." *Delta* (Montpellier), XXIII (1986), 1–17.

White, John. "The Novelist as Historian: William Styron and American Negro Slavery." *Journal of American Studies*, IV (1971), 233–45.

Index